The book of Isaiah and God's kingdom

NEW STUDIES IN BIBLICAL THEOLOGY 40

Series editor: D. A. Carson

The book of Isaiah and God's kingdom

A THEMATIC–THEOLOGICAL APPROACH

Andrew T. Abernethy

APOLLOS

INTERVARSITY PRESS
DOWNERS GROVE, ILLINOIS 60515

APOLLOS (an imprint of Inter-Varsity Press, England)
36 Causton Street
London SW1P 4ST, England
Website: www.ivpbooks.com
Email: ivp@ivpbooks.com

InterVarsity Press, USA
P.O. Box 1400
Downers Grove, IL 60515, USA
Website: www.ivpress.com
Email: email@ivpress.com

First published 2016

Set in Monotype Times New Roman

Typeset in Great Britain by CRB Associates, Potterhanworth, Lincolnshire

USA ISBN 978-0-8308-2641-4 (print)
USA ISBN 978-0-8308-9449-9 (digital)

UK ISBN 978-1-78359-428-3 (print)
UK ISBN 978-1-78359-497-9 (digital)

British Library Cataloguing-in-Publication Data

A catalogue record for this book is available from the British Library.

Library of Congress Cataloging-in-Publication Data

A catalog record for this book is available from the Library of Congress.

P 25 24 23 22 21 20 19 18 17 16 15 14 13 12 11 10 9 8 7 6 5 4 3 2 1
Y 37 36 35 34 33 32 31 30 29 28 27 26 25 24 23 22 21 20 19 18 17 16

Contents

Series preface

New Studies in Biblical Theology is a series of monographs that address key issues in the discipline of biblical theology. Contributions to the series focus on one or more of three areas: (1) the nature and status of biblical theology, including its relations with other disciplines (e.g. historical theology, exegesis, systematic theology, historical criticism, narrative theology); (2) the articulation and exposition of the structure of thought of a particular biblical writer or corpus; and (3) the delineation of a biblical theme across all or part of the biblical corpora.

Above all, these monographs are creative attempts to help thinking Christians understand their Bibles better. The series aims simultaneously to instruct and to edify, to interact with the current literature, and to point the way ahead. In God's universe, mind and heart should not be divorced: in this series we will try not to separate what God has joined together. While the notes interact with the best of scholarly literature, the text is uncluttered with untransliterated Greek and Hebrew, and tries to avoid too much technical jargon. The volumes are written within the framework of confessional evangelicalism, but there is always an attempt at thoughtful engagement with the sweep of the relevant literature.

Anyone who has tried to teach or preach through the prophecy of Isaiah has felt a powerful strain – the tug between, on the one hand, the soaring imagination and evocative phrasing of passage after passage in this magnificent book, and, on the other, the challenge of fitting the book together and grasping with confidence the referents Isaiah has in mind. In a well-written and remarkably comprehensive treatment, Dr Andrew Abernethy takes us through the book by unfolding the way God and his kingdom are presented in each of the three major sections of the prophecy, and then by outlining the way this reigning God uses agents to accomplish his purpose. Dr Abernethy undertakes all of this exegetical and theological exploration with an eye peeled for the way New Testament writers, seven centuries later, pick up on these trajectories to bring us to Christ. One need not agree with every exegetical decision to be profoundly grateful for the sweep and comprehensiveness of the treatment.

D. A. Carson
Trinity Evangelical Divinity School

Author's preface

The book of Isaiah has nourished the church throughout the centuries. Jerome (AD 342–420) stated that Isaiah's message so clearly conveyed the gospel that Isaiah 'should be called an evangelist rather than a prophet'.[1] Few today, however, have such strong affections for Isaiah. For many, Isaiah seems like an intimidating mountain – massive in scale, difficult to ascend, complex in its terrain and shadowy. There is great reward, however, for those who set out to climb Isaiah, as glorious vistas await them along the arduous trek. While the *main* purpose of commentaries is to help readers navigate individual parts of the mountain, a work of biblical theology – such as this one – primarily aims to offer an orientation for the whole mountain (Isaiah) in the light of the entire range (canon). My conviction is that pastors, students and educated laity need resources like this one, as a sense for the overarching message of Isaiah within the context of the canon is vital for reading and teaching from individual passages. It is my hope that this study on kingdom in Isaiah will help the church to share with Jerome in savouring the 'gospel' in Isaiah.

Midway through writing this book John Goldingay published a short volume on Isaiah's theology.[2] This led me to fear that my project was unnecessary. Upon reading his book, I was relieved to see that there is quite a difference between our audiences and the way we package Isaiah's theology. Goldingay, primarily writing for laypeople, makes little attempt to integrate his reflections on a wide range of themes and topics from each part of the book. I, on the other hand, am writing for pastors and advanced college and seminary students and am attempting to use 'kingdom' as a unifying concept. I think that a range of readers will find benefit from both approaches and find that they complement one another.

This book is the result of a lengthy process, so a number of acknowledgments are in order. Willem VanGemeren deserves special

[1] Sawyer 1996: 1.
[2] Goldingay 2014.

recognition, as his lectures on the prophets were my first exposure to how the concept of the kingdom of God might be an avenue for conceptualizing the message of the prophets. He also graciously took time to read through my manuscript. Also, the students and faculty at Ridley College (Melbourne) deserve thanks for providing input and encouragement as I began testing ideas in the classroom and in the initial stages of writing. Additionally, Wheaton College's Alumni Association awarded me a Junior Faculty Development Grant, which served to fund my research. Furthermore, there are a number of pastors and scholars who deserve recognition for reading through parts of this book: Aaron Baker, Joe Bartemus, Brandon Crowe, Greg Goswell, Charlie Trimm and particularly Richard Schultz. My teaching assistants, Jonathan Wright and Stephen Wunrow, also improved this manuscript through their proofreading, attention to style and insights. Stephen undertook the taxing project of creating the indices. Furthermore, I would like to thank the editors, D. A. Carson and Philip Duce, for accepting this book into the NSBT series and for their patience and input along its way to publication. Eldo Barkhuizen, the copy editor, was a tremendous help in polishing this book. Finally, I would like to thank my wife, Katie, and our two daughters for the joy, support and perspective that they have brought to me throughout the course of this project.

Abbreviations

AB	Anchor Bible
ABD	*Anchor Bible Dictionary*, ed. D. N. Freedman, 6 vols., New York: Doubleday, 1992
AJSL	*American Journal of Semitic Languages and Literature*
ANE	ancient Near East(ern)
AOAT	Alter Orient und Altes Testament
AV	Authorized (King James) Version
BBR	*Bulletin for Biblical Research*
BETL	Bibliotheca ephemeridum theologicarum lovaniensium
BI	*Biblical Interpretation*
Bib	*Biblica*
BIS	Biblical Interpretation Series
BSac	*Bibliotheca sacra*
BTB	*Biblical Theology Bulletin*
BZAW	Beihefte zur Zeitschrift für die alttestamentliche Wissenschaft
BZNW	Beihefte zur Zeitschrift für die neutestamentliche Wissenschaft
CANE	*Civilizations of the Ancient Near East*, ed. J. M. Sasson, 4 vols., Peabody: Hendrickson, 1995
CBQ	*Catholic Biblical Quarterly*
CBQMS	Catholic Biblical Quarterly Monograph Series
CBR	*Currents in Biblical Research*
CC	Continental Commentaries
ConBOT	Coniectanea biblica: Old Testament Series
CTJ	*Calvin Theological Journal*
CTR	*Criswell Theological Review*
DOTP	*Dictionary of the Old Testament Pentateuch*, ed. T. D. Alexander and D. W. Baker, Downers Grove: InterVarsity Press, 2003
DTIB	*Dictionary for Theological Interpretation of the Bible*, ed. K. J. Vanhoozer, C. G. Bartholomew, D. J. Treier and N. T. Wright, Grand Rapids: Baker, 2005

EgT	*Eglise et théologie*
ESV	English Standard Version
ETL	*Ephemerides theologicae lovanienses*
ExAud	*Ex auditu*
ExpTim	*Expository Times*
FAT	Forschungen zum Alten Testament
FOTL	Forms of Old Testament Literature
HCOT	Historical Commentary on the Old Testament
HSM	Harvard Semitic Monographs
HTKAT	Herders theologischer Kommentar zum Alten Testament
HTR	*Harvard Theological Review*
HUCA	*Hebrew Union College Annual*
ICC	International Critical Commentary
JAOS	*Journal of the American Oriental Society*
JBL	*Journal of Biblical Literature*
JESOT	*Journal for the Evangelical Study of the Old Testament*
JETS	*Journal of the Evangelical Theological Society*
JNES	*Journal of Near Eastern Studies*
JPS	Jewish Publication Society translation
JQR	*Jewish Quarterly Review*
JR	*Journal of Religion*
JSNTSup	Journal for the Study of the New Testament, Supplement Series
JSOT	*Journal for the Study of the Old Testament*
JSOTSup	Journal for the Study of the Old Testament, Supplement Series
JSS	*Journal of Semitic Studies*
JSSM	Journal of Semitic Studies Monograph
LHBOTS	Library for the Hebrew Bible / Old Testament Series
LNTS	Library of New Testament Studies
LXX	Septuagint
NAC	New American Commentary
NASB	New American Standard Bible
NCBC	New Century Bible Commentary
NIBC	New International Biblical Commentary
NICNT	New International Commentary on the New Testament
NICOT	New International Commentary on the Old Testament

NIDOTTE   *New International Dictionary of Old Testament Theology and Exegesis*, ed. W. A. VanGemeren, 5 vols., Grand Rapids: Zondervan, 1997

NIGTC   New International Greek Testament Commentary

NIV   New International Version

NRSV   New Revised Standard Version

NSBT   New Studies in Biblical Theology

NT   New Testament

OBT   Overtures to Biblical Theology

OT   Old Testament

OTL   Old Testament Library

OTS   *Oudtestamentische Studiën*

OtSt   Oudtestamentische Studiën

PNTC   Pillar New Testament Commentary

PRS   *Perspectives in Religious Studies*

RevExp   *Review & Expositor*

RIMA   The Royal Inscriptions of Mesopotamia, Assyrian Periods

SBS   Stuttgarter Bibelstudien

SBTS   Sources for Biblical and Theological Study

SJOT   *Scandinavian Journal of the Old Testament*

SJT   *Scottish Journal of Theology*

STI   Studies in Theological Interpretation

STR   *Southeastern Theological Review*

TDOT   *Theological Dictionary of the Old Testament*, ed. G. J. Botterweck and H. Ringgren, tr. J. T. Willis, G. W. Bromiley and D. E. Green, 8 vols., Grand Rapids: Eerdmans, 1974–

Them   *Themelios*

TrinJ   *Trinity Journal*

TynBul   *Tyndale Bulletin*

VT   *Vetus Testamentum*

VTSup   Supplements to Vetus Testamentum

WBC   Word Biblical Commentary

WMANT   Wissenschaftliche Monographien zum Alten und Neuen Testament

WTJ   *Westminster Theological Journal*

ZAW   *Zeitschrift für die alttestamentliche Wissenschaft*

ZRG   *Zeitschrift für Religions- und Geistesgeschichte*

Introduction

My wife and I arrived in Melbourne as strangers, aliens in the land of Australia. It was only three months earlier in Chicago that I had located Melbourne on a map. With our plane on the ground, this foreign metropolis was now our home. Tim, the director of the college, was our tour guide from the airport to Ridley College, where we would live for the next three and a half years. Along the way, he noted a massive Australian Football League stadium and explained how fanatical Melbournians are about 'footy'. He then drew our attention to Flinders Street Station, a hub for public transport and an orientation point if we were ever lost. Finally, he told us about a local café, which began a conversation about Melbourne's coffee culture. By instinct Tim knew it would be of little benefit to comment on the hundreds or even thousands of streets, landmarks, stores, buildings and homes in Melbourne. What he gave us were some points of reference to gain perspective on what makes Melbourne what it is.

As with encountering a new city, points of orientation are invaluable for navigating a book like Isaiah.[1] Isaiah's massive size is intimidating. Its historical setting seems distant, opaque and varied. Its organization and composition seem disjointed and fragmented. Its abundance of terse, poetic language can make the book's message seem veiled. Where are all of those explicit prophecies about Christ? These are typical experiences for many who try to read, let alone teach or preach, through Isaiah; student, pastor and scholar alike.

My conviction is that thematic points of reference can be of great help in encountering Isaiah and its rich theological message. While there are a number of beneficial commentaries on Isaiah, it is rare for someone to read through an entire commentary, and, as a result, there is very little sense of the big picture themes and message that unfold throughout the book. The concept of 'kingdom' will be our entry point for organizing the book's major themes, which should prove helpful in navigating the difficult, though splendid, terrain of Isaiah.

---

[1] 'Landscape' is a comparable metaphor for OT theology; see Goldingay 1987: 115.

Kingdom, Isaiah and canon

Why use the concept of 'kingdom'? Though the term 'kingdom' occurs infrequently in Isaiah, the concept is integral throughout.

First, the book regularly refers to God with titles like 'king' (*melek*),[2] 'lord' (*'ădōnāy*)[3] and 'YHWH (Lord) of hosts' (*yhwh ṣĕbā'ôt*).[4] Second, concepts related to kingdom, such as the throne, tribute, warfare, glory, and justice and righteousness, arise throughout Isaiah. Third, passages highlighting God's kingship occur at strategic points throughout Isaiah, indicating the concept's structural importance (Isa. 6; 24 – 25; 33; 40; 52; 59:15 – 63:6; 66). Fourth, the book of Isaiah addresses a people living amid a long trajectory of empires – Assyria, Babylon and Persia – so it is no surprise that Isaiah casts its message in the light of the notion of kingdom.[5] In many respects, Isaiah provides a people living amid imperial contexts with a theological interpretation of these situations in the light of YHWH's past, present and future sovereign reign. While the points above will be more fully developed throughout this book, there is little doubt that kingdom is fundamental to the book of Isaiah's message.

There are four features of kingdom in Isaiah that will frame our study: (1) God, the king, (2) the lead agents of the king, (3) the realm of the kingdom, and (4) the people of the king.[6] A number of scholars have recognized the importance of God's kingdom in Isaiah, though

---

[2] Isa. 6:5; 33:17, 22; 41:21; 43:15; 44:6; cf. verb *mlk* (to reign) 24:23 and 52:7.

[3] Isa. 3:15, 17–18; 4:4; 6:1, 8, 11; 7:7, 14, 20; 8:7; 9:7, 17; 10:12, 23–24; 11:11; 21:6, 16; 22:5, 12, 14–15; 25:8; 28:2, 16, 22; 29:13; 30:15, 20; 37:24; 38:14, 16; 40:10; 48:16; 49:14, 22; 50:4–5, 7, 9; 52:4; 56:8; 61:1, 11; 65:13, 15. 'Lord YHWH' is especially prominent in Isa. 65 – 66.

[4] Isa. 3:15, 17–18; 4:4; 6:2, 5, 11; 7:7, 14, 20; 8:7; 9:7, 17; 10:12, 23–24; 11:11; 21:6, 10, 16; 22:5, 12, 14–15; 25:6; 28:5, 16, 22; 29:13; 30:15, 20; 37:24; 38:14, 16; 40:10; 48:16; 49:14, 22; 50:4–5, 7, 9; 52:4; 56:8; 61:1, 11; 65:13, 15. Irsigler (1991: 154) states that Isaiah of Jerusalem uses this title exclusively for YHWH, while *melek* (king) could be applied to human rulers.

[5] References to kings from these empires and other nations arise throughout the book. The term *melek* (king) applies to rulers from Assyria (7:17, 20; 8:4, 7; 10:12; 20:1, 4, 6; 36:1, 2, 4, 8, 13, 14, 15, 16, 18; 37:4, 6, 8, 11, 18, 21, 33, 37, 38; 38:6), Babylon (14:4; 39:1, 7), Aram (7:11), Cush (37:9), Israel (7:1), Judah (1:1; 6:1; 7:1; 30:33?; 36:1, 21; 37:1, 5, 10; 38:9; 39:3), and the nations generally (14:9, 18; 19:11; 24:21; 41:2; 45:1; 49:7, 23; 52:15; 60:3, 10, 11, 16; 62:2; cf. 37:13).

[6] A fifth category could be 'God's law', as law is a common feature of kingdom. As will be evident, God's law overlaps the four other categories. When considering God's role as king in Isa. 1 – 12, we will see that God as king issues his instruction from Zion (e.g. 2:2–4). God's agents, his Davidic ruler and the servant, are to be agents of conveying and enforcing God's torah both at home and abroad. God's people are those who obey and tremble at his instruction.

most studies focus only on one feature of God's kingdom, such as God's kingship or his leaders, and are written primarily for academic audiences.[7] Williamson's book *Variations on a Theme* was a significant starting point in my own journey towards conceptualizing the book's message around kingdom.[8] After spending about twenty-five pages on God's kingship and exaltation in select passages from Isaiah 1 – 39, he devotes the rest of the book to tracing how Immanuel, the Davidic ruler, the servant, and then God's servants feature in an evolving portrait of leaders who are to serve in the establishment of God's kingdom. Though his work was groundbreaking for me, one can take Williamson's schema further. How does God's kingship feature in other parts of Isaiah 1 – 39 and Isaiah 40 – 66? Is he correct that promises regarding a Davidic ruler from earlier in the book are left behind and democratized in the latter part of the book? Does the suffering servant (52:13 – 53:12), whom Williamson bypasses, fit into the schema? What about other features of a kingdom, such as its realm and its people? By offering a study that coordinates God's kingship, his lead agents, the realm of the kingdom, and the people of the kingdom into one volume, my hope is that an integrated vision will prove valuable for attaining a more comprehensive sense of the totality of Isaiah's kingdom message.

Though my primary focus will be upon unveiling the dynamics of kingdom in Isaiah in its OT context, I will not be treating the OT in an ancient vacuum, in isolation from its role in a two-testament canon. Within OT scholarship many Christian interpreters, myself included

---

[7] Among the most significant studies on kingship in Isaiah, see Irsigler (1991), who explores how Isaiah's vision of YHWH as king in Isa. 6 impacts 'eighth-century' texts; Mettinger (1997: 143–154) and Berges (2011: 95–119), who argue for the centrality of God's kingship in Isa. 40 – 55; Blenkinsopp (2003: 80–81), who does the same for 40 – 66; Beuken (2009), who considers the strategic placement of climactic announcements of YHWH's kingship at Zion throughout Isaiah (24:23; 52:7–10; 66:15–24); Schultz (1995), who clarifies how consistent emphases on YHWH's reign throughout Isaiah's various sections grant perspective on the place of human agency in the book; Houston (1993: 34), who wrestles with the already and not-yet nature of the kingdom in Isaiah and argues that the essence of Isaiah is 'the kingship of God now visible to the eye of faith and to be made visible to all in the new world that is about to dawn'; Schmid (2005), who argues that the entire book of Isaiah – and not simply individual, isolated verses – presents YHWH's kingship as its central hope, with Davidic kingship fading and God's kingship becoming more pronounced; McCann (2003), who offers a brief, though helpfully integrated, reflection on God's sovereignty in Zion and with his people; Roberts (1983a), who explores the place of the human king, ministers and the people in the future era of salvation according to Isa. 1 – 39.

[8] Williamson 1998a; cf. 1998b.

at times, are afraid that the scholarly guild will blow the whistle, accusing us of violating the rule that Christ and the NT must not intermingle with our examinations of OT texts. While I affirm that there is a place for limiting one's interpretative focus to OT texts in their original setting, as is evident in a number of my other publications, the reception of the OT by the church as Christian scripture should ultimately lead Christian interpretations to probe how the OT bears witness to Jesus Christ. The abundant quotations, allusions and echoes from and to Isaiah in the NT demonstrate how vital Isaiah was for the church in their conceptualization of how the kingdom of God had come and will come in Christ. If the divine author of Isaiah is also the author of the entire canon, then we should weigh how God may have providentially inspired the human words, including a book's arrangement, in an initial context to play a role in the larger canonical witness to Jesus Christ and God's redemptive plan, even if the human writers were not fully cognizant of the way in which their contextually tailored utterances, or the book's arrangement, would function as part of a larger whole and address later audiences of God's people. One, however, must be careful to not impose the New on the Old to such an extent that this mutes the discrete witness of the OT.⁹ If all one is left with in the interpretative process is something one could have read in the NT, the OT is not even necessary.¹⁰ The key issue is to allow an OT text to sound its own discrete voice while also factoring in how this joins in with the NT as they jointly bear witness to Christ and God's redemptive plan. As Vanhoozer puts it, 'Theological interpretation is not a matter of breaking some code ("this is what it means") but of grasping everything God is doing in and with the various strata of biblical discourse.'¹¹ Throughout each chapter I will probe how the theme of kingdom in Isaiah bears witness to Christ and God's ways with his church and the world today, while primarily focusing on kingdom within Isaiah.

What we have before us, then, is an attempt to offer an integrated vision of the message of Isaiah through the concept of kingdom. While our primary interest will be to make the case for how

---

⁹ This is the regular cry of Goldingay (cf. 2003: 20): 'I want to try to write on the Old Testament without looking at it through Christian lenses or even New Testament lenses.' He does reserve a place for reading the OT in the light of the NT, as long as one recognizes the need to read the NT in the light of the OT, as well.

¹⁰ See Seitz (2001: 103–116; 2011), who persuasively points to how the OT, and especially Isaiah, was the early church's scriptural witness to Jesus Christ.

¹¹ Vanhoozer 2006: 71. For an introduction to the theological interpretation of Scripture, see Treier 2008; Vanhoozer 2005a.

kingdom is fundamental to Isaiah when understood within its OT context, the interspersed canonical reflections will assist those who are wrestling with how Isaiah might be read as Christian scripture in and for the church.[12] I expect that scholars will benefit from this book, but the primary audiences I have in mind are pastors and students engaged in biblical and theological training.[13]

Biblical theology

How does our study fit within biblical theology? The history and challenges of biblical theology have been traced repeatedly and need not occupy our attention here.[14] Boda's definition is a sufficient starting point: 'Biblical theology is a theological discipline that reflects on the theological witness of the Bible in its own idiom with attention to both its unity and diversity.'[15] Reflections on several elements in Boda's definition will set the stage for our investigation.

Biblical theology is a 'theological discipline'. While affirming that the Bible is theological (it reveals God), biblical theology is a human enterprise – a discipline – that attempts to describe what the Bible has to say about God. In this sense, biblical theology is 'extrabiblical', 'extra-textual'. As Möller observes, biblical theology is really 'second-level discourse' based upon 'first-level discourse' (the Bible).[16] While biblical theology aims to ring true to what one finds in Scripture, it is nonetheless a productive endeavour, producing discourse of a different order. By using the 'kingdom schema' I recognize that I am offering my own non-exhaustive and provisional avenue for understanding Isaiah's message. The goal of these suggested avenues is to 'enable readers to navigate the biblical landscape [of Isaiah] in all its stunning beauty and surprising (and perhaps even frustrating) jaggedness'.[17] As the preface of this series states, 'Above all, these monographs are creative attempts to help thinking Christians understand their Bibles better.'

---

[12] Seitz 2001; 2011.

[13] Readers will find the approach here to be different from Goldingay's (2014) concise and helpful introduction to the theology of Isaiah. He makes little attempt to integrate the theology of Isaiah around one concept, so our studies complement one another.

[14] For a thorough overview, see Barr 1999. For a brief, recent overview with an evangelical focus, see Köstenberger 2012.

[15] Boda 2012: 122–123.

[16] Möller 2004: 60.

[17] Ibid. 62.

Along with being a human enterprise, biblical theology aims to use the Bible's 'own idiom'.[18] The qualifier 'own idiom' is probably more contrastive and idealistic than descriptive and realistic.[19] In the attempt to follow the Bible's own idiom, biblical theologians contrast their work with systematic theology by focusing on the dynamics in the biblical text rather than repackaging them in the light of contemporary questions and the logical categories of systematic theology.[20] Most biblical theologians, however, recognize that they are still producing second-level discourse, while aiming to ring true to how the Bible presents its own message. One can never attain the lofty ambition of using only the Bible's own idiom; otherwise all one could do is quote Scripture.[21] Nevertheless, the decision to use 'kingdom' in this study derives from the conviction that the notion stems from Isaiah itself, its own idiom if you will, while recognizing that this study remains second-level discourse.

Biblical theology also pays attention to the Bible's 'unity and diversity'. On the one hand, with the triune God as the Bible's unifying centre, one rightly expects to find unity within the Bible. Additionally, since the book of Isaiah was arranged intentionally, a reader can rightly expect to establish networks of coherence between texts across a book for conceptualizing its message. On the other hand, the complexity of this triune God's work through various phases in redemptive history, discontinuities between the testaments, and the diversity of ideas within each biblical book and corpus call for recognizing the Bible's diversity amid its unity. Does Isaiah give a uniform portrayal of God as king? Do the different parts of Isaiah offer identical messages about Davidic kingship? Is the use of the 'kingdom of God' in the Gospels the mould within which the kingdom of God in Isaiah must fit? As we utilize the concept of 'kingdom' to integrate various themes in Isaiah, preserving what each topic and relevant passage uniquely offers will be prioritized. A good 'biblical theology' should

---

[18] Bartholomew (2004: 1) emphasizes this when he states, 'Biblical theology is, in my opinion, the attempt to grasp Scripture in its totality *according to its own, rather than imposed, categories*' (my emphasis).

[19] Barr 1999: 6. Watson (1997: 2–9), however, challenges whether a division between biblical and systematic theology is legitimate. This distinction traces back to the 1797 lecture by Gabler (2004).

[20] Scobie 1991: 50–51. Shead's (2012) study in this series does branch into doctrinal discussion on inspiration in the light of Jeremiah.

[21] Möller 2004: 56. C. J. H. Wright (2006: 68–69) introduces the metaphor of a map: maps do not reproduce the world exactly as it is in all of its dimensions, but a map 'provide[s] a way of seeing the whole terrain, a way of navigating one's way through it, a way of observing what is most significant'.

be more like a menu at a restaurant than a puree soup. In a puree soup many vegetables are blended together to such an extent that each vegetable is unidentifiable to the eye, with the most colourful vegetable becoming the dominant hue. There is danger in harmonizing passages in Isaiah and between Isaiah and the larger biblical canon to such an extent that the unique contributions of Isaiah's witness are erased. This is why a 'menu' analogy is preferable. On a menu, each dish has the signature of the restaurant (unity) and is strategically chosen in the light of how it corresponds with the other items on offer, yet its distinctness from other dishes both in terms of its place on the menu and its ingredients is still quite apparent (diversity). The aim of this study is to treat themes related to 'kingdom' in Isaiah in such a way that unity and diversity are maintained within Isaiah and the canon.

A final observation on biblical theology is related to the preface to this series. The second of three noted contribution areas for this series is 'the articulation and exposition of the structure of thought of a particular biblical writer or corpus'. Though this study pays some attention to how passages and themes in Isaiah fit within the canon, the bulk of our focus will be upon the book of Isaiah.

In summary, under the purview of biblical theology, our study is second-level discourse that uses kingdom, a concept from Isaiah, as a means of approaching the unified and diverse theology in the book of Isaiah with an eye towards its role in the canon.

Approaching Isaiah and kingdom

The two most prominent approaches that scholars adopt in studying Isaiah are *diachronic* and *synchronic*.[22] A *diachronic* (through time) approach attempts to provide historical classifications of texts in Isaiah and explain the historical process by which these texts were gathered and organized (redaction). Generally speaking, there are two main diachronic explanations of Isaiah's formation. One explanation holds that the prophecies in Isaiah derive almost entirely from the eighth-century prophet and were arranged by the hand of the prophet or by later editors into book form.[23] Another explanation, which is the

---

[22] For an overview of scholarly approaches, see Stromberg 2011a. One may add what Gorman (2009: 17–23) calls 'an existential approach' within which he groups theological interpretation and ideological readings.

[23] An example of this is Wegner's (1992a) study on human kingship in Isa. 1 – 35, where he tries to determine the historical origin of a given passage and then the editorial process by which it came to be placed where it is in the book.

critical consensus, is that the book of Isaiah contains some prophecies from the eighth-century prophet, along with writings from other authors from the later pre-exilic, exilic and post-exilic eras. While the latter view has been popularized into a schema of three books (1 – 39; 40 – 55; 56 – 66), three eras (pre-exilic, exilic, post-exilic) and three prophetic figures (First Isaiah, Deutero-Isaiah, Third Isaiah), theories are far more complex, with scholars arguing for many hands at work in every section of the book over many centuries.[24] The aim of the *diachronic* approach, among both conservative and critical explanations, is to uncover the historical process behind how the various passages originated and then came to be part of the book of Isaiah.

A *synchronic* approach interprets a work of literature as a literary whole, without probing its historic formation. Conrad is the most extreme advocate of this approach. He argues that a *synchronic* reading 'relat[es] parts of the text not to a world external to it (its historical background or its history of literary development) but to the literary world of the text itself'.[25] Though Conrad's sensitivity to the literary dimensions of the text and his prioritization of the literary context in interpretation is compelling, his disregard for the role of historical and cultural contexts surrounding the text is questionable. Darr's synchronic approach is more moderate, as she allows historical information to inform one's reading because all texts are produced in historical contexts;[26] texts invite readers to draw upon historical settings for understanding. *Synchronic* approaches to Isaiah have uncovered strategic networks of literary association throughout the book that contribute to the book's coherence.[27]

While *diachronic* approaches have their place in the field of biblical studies, a *synchronic* (literary) approach will be used here.[28] A

---

[24] E.g. P. A. Smith's (1995) theory on the formation of Isa. 56 – 66 identifies four sources that make up 'Trito-Isaiah', which is tame compared to Steck's (1991) explanation of Isa. 56 – 66 as the product of many sources that came to completion during the Greek era. For strategic insertion of materials into earlier parts of the book and on writing with conscious awareness of earlier prophecy, see Rendtorff 1993c: 181–189; 1993a: 146–169; Stromberg 2011b; Williamson 1994.

[25] Conrad 1991: 20.

[26] Darr 1994: 25.

[27] Along with Conrad and Darr, see helpful introductions to synchronic studies of Isaiah by Webb (1990) and Schultz (2005).

[28] Scholars often fuse the two approaches together. On the theme of justice, see Leclerc 2001. In this volume I will often avoid saying 'Isaiah says', primarily because I want to recognize the important role that the later authors/redactors played in arranging the oracles into book form over a long period of time. My primary interest is in what the book in its final form may be communicating in view of the arrangement of its materials.

synchronic approach is more akin to how the original recipients of the book would have read Isaiah. The faith community would not have read Isaiah with an interest in diachronic development.[29] Even if the book of Isaiah contains many passages from various phases of an individual prophet's ministry or from many different authors throughout many eras (views impossible to prove or disprove decisively), the original setting of each isolated prophecy has been removed and the possible fingerprints of other prophets are now gone. The book itself names only one prophet in its superscript (1:1). This results in the book's being presented as a literary whole, with God's speaking through Isaiah to address the Assyrian, Babylonian and Persian eras, even through to the eschaton. Furthermore, the logic internal to the book is that God is able to speak of events before they come about as proof of his exclusivity among the gods (e.g. Isa. 41:21–29; 45:21; 48:3–8). The book itself invites readers to interpret it as God's voice through Isaiah to various eras, as impossible as this may seem. This is why Ben Sira c. 200 BC could speak in the following way about Isaiah's ministry:

> For Hezekiah did what was right and held fast to the paths of David, as ordered by the illustrious prophet Isaiah, who saw truth in visions. In his lifetime he turned back the sun and prolonged the life of the king. By his powerful spirit he looked into the future and consoled the mourners of Zion; He foretold what would happen till the end of time, hidden things yet to be fulfilled. (Sirach 48.22–25)

Ben Sira speaks of how Isaiah addresses pre-exilic times with Hezekiah (c. 700 BC), exilic times following Zion's destruction by Babylon (post-586 BC), and the 'end of time'. It seems optimal, then, to employ a synchronic approach in this study of Isaiah as we seek to synthesize the theology communicated in the final form of the book.[30]

This does not mean that history is unimportant in a synchronic reading of Isaiah. While setting aside questions concerning the historical process behind the book's composition, the book itself invites us to adopt a particular view of history.[31] Isaiah 1 – 39 is set primarily

---

[29] Williamson 1999: 194; Steck 2000: 29.

[30] My claim is not that the formation of the book of Isaiah was insignificant theologically, as God himself was guiding the editors of the book to arrange the materials as they are. The challenge is that this process is impossible to reconstruct and that the final form of the book has little interest in unveiling the process.

[31] For a similar argument on the Book of the Twelve, see Seitz 2007: 189–219.

in the Assyrian era,[32] where God uses Assyria to judge Israel and Judah while also anticipating Assyria's own experience of judgment (Isa. 10), which will result in YHWH's using Babylon to take Jerusalem into exile (Isa. 39). Isaiah 40 – 55 primarily addresses a context following Jerusalem's fall at the hands of Babylon with an eye towards God's using a Persian king (Cyrus) to rebuild Zion (Isa. 44 – 45). Isaiah 56 – 66 wrestles with exilic and perhaps post-exilic concerns in the light of the eschaton. This results in a general impression of temporal movement in Isaiah (see the figure below).

Assyrian era → Babylonian era → Persian era → Eschatological era[33]

This establishes what Steck refers to as a 'metahistory' whereby future readers discern in historical addresses to the Assyrian, Babylonian and Persian eras patterns of divine and human action that will recur until the eschaton.[34] Similarly, Seitz argues that Zion's lack of final restoration at the close of the book leaves Isaiah's message open, enabling later readers to identify their place within the story of God's unfolding word.[35] Our approach to Isaiah, then, is to read it in its final form while being mindful that the book itself establishes a 'metahistory' through which future readers appropriate its message about God's recurring ways in the light of where they fit within Isaiah's narrative.

Overview of the book

As we venture into our study, here is an overview of what is to come. Chapters 1–3 will argue that God's rule is central to the three major sections of Isaiah. Within Isaiah 1 – 39 a vision of the holy king who must judge Judah (ch. 6), an eschatological scene of God's rule on Zion resulting in cosmic judgment (24:21–23) and an international feast (25:6–8), the hope of seeing the king in his beauty (33:17, 22), and a historical account of YHWH defeating Sennacherib (chs. 36–37) sit strategically within the subsections of Isaiah 1 – 39 (1 – 12;

---

[32] There are, of course, numerous passages that envisage different eras in Isa. 1 – 39 (2:2–4; 4:2–6; 12:1–6; 13 – 14; 24 – 27; 34 – 35), but the repeated mention of Assyria and its kings along with the historical narratives of Isa. 7 and 36 – 38 provide ample support for Assyria's being the prominent setting for Isa. 1 – 39.

[33] For helpful overviews of these historical periods, see Kelle 2012: 402–417; Provan, Long and Longman 2003: 266–303; Miller and Hayes 2006: 360–540.

[34] Steck 2000: 20–65.

[35] Seitz 1988: 123.

13 – 27; 28 – 33; 34 – 39) to establish God's kingship as an integral part of the first half of the book. Within Isaiah 40 – 55 God's kingship is also extremely important, as an arch from 40:9–11 and 52:7 presents the gospel of God's coming reign as king as fundamental to this section of the book. Within Isaiah 56 – 66 God's kingship is at the centre of its chiastic arrangement, where there is the expectation that upon coming as a warrior king (59:15–20; 63:1–6) God will reside as an international King of glory in Zion where he will receive tribute from all nations (60 – 62). The book concludes on a similar note in Isaiah 66:1–2 and 18–24 by presenting God as the cosmic king who will reign in Zion, with all nations journeying to his glory. The strategic placement of passages pertaining to God's kingship within the major sections of Isaiah places a spotlight on God as the king in Isaiah, both now and in the future.

Chapter 4 will probe how God's lead agents fit into Isaiah's vision of the kingdom. With each section of the book firmly anchored in God's kingship, lead agents in establishing and maintaining the divine king's ideals arise. In Isaiah 1 – 39 the Davidic ruler (9:1–7; 11:1–10; 16:5; 32:1) is God's leading agent who promotes justice and righteousness through God's empowering Spirit. In Isaiah 40 – 55 the servant of the Lord (49:1–7; 50:3–9; 52:13 – 53:12) takes up the mantle of Israel (42:1–4), the faltering servant nation, and brings light to Israel and the nations through suffering sacrificially to restore humanity to God. In Isaiah 56 – 66 the Spirit empowers an anointed messenger (61:1–3) to proclaim comfort to the disenfranchised as God's kingdom is about to break into the world. These are three distinct agents of God who will carry out unique tasks in the promotion of God's kingdom.

Chapter 5 will investigate how the realm and the people of God's kingdom intertwine. The realm of God's kingdom should be understood from a bifocal perspective. God's reign is everywhere, since heaven is his throne and the earth is his footstool (66:1). Yet God's reign is particularized in Zion, the hub of an international kingdom. The people of God who inhabit these realms will consist of people from Israel and the nations who have experienced God's salvation and who obey God through practising justice. A conclusion will ponder the kingdom vision that Isaiah invites us to imagine.

The kingdom theme currently enjoys much attention among evangelicals. Numerous recent 'whole Bible' biblical theologies employ 'kingdom' as a central paradigm for conceptualizing the Bible's message.[36] Furthermore, the provocative and inspiring books by J. K. A. Smith *Desiring the Kingdom* and *Imagining the Kingdom* have catapulted kingdom back into liturgical practice. Smith challenges readers to recognize that the imagination is integral for becoming those who desire the kingdom: 'We become a people who *desire* the kingdom (or some other, rival version of "the kingdom") insofar as we are a people who have been trained to *imagine* the kingdom in a certain way.'[37] For Smith, it is through aesthetics, not simply propositional knowledge, that one comes first to 'imagine' and then to desire the kingdom. The prophets would agree, though surely retaining a place for propositional knowledge too. It is through poetry and narrative that Isaiah's kingdom message confronts and dismantles imagined rival kingdoms and entices us to imagine the true kingdom of God and trust him as king. My hope is that this study will contribute in some small way to the recovery of how Isaiah contributes to the biblical vision of God's kingdom.

[36] Goldsworthy 1981; Bartholomew and Goheen 2004; Gentry and Wellum 2012; Morgan and Peterson 2012.
[37] J. K. A. Smith 2013: 125, emphases original.

Chapter One

God, the king now and to come in Isaiah 1 – 39

After preaching from Isaiah 6, I vividly remember a very spiritual woman – the sort who raises her hands in praise, even in a reformed Anglican church – thanking me for my sermon. When I asked her what she found helpful, her answer surprised me. She said, 'I don't often think about God in his greatness. I usually think of God as a friend, which is true, but it is so helpful to step back and see God in his greatness, as the holy king.' This godly woman's honest comment captures my own experience, and also the reason why I have been attracted to the book of Isaiah. Since I naturally gravitate towards the comfort of God's immanence in Christ, I have found that a regular diet of passages that speak of God's transcendence expands my view of God and reminds me that the God who is near is also the holy king of the universe.

In the time of Isaiah, as well as in our own, orienting God's people around God as king was vital. Without a king, there is no kingdom. If this king fails to capture the allegiance of the people, the kingdom disintegrates. The book of Isaiah endeavours to orient the allegiance of its readers around a king, namely YHWH. As we work our way through important passages (6, 24 – 25, 33, 36 – 37) pertaining to God's kingship from Isaiah 1 – 39 in this chapter, and from 40 – 55 and 56 – 66 in subsequent chapters, we will find our view of God, and indeed our view of him as king, becoming more well rounded and nuanced. God's kingship in Isaiah 1 – 39 takes on many different textures and temporal frames. Some passages depict God's kingship through narrative (Isa. 6; 36 – 37), and others through poetry (24 – 25; 33). Some texts place more weight upon God as a king who judges (Isa. 6; 24), and others upon God as a king who saves (25; 33; 36 – 37). A variety of imagery – palatial (Isa. 6), banqueting (25:6–8) and political (36 – 37) – is utilized to portray YHWH as king. Some passages have more of an eighth-century outlook (Isa. 6; 36 – 37), and others are more eschatological in nature (24 – 25; 33). Just as a lawyer may use different lines of evidence to make a case, so Isaiah 1 – 39 argues for YHWH's supreme sovereignty from a variety of angles to impress a wide-ranging sense of God's kingship upon the hearts and minds of its readers.

The holy king in Isaiah 6

While other passages in Isaiah direct our gaze to YHWH's future reign or assuage wounded souls with comforting assurances that YHWH will save, the vision of YHWH as king in Isaiah 6 is far more disconcerting, far more unsettling, a present reality that one cannot ignore. Since this terrifying and purifying vision of the holy king is set strategically at the heart of the opening section of the book (Isa. 1 – 12), it is not an overstatement to claim that the book of Isaiah wants to humble us before God's throne from the start, establishing a gateway into the rest of the book through a recognition of the present reign of a holy king. Why is this important? The vision of YHWH as a holy king casts *narrative* light upon the five poetic chapters that open the book. The story of Isaiah's vision enables readers to receive the book's message of judgment and hope. How can an audience tolerate God's depicting his people as being stupider than an ox or donkey (1:3), as a prostitute (1:21), enemies (1:24) or a vineyard producing putrid grapes (5:1–7)? How can they bear the thought of God's starving his city amid a blockade (3:1), coming in such fury that people will try to hide in caves (2:19) or using a foreign empire like a rod to punish his own people (10:5)? The vision of the holy king in Isaiah 6 grants a glimpse of God, albeit terrifying with a lining of hope, that not only enables us to make (some) sense of God's difficult words in the book, but also invites us to examine ourselves personally and corporately and to revere the holy king who stands behind the utterances in Isaiah 1 – 12 and the entire book.

A vision of the king

During a time when an earthly king, Uzziah, takes his final breath (6:1; 740 BC) and when a distant and ancient kingdom, Assyria, is again on the rise under Tiglath-pileser III,[1] Isaiah reports, 'I saw the Lord' (6:1b).[2] This verb of perception piques our interest, inviting us

---

[1] On the Assyrian threat in this context, see Isa. 5:26–30; 7:17–18, 20; 8:4, 7.

[2] I divide Isa. 6 between vv. 1–7 and 8–13 due to the transition from 'seeing' to 'hearing' (Beuken 2004: 74; Oswalt 1986). See alternatives in Magonet 1986: 94–95; Sweeney 1996: 132–134. Some argue that all of ch. 6 may date to the eighth century (Evans 1986; Seitz 1993: 59; Sweeney 1996: 138–139); others assign parts of the passage to pre-exilic (vv. 1–11), exilic (vv. 12–13a) and post-exilic (v. 13b) sources (Beuken 2003: 164).

to join in perceiving what was seen, now through the written word. The first four verses attempt to portray this ineffable vision. The account begins with the 'who', the main focus of what Isaiah saw: 'the Lord'. While those reading in English might quickly bypass 'Lord', the use of 'Lord' (*'ădōnāy*), not 'LORD' (*yhwh*), is telling. Having just set this vision during the death year of a 'king' (*melek*), the prophet uses the title 'Lord' to highlight God's sovereignty.[3] In fact, six of the seven titles for God in Isaiah 6 derive from the domain of dominion, indicating that the choice of 'Lord' in 6:1 is not incidental.[4] This is a vision and a message about God, the sovereign Lord, during a time when a human king was dying or had died.

The 'Lord' is 'sitting upon a throne' (6:1). Sitting upon a throne is a common expression of royal authority.[5] For example, when Zimri assassinates King Elah, son of Baasha, he 'seated himself on his throne' (1 Kgs 16:11) to signal his new-found power (cf. 2 Kgs 11:19). Another instance of this is when kings Ahab of Israel and Jehoshaphat of Judah meet together: they both sit on thrones while dressed in their royal garb to indicate that both kings remain equally in power (1 Kgs 22:10). Ironically, in that same chapter, a prophet named Micaiah has a vision very similar to Isaiah's: 'I saw the LORD sitting on his throne' (1 Kgs 22:19). Similar to Isaiah's contrast with King Uzziah, Micaiah's vision of God sitting upon a throne rhetorically contrasts with the presumed authorities seated on their thrones (22:10) – Ahab and Jehoshaphat – who are destined for judgment. Unique to Isaiah, however, is the use of 'Lord' (*'ădōnāy*) rather than 'LORD' (*yhwh*; 1 Kgs 22:19) to name the one on the throne. This highlights the rhetorical emphasis of Isaiah 6 to capture YHWH's sovereign kingship further. Referring to God as sitting upon the throne is not unique to Isaiah and 1 Kings, as the Psalms (47:8[9]; cf. 9:4[5], 7[8]) and Lamentations (5:19) do so as well.

'Sitting upon a throne' does more than indicate a king who is in power. The throne is the place for executing judgment. As Brettler puts it, 'God's throne is specifically associated with his role as judge.'[6] On several occasions Psalms speaks of God's 'throne' (*kisē'*) as a place of 'judgment' (*mišpāṭ*):[7]

---

[3] On the correspondence between a human *'ădōnāy* and YHWH, see Brettler 1989: 40–44.

[4] Lind (1997: 320) suggests that Isaiah is the 'first to use [Lord] freely of Yahweh'.

[5] Occasionally, priests sit upon a throne (1 Sam. 1:9; 4:13). On the throne and royalty, see Brettler 1989: 81–85.

[6] Ibid. 82.

[7] See also Pss 89:14[15]; 97:2. See Knierim (1968: 54–55), who notes Pss 11:4–7; 45:6–7; 82:8; 98:9; 1 Kgs 22:19; Dan. 7:9; Amos 1:2; Mal. 3:1–5.

> you have sat on the throne, giving righteous judgment.
> (Ps. 9:4[5])[8]

> But the LORD sits enthroned for ever,
> he has established his throne for judgement.
> (Ps. 9:7[8], NRSV)

The same intersection of the throne and judgment occurs in the realm of human kingship as well:

> There thrones for judgement were set,
> the thrones of the house of David.
> (Ps. 122:5; cf. Prov. 20:8)

> And he made the Hall of the Throne where he was to pronounce judgement, even the Hall of Judgement. (1 Kgs 7:7; cf. 1 Kgs 10:9; 2 Chr. 9:8)

Similarly, the book of Isaiah regularly associates the *throne* of the Davidic king with the role of executing justice (9:7[6]; 16:5; cf. Jer. 22:2).[9] Sitting on a throne, then, can connote a context where the sovereign power is about to execute judgment. In this way, the throne signals the place from which the authority of the office of king is, or at least should be, carried out. Isaiah's vision of the Lord sitting upon a throne is not a generic statement that YHWH is king; fundamental to this vision is that the king is about to exact judgment.

The descriptors 'high and lifted up; and the train of his robe filled the temple' (6:1b) heighten this royal portrait. In his extensive study on throne imagery in the ANE, Metzger (1985) details how tiered platforms were often built to elevate a throne to the highest point within a royal or temple dwelling. This conveyed the power of the ruler or deity. As Blenkinsopp notes, 'Perhaps the author had in mind something similar to the depiction of Assyrian kings of gigantic proportions compared to those of pygmy size who attended them or the prisoners paraded before them.'[10] With Isaiah's seeing the hem of his *robe* filling the temple, which itself resembles a royal house,[11] Metzger suggests that Isaiah 6 presents YHWH's throne as towering even over

---

[8] All Scripture citations are from the ESV, unless otherwise noted.
[9] On the divine king as judge, see Brettler 1989: 44–45, 81–85, esp. 109–116.
[10] Blenkinsopp 2000: 225.
[11] Brettler 1989: 90–92. See 1 Kgs 7:1–12; 9:1; 21:1.

the temple itself, with the tip of the robe filling it.[12] While it is unclear if Isaiah 6 envisages the throne to be towering over the temple or if the throne is towering within the temple,[13] the description of the throne as 'high and lifted up' conveys the supremacy of the one sitting upon it – the Lord.

Isaiah goes on to describe what was taking place around the throne: 'Above him stood the seraphim.' Three points about the seraphim are relevant here. First, the use of 'seraph' probably brings to mind judgment, which the verbal root *śārap* (to burn) may imply. In Numbers 21 seraphim were snake-like figures sent to bite the people of Israel, leading to the death of many (21:6, 8). Later in Isaiah 14:29 and 30:6, a seraph is also pictured as a snake bringing destruction; these snakes, however, are able to fly, just as in Isaiah 6:2. Since punishment accompanies every mention of seraphim in the OT, this vision of seraphim would send shivers down one's spine: judgment is looming. Second, though seraphim are rare in the OT, the imagery of winged creatures around the throne of a deity or king is common throughout the ANE and surfaces with the cherubim in the OT.[14] Metzger identifies three roles for these winged creatures in the ANE: (1) destroyers of enemies, (2) destroyers of the unsuspecting, and (3) protectors of what is important.[15] The first and last of these roles may be called to mind here. If 14:29 and 30:6 are any indication, these seraphim will be agents of judgment. This is confirmed by referring to these creatures as seraphim when one would expect cherubim, for it is the cherubim who surround the ark as pointers to the heavenly reality (cf. Exod. 24:10; 25:9).[16] The seraphim are also protectors of the sancta, as is evident when they purify Isaiah. Thus the seraphim present a sense of danger here, as guardians of the holy and agents of judgment.

It is worth pausing at this point to ask, what have we actually been able to see? While Isaiah 6:1 says, 'I saw the Lord', the account describes no feature of God, aside from noting his hem, having a centrifugal focus on features surrounding the king.[17] Though we are

---

[12] Metzger 1985: 349.

[13] Knierim (1968: 53–54) argues that reference to YHWH's throne 'belongs to the conception of Yahwe as king of heaven' because of references to the king of heaven in the OT (1 Kgs 22:19; Pss 82:1; 89:6–8) and similarities in Canaanite myths.

[14] For images of cherubim around thrones, see Mettinger 1982: 114–115.

[15] E.g. Exod. 25:18–22; Num. 7:89; 1 Sam. 4:4; 1 Kgs 6:23–35; Pss 80:1[2]; 99:1; Ezek. 10. Metzger 1985: 320–321; Beuken 2003: 171; Sweeney 1996: 139.

[16] Irsigler 1991: 141.

[17] Landy 1999: 61–62.

prepared to see YHWH, the depiction blocks a direct glimpse of him. Even the seraphim hovering around the Holy One veil their faces with their wings (6:2). This results in a 'converg[ence] in the reader's imagination, to emphasise the gap between the seraphim and God and the seraphim and ourselves'.[18] Isaiah 6 offers more of a 'sense' of the Lord through envisioning what is transpiring around him than an actual description of the Lord. As Moberly explains, 'Isaiah's vision is of YHWH as king – though with characteristic Hebrew reserve the account makes no attempt to depict YHWH in himself, for YHWH is primarily depicted by what is seen and said around him.'[19] We learn about the king by sensing the need of being shielded from his person and by considering the splendid, yet alarming, features around him.

The cry of the seraph maintains a focus on the nature of the one on the throne: 'Holy, holy, holy is the LORD of hosts' (6:3). The threefold declaration – unique within the OT and thus highlighting how superlative YHWH is – of the Lord's holiness emphasizes the incomparable, inexhaustible and incomprehensible nature of YHWH. With God's kingship already in mind from 6:1–2, this declaration by the seraphim conveys that 'God's kingship entails his holiness.'[20] While holiness is often defined as having the quality of being 'set apart' or 'other', this is just one aspect of a more complex reality. Holiness is a quality that belongs exclusively to God, whereby the holiness of any other person or object is derivative from being in relation to the Holy One, the source of holiness.[21] Furthermore, the Lord's holiness is active, not merely static. As Wildberger states, 'Yahweh's holiness is a completely dynamic reality, not a static "quality". It is seen in action when it destroys all the opposition which human beings set up over against God.'[22] By declaring that YHWH is thrice-holy the seraphim are exclaiming that holiness is so essential to YHWH's very being that not only are they in danger while in his presence – as is evident in their covering their eyes and feet – but they are moved to extol him because of it. Isaiah's exposure to such a sight moves him to acknowledge that he and the people are 'unclean' (*ṭāmē*; 6:5), a term often contrasted with holiness.[23] This distinctively

---

[18] Ibid. 64.
[19] Moberly 2003: 124.
[20] Ibid. 126.
[21] See Hartley (2003: 420–431, esp. 420) for an evaluation of defining holiness as separation. See also Naudé 1997: 3:877–887.
[22] Wildberger 1991: 266.
[23] Naudé 1997: 3:878. Cf. Isa. 52:1.

marks the rest of Isaiah's message, as references to YHWH as 'the Holy One of Israel' recur throughout the book. As Oswalt notes, 'Whatever else this experience did for Isaiah, it convinces him that God alone is holy.'[24]

The title used by the seraphim for the one extolled as holy, holy, holy is 'LORD of hosts' (*yhwh ṣĕbā'ôt*). This title occurs 259 times in the OT, with 237 of them occurring in the latter prophets, though curiously with no uses in Ezekiel. Williamson notes that the title 'was associated with the notion of God as king, dwelling enthroned in his royal palace',[25] and can be associated with ark traditions.[26] Similarly, Mettinger notes how *yhwh ṣĕbā'ôt* may derive from an understanding of YHWH's rule over the heavenly council.[27] In the case of Isaiah 6 the heavenly court is clearly present when YHWH asks whom to send (6:8). This parallels the presence of a king amid a royal court.[28]

Not only does the title 'LORD of hosts' emphasize YHWH's rule, but the second half of verse 3, 'the whole earth is full of his glory', does too. Lind argues that the reference to glory 'belongs to the word-field of human and divine kingship' in the light of Psalm 21:5[6].[29] There are numerous places throughout the OT where kingship intersects with glory. One thinks, for example of the five uses of 'king of glory' in Psalm 24:7–10. In Isaiah it is said that God will bring 'the king of Assyria and all his glory' to judge his people (8:7). In 24:23 'the LORD of hosts reigns [*mālak*] . . . and his glory will be before his elders'. The announcement that YHWH's glory fills the earth in 6:3 highlights the prominence, or weightiness, of the king's splendour, which pervades all of creation. The seraphim cannot help but shout about this. By drawing us into the vision, though, the implication is not necessarily that we join in these shouts immediately. Initially, as one sees in Isaiah's own response, the aim of these words of the seraphim is to force us to encounter, be struck by and reckon with God's holiness and the extent of his glory. It will only be as we come to terms with and find resolution concerning our own uncleanness in the presence of the Holy One that the words of the seraphim can resound from our lips.

[24] Oswalt 1986: 180.
[25] Williamson 2006: 72.
[26] Lind 1997: 319.
[27] Mettinger 1982: 123–128.
[28] Brettler 1989: 103.
[29] Lind 1997: 319.

The cries of the seraphim are so great that the posts of the temple are shaking (6:4). Simultaneously, smoke fills the temple. This 'smoke' (*'āšān*) is not to be confused with cultic incense or the aroma of burning sacrifices in the temple; the term *'āšān* is never used in a cultic sense elsewhere in the OT.[30] Instead, *'āšān* is a common symbol for God's theophanic presence (e.g. Exod. 19:18; 20:18; Ps. 104:32; Isa. 4:5) or his anger (e.g. 2 Sam. 22:9; cf. Ps. 74:1; Isa. 14:31; 34:10; 65:5; Joel 3:3; Nah. 2:13). It is likely, then, that a reader would associate this smoke with God's weighty presence in the temple, as it was upon Sinai, and perhaps even his anger which could break out like fire (cf. Isa. 10:17). This is now our third occurrence of the root for 'filling' (*ml'*), giving a sense of the expansiveness of YHWH. His majesty is so extensive that his robe fills the temple (6:1), his glory pervades all of creation (6:3), and smoke fills the temple (6:4).[31] God is so great that he is all encompassing, filling all with which he is in contact.

Before we consider Isaiah's response (6:5–7), the overall impression of this vision can be summarized. The two titles used for God in 6:1–4 are 'Lord' (*'ǎdōnāy*) and 'LORD of hosts' (*yhwh ṣěbā'ôt*); both belong to the sphere of royal sovereignty. The depiction of his 'sitting upon the throne' and the mention of his 'glory' also signal an emphasis on YHWH's kingship. This is not, however, a neutral vision of a divine king. This portrayal is infused with overtones of impending judgment: the throne is where judgment issues forth; seraphim are dangerous protectors of a holy God, even agents in judgment; YHWH's absolute holiness demands purging; smoke is filling the temple. A cosmic king, utterly holy, is on the brink of breaking forth in purifying judgment.

The prophet's response to this encounter is fitting: 'Woe is me!' (6:5). A vision of the Holy One does not result merely in meditative awe. God's holiness creates a crisis for Isaiah; it demands personal and corporate assessment. His unclean lips and those of his people place them all in grave danger. The prophet's ultimate reasoning behind his woeful status becomes apparent at the end of verse 5. The Hebrew word order of this clause is significant as is reflected in my word-for-word translation: 'for the king, the LORD of hosts, my eyes have seen'.

---

[30] A cultic context could come to mind through the coal coming from the altar (6:6).
[31] The use of 'full' in 6:3 contrasts with the empty land in 6:12 (Magonet 1986: 92–93).

Typical Hebrew word order would place either the verb or the subject first ('my eyes have seen') in a clause, but here the object, 'the King, the LORD of hosts', occurs first for emphasis. For the first time in Isaiah 6 and the book of Isaiah, YHWH receives the title 'King'.[32] This is a fitting title in the light of Isaiah 6:1–4. By using the appellation 'the King [*hammelek*] the LORD of hosts [*yhwh ṣĕbā'ôt*]', a contrast occurs with the opening of chapter 6, which places the vision during the year when 'the King [*hammelek*], Uzziah' died. This contrast highlights YHWH's eternal, unchanging nature, over against Uzziah's transience. Though the death of *hammelek* Uzziah (6:1) threatens the nation's stability, the reign of *hammelek*, the Lord of hosts (6:5), is unthreatened and immovable.[33] Not only do 6:1 and 6:5 share the term *hammelek*; they both use the verb *rā'â* (to see): 'I saw the Lord . . . my eyes have seen the King' (6:1, 5). These statements frame verses 1–5 to conceptualize the vision: seeing God as king (*'ădōnây*; *hammelek*).[34] Isaiah's short statement explains why he is undone, interprets what he saw in 6:1–4, and hence the impression a reader should take away – that YHWH is king.[35]

Tension within this narrative is at its height in Isaiah 6:5. What will the outcome be for Isaiah? Along with the prophet's individual predicament, the people are in grave danger too, even though the people have not seen this king. In a surprising move, one of the seraphim touches Isaiah's lips with a burning coal, signifying the atoning of his sin (6:6–7).[36] This glimmer of hope quickly fades in the second half of this chapter, after the shift from seeing (6:1–7) to hearing (6:8–13). Isaiah can now hear 'the Lord ['*ădōnây*]', and he receives a commission to speak to a people, who unlike Isaiah will neither hear nor see (6:9) – judgment is set against this people. In fact, when Isaiah asks the 'Lord ['*ădōnây*]' how long the people are condemned to unreceptivity, the answer is bleak: it will last until cities, houses and the land become desolate (6:11–12). It is fixed; the holy Lord is bent on bringing desolation and exile to his people and his land. The danger Isaiah sensed when he saw the king will become a reality, and he will participate in the process as a prophet who

---

[32] Isa. 6:5 could be the earliest use of *melek* for YHWH in the OT, though the concept has a long prehistory. See Irsigler 1991: 128; Eissfeldt 1962a: 192–193.

[33] On the longevity of kingship and stability for a people, see Brettler 1989: 50–53.

[34] Irsigler 1991: 130, 133–135.

[35] Beuken 2004: 75; Moberly 2003: 125.

[36] Calvin (1979a: 7.210–211) notes that the seraph symbolizes atonement but is not the author of atonement.

hardens the people. A sliver of hope emerges in the final clause of verse 13, for in the aftermath of various phases of judgment there will be a holy seed, a purified remnant.[37]

While the dramatic narrative of Isaiah's call informs us about the prophet and his mission, its central purpose is to bring readers through the story of the prophet into God's very presence (albeit shielded), the God who stands behind the prophet's awful messages of judgment and condemnation and occasional messages of hope. Purifying judgment will result in a pure remnant. The prominent mode of conceptualizing the ineffable God in Isaiah 6 is through the lens of kingship. As Moberly explains, 'in one way or other the symbolism, assumptions and language of the narrative consistently envisage the kingly nature of YHWH'.[38] Table 1.1, which looks at God as king in Isaiah 6, summarizes the indications in the text that point to God as king.

Table 1.1 God as king in Isaiah 6

Royal titles	Royal surroundings	Royal characteristics
Lord (*'ădōnây*; 6:1, 8, 11)	Throne (6:1)	Issuing judgment (6:9–12)
King (*hammelek*; 6:5)	Seraphim (6:2)	Seeking counsel (6:8)
LORD of hosts (*yhwh ṣĕbā'ôt*; 6:3, 5)	Temple/house (6:1, 4)	Glory (6:3)

Isaiah 6 is crafted to leave an impression that the holy God reigns as the king and that he has decreed purifying judgment. Isaiah's experience of pardon (6:6–7) and the anticipation of a holy remnant (6:13), however, shine like dim stars on a dark night. Through this vision of the thrice-holy Lord (6:1–7) we can understand what we hear (6:8–13); judgment has to come now, initially in the eighth-century BC context and later in the sixth century BC, though glimpses of mercy keep embers of hope aflame, even if barely.

The vision of the king within Isaiah 1 – 12

Isaiah 1 – 12 can be divided into two major sections, chapters 1–5 and 7–12, with chapter 6 operating as a linchpin between them. The

---

[37] Isa. 6:13 is a difficult verse to translate and interpret; see Emerton 1982. Beale (1991) argues that the 'holy seed' in 6:13 is a negative statement concerning how the nation that was supposed to be 'holy' is actually the very pillar of idolatrous practice. While Beale's contention is possible, the remnant motif in the early chapters of Isaiah, particularly in 4:3 where the remnant is called 'holy', seems to have a stronger force in this context, namely God's judgment will result in a purified remnant. For an overview on the remnant in Isaiah, see King 2015.

[38] Moberly 2003: 125.

question now is why the vision of YHWH as a holy king in Isaiah 6 appears where it does. Why not open the book with this vision and prophetic call, akin to Jeremiah and Ezekiel? Answers to this question vary. There are those who argue that Isaiah 6 is not Isaiah's inaugural call, so it does not belong at the start of the book. To cite several interpreters, Calvin thinks Isaiah 1 – 5 consists of oracles from the reign of Uzziah, with the divine encounter in Isaiah 6 affirming Isaiah in his already existent calling amid a lack of success (Isa. 1 – 5).[39] Blenkinsopp, Smith and Williamson believe Isaiah's commission in Isaiah 6 to harden the people is limited to the Syro-Ephraimite crisis depicted in Isaiah 7 – 8.[40] Others argue that Isaiah 6 represents Isaiah's inaugural call and offer various reasons for the chapter's present placement. For example, Oswalt argues that Isaiah 6 plays an important role in answering the question arising from Isaiah 1 – 5 of how God's rebellious people can become a light to the nations (2:2–4). The answer is 'when the experience of Isaiah becomes the experience of the nation'.[41] House maintains that the prophetic call in Isaiah clarifies 'the difficulty of the prophet's message in Isaiah 1–5 and the difficulty of the prophet's ministry in Isaiah 7–12'.[42]

In my estimation it is impossible to determine with certainty whether Isaiah 6 recounts the prophet's inaugural call, a commission to a specific task or an encouragement to continue in the ministry. The role of Isaiah 6 within the final form of the book, however, does not require an answer to this question if its main aim is to introduce its readers to the holy king. Even if Isaiah 6 recounts a commission for a limited phase of the prophet's ministry, the God we encounter in this chapter is the holy king who speaks throughout the book.[43] This is evident with the repeated use of 'Holy One of Israel' as a title for YHWH throughout the book, which is fairly unique to Isaiah.[44] To illustrate the point being made here, one can think of a guest conductor for an orchestra. Even if an orchestra plays only one symphony by Beethoven under that conductor, they would have a sense of that conductor's style, technique and how he or she would

---

[39] Calvin 1979a: 7.198–199.

[40] Williamson 1998b: 84–86; Blenkinsopp 2000: 223; G. V. Smith 2007: 184.

[41] Oswalt 1986: 174–175. I think a reader would be asking a different question: What kind of God would convey such a message of judgment, with a lining of hope?

[42] House 1993: 207–222.

[43] On Isa. 6 within the entire book of Isaiah, see Rendtorff 1993b: 170–180.

[44] 2 Kgs 19:22; Pss 71:22; 78:41; 89:18; Isa. 1:4; 5:19, 24; 10:20; 12:6; 17:7; 29:19; 30:11–12, 15; 31:1; 37:23; 41:14, 16, 20; 43:3, 14; 45:11; 47:4; 48:17; 49:7; 54:5; 55:5; 60:9, 14; Jer. 50:29; 51:5.

interpret other pieces by Beethoven. Similarly, the vision of God in Isaiah 6 leaves an impression concerning the holy king who resides behind all parts of the book, even if the Syro-Ephraimite crisis is the specific focus of Isaiah 6. This makes Isaiah 6 an appropriate point of orientation for understanding the messages found in 1 – 12 and the entire book.

Instead of beginning the book with Isaiah 6, the book wants us to begin by encountering the message of God in the first five chapters. How does Isaiah 6 coordinate with and complement the messages introduced in Isaiah 1 – 5? To begin, it is significant that the vast majority of chapters 1 – 5 is poetic (but cf. 4:2–6). While Hebrew poetry packs a hard punch, it can also be extremely terse and opaque. For this reason narratives are interspersed amid poetic texts from time to time in prophetic literature to establish coherence through narratival perspective (e.g. Jer. 3:6–12, 15–18; Hos. 3; Amos 7:10–15). Isaiah 6 offers an account and vision of YHWH that forces a reader to come more fully to terms with the Holy One (1:4; 5:19, 24), who is speaking throughout the first five chapters. After being assaulted by a diverse array of poetic arsenal in the first five chapters, the narrated account of Isaiah's encounter with the holy king who commissions his prophet to speak such words of judgment enables the reader to grasp the poetic messages better.

It even seems that the materials in Isaiah 1 – 5 have been selectively chosen and arranged to find coherence through the vision of Isaiah 6. The expression 'despised . . . the Holy One of Israel' opens Isaiah 1 (v. 4) and concludes chapter 5 (v. 24).[45]

> Ah, sinful nation,
>> a people laden with iniquity,
> offspring of evildoers,
>> children who deal corruptly!
> They have forsaken the LORD,
>> they have despised the Holy One of Israel,
> they are utterly estranged.
>
> (Isa. 1:4)

> Therefore, as the tongue of fire devours the stubble,
>> and as dry grass sinks down in the flame,

---

[45] Goldingay 2014: 24. Liebreich (1954: 37–38) notes the repetition of the title but overlooks the repetition of *n'ṣ* (to reject).

so their root will be as rottenness,
  and their blossom go up like dust;
for they have rejected the law of the LORD of hosts,
  and have despised the word of the Holy One of Israel.
(Isa. 5:24)

By framing Isaiah 1 – 5 with this repeated expression, the many condemning accusations against the people for injustice (1:15, 21; 3:14; 5:7, 23), idolatry (1:29–31; 2:8, 20), greed (5:8), drunkenness (5:11, 22) and arrogance (2:11, 17; 5:15; cf. 5:21) are understood as indictments for despising the Holy One of Israel and his word. These are not merely unrelated episodes of sin: they are subsumed, or interrelated, for Isaiah under the broader rubric of spurning the Holy One. Through this framing technique we are prepared to continue conceptualizing the messages of indictment in chapters 1–5 in the light of the storied vision of the thrice-holy king of Isaiah 6.

Along with the title 'Holy One of Israel' preparing for Isaiah 6, the notions of 'high' and 'lofty' in chapter 2 do as well. Isaiah 2 opens with a vision where the mount of YHWH's house will be 'lifted up above the hills' (2:2), which is a fitting destiny for Zion – the place YHWH dwells. In contrast to YHWH's mountain being 'lifted' (*nś'*) above all others, those arrogant people who are described as 'high' (*rwm*) and 'lofty' (*nś'*) in 2:11–14, 17 will be brought low, for YHWH alone will be exalted (2:11, 17):

> For the LORD of hosts has a day
>   against all that is proud and lofty [*rwm*],
>   against all that is lifted up [*nś'*] –
>   and it shall be brought low . . .
> (Isa. 2:12)

For Isaiah, this message of levelling is not as simple as arrogant people being judged; the reason arrogance must be levelled is because the Lord alone is to be exalted, which the vision of the Lord and his throne being 'high' (*rwm*) and 'lofty' (*nś'*) in 6:1 reiterates.[46]

Furthermore, Isaiah 1 – 5 contains many titles for YHWH also occurring in chapter 6 that pertain to the realm of sovereignty: 'Lord'

---

[46] Cole 2011: 167, 169–170. On God's levelling all that is high and exalted in Isa. 2 and other parts of 1 – 12, see Moberly 2003: 166–168; Williamson 1998b: 12–29.

('ădōnây; 3:15, 17, 18; 4:4), 'LORD of Hosts' (yhwh ṣebā'ôt; 1:9, 24; 2:12; 3:1, 15; 5:7, 9, 16, 24) and 'the Lord . . . LORD of Hosts' (hā'ādôn yhwh ṣebā'ôt; 1:24; 3:1). These titles are embedded within the fearful reality of impending judgment, envisaged as God's devouring sinners by the sword (1:20), besieging his own city (3:1), causing poor yields for crops (5:10), forcing exile (5:13) and coming in burning anger (5:25). Since these titles from chapters 1–5 correspond to the ones occurring in Isaiah 6, the narrative vision of YHWH as king confirms that the sovereign, holy king is the one who stands behind the dreadful anticipation of judgment in Isaiah 1 – 5.

While the overwhelming impression of Isaiah 1 – 5 is negative, there are glimmers of hope in Isaiah 1:19, 26, 27; 2:1–4; and 4:2–6. These too find a point of orientation in Isaiah 6. As noted above, the expectation that God's mountain will be 'lifted' (nś') above all other mountains as all nations stream to Zion in 2:2–4 is a fitting corollary to the heavenly vision of God's exaltation in Isaiah 6. It will be from Zion, the place where heaven and earth meet, that God the king will issue his judgments for the nations that will result in peace (2:4). This motif of God bringing justice as a universal king resonates with numerous psalms (e.g. 72:1–7; 96:10–13; 97:2; 98:6–9; 99:4).[47] Furthermore, with the Holy One promising to leave a holy seed (6:13), the promise of a holy remnant in 4:3 coordinates with chapter 6. Just as God's smoke fills the temple (6:4) and his glory is said to fill the earth (6:3) in chapter 6, so the glory and the weighty smoke of God's presence will be evident specifically in Zion with this remnant (4:2, 5). These glimmers of hope in Isaiah 1 – 5 make more sense in the light of Isaiah 6, where the seraphim declare that God's glory fills the world and Isaiah experiences forgiveness and hears of God's plan to create a holy remnant after purging.

Thus it seems likely that the vision of YHWH as a holy king who is bringing judgment with a lining of hope in Isaiah 6 offers a story that enables readers to apprehend the messages of judgment and hope in Isaiah 1 – 5 better. How can a people despise a thrice-holy king through their injustice, greed and idolatry and not be judged? YHWH's threats are not empty. How can there be hope beyond such judgment? The thrice-holy king also forgives and desires a holy remnant.

Not only does Isaiah 6 establish frames of reference for understanding chapters 1–5; it does the same for chapters 7–12. The title 'Holy One' is also important in the second half of this opening subsection

---

[47] McCann 2003: 91.

of the book. While chapters 1–5 evoke the title 'Holy One of Israel' when declaring God's judgment against Israel for rejecting him, Isaiah 10:17 utilizes the title to depict the Holy One as a flame, bringing burning judgment against Assyria (10:17; cf. *b'r*, 'to burn', in 1:31; 6:13).[48] This will result, positively, in God's people trusting in 'the Holy One of Israel' (10:20). Furthermore, Isaiah 12 concludes by envisaging Zion rejoicing because 'great in your midst is the Holy One of Israel' (12:6). This frames Isaiah 1 – 12 around a movement from condemnation of Israel for despising the Holy One to a wonderful future following the purifying judgment of Israel and Assyria when the Holy One will be in Zion.[49] The great hope is that the holy king seen in Isaiah 6 will reside among a purified people in Zion.

The motif of 'kingship' in chapter 6 has far greater resonance with human kings in chapters 7–12 than in chapters 1–5. As noted above, the vision of YHWH in his royal glory contrasts with the temporal setting of the death of King Uzziah in chapter 6. Contrast with human kings continues in the following chapters. King Ahaz is portrayed as faithless and faltering amid the threat of invading kings (7:2, 12). Those 'kings' (*mĕlākîm*) – Rezin of Aram and Pekah of Israel – who are threatening to depose Ahaz and replace him with a different 'king' (*melek*) hold little sway in YHWH's plans (7:1, 6), for the land of these 'kings' (*mĕlākîm*) will be abandoned (7:16). These two smouldering stubs of firewood will be snuffed out. In fact, YHWH will use the 'king' (*melek*) of Assyria to execute judgment on Aram, Israel and Judah (7:17, 20; 8:4).[50] Though Assyria, YHWH's instrument of judgment against his people, boasts that its commanders are 'kings' (*mĕlākîm*; 10:8) and its 'king' (*melek*) is proud (10:12), they will have a day of reckoning with YHWH, who will level them, which will lead to the establishment of God's Davidic king (Isa. 9:1–7; 11:1–10). As an alternative to the failing and threatening kings, Isaiah 7 – 8 offers the hope of 'God with us' (*'immānû 'ēl*; 7:14; 8:10);[51] they are to stand fearlessly in the face of what all others fear (7:4, 9; 8:12–13), consecrate YHWH alone (8:13) and find that he is their sanctuary (8:14) while others stumble. Thus YHWH's kingship becomes the lens for

---

[48] On the relationship between 6:13 and 1:29–31, see Williamson 1997: 119–128.

[49] See Bartelt 2004: 316–335, esp. 324–335, who in a circuitous way argues that 'The presence of the holy God in the midst of His people is one of the major themes of the whole of chapters 2–12.'

[50] See Liebreich 1954: 39–40. On the political implications of Isa. 6 with 7 – 8, see Lind 1997: 323–328.

[51] See the more detailed discussion of Immanuel in chapter 4.

viewing incursions of foreign kings into the land and initiatives of YHWH in promising future kings for Judah for the benefit of all nations.

In summary, Isaiah 6 sits at the centre of Isaiah 1 – 5 and 7 – 12 like a stadium light casting light by means of a narrative upon all around it. Isaiah 6 invites us into a vision of God, the holy king, so that we might encounter the thrice-holy king who has no rival at home or abroad and thus grasp better and respond to the searing messages of indictment and judgment and the faint embers of hope in chapters 1–12. This is a holy king who reigns now, who cannot tolerate sin, who must bring judgment, though still holding out hope beyond judgment. As a story that operates as a frame of reference for understanding the messages in both Isaiah 1 – 12 and the entire book, a vision of God as the holy king should not simply help us to understand these messages. It also should force us to grapple personally and corporately with and respond to this dreadful reality of a holy king, while not losing sight of the ultimate aim of his purifying judgment – a holy seed.

Isaiah 6 and canon

While Isaiah 6 is set historically during the time of King Uzziah's death (740 BC) and addresses God's plans for judgment during the eighth century, it speaks canonically beyond this setting. As is evident from above, Isaiah 6 rests strategically in the midst of Isaiah 1 – 12 to enable their messages of judgment and salvation to bear theological witness to the God behind the messages who will continue to act beyond the initial purview of the Assyrian era. This is part of a larger strategy within Isaiah 1 – 39 of utilizing messages from the Assyrian era to serve as 'types' for the Babylonian era and beyond.[52] By asking about the enduring historical, theological or canonical relevance of Isaiah 6, we are not asking, then, a question foreign to the aims of the book of Isaiah itself.[53] The canonical assumption is that Isaiah 6 (and any other passage in Isaiah) will speak as God's word to God's people in future times.[54]

These initial reflections are vital to keep in mind as we turn to two representative instances where the NT quotes from Isaiah 6. When

---

[52] See Laato (1998: 57–61), who understands Assyrian material typologically in the organization of Isaiah.

[53] For a similar claim on Jeremiah, see Abernethy 2014b.

[54] Here and throughout this book I have been greatly influenced by C. R. Seitz (1998; 2001; 2011).

probing how Isaiah 6 bears witness to Christ, the logic here is not 'Let's look at how the NT views Jesus, and then reread Isaiah 6 in that light to understand how it speaks of Christ.' This is not even the logic of the NT writers, who believed that Jesus was one with the Father and that by implication the God spoken of in the OT is indeed the triune God. If Jesus is one with the Father, then there must be accordance between the literal sense of the OT and God's ways in Christ and the church. Just as Isaiah 6 bears witness to a holy God who would judge and save during the Assyrian era, the Babylonian era, and even beyond the Persian era, so Isaiah 6 bears witness figurally to future eras of God's work, including Christ's first and second comings.

John 12:37–41 quotes from Isaiah 53:1 and 6:9–10, as both speak of a lack of response to God's word, to offer a theological assessment for why so few Jews were responding to Jesus' miraculous signs (cf. John 12:42, however). Following these quotations, John states, 'Isaiah said these things because he saw his glory and spoke of him' (John 12:41). The use of the plural 'these things' (*tauta*) makes it most likely that John is referring to both passages from Isaiah.[55] The reference to Isaiah's 'seeing his glory', however, explicitly points to Isaiah 6, where Isaiah 'sees' the Lord (6:1) and the seraphim declare that the entire earth is full of 'his glory' (6:3). In what sense did Isaiah 'see' Jesus' glory in Isaiah 6? Some argue that the vision of Isaiah 6 is a direct prophecy of 'the future glory of the incarnate Christ'.[56] This is a difficult position to defend because of how deeply rooted Isaiah 6 is within the context of Isaiah's time. Isaiah sees a vision of God seated on the throne during his own time, who will bring judgment in the immediate context. Instead of treating Isaiah 6 as direct prophecy, it seems most likely, with the majority of scholars, that John is analogically relating 'Jesus' glory as king to Yahweh's glory as king'.[57] Carson summarizes John's reasoning well:

> if the Son, the Word, was with God in the beginning, and was God, and if he was God's agent of creation, and the perfect revelation of God to humankind, then it stands to reason that in those OT passages where God is said to reveal himself rather spectacularly to someone, it must have been through the agency of his Son, his Word, however imperfectly the point was spelled out at the time.[58]

---

[55] Brendsel 2014: 123–125.
[56] Ibid. 126–130, esp. 126. See also Cole 2011: 166.
[57] Stovell 2012: 264.
[58] Carson 1991: 450.

While John is claiming more about the glory that Isaiah saw by blending Isaiah 6 with Isaiah 53, Isaiah 6 helps John and the early church 'read' Jesus and various responses to him. Since people in Isaiah's time ignored the holy king, it is not surprising that this would continue when the holy king, the one Isaiah spoke about, was incarnate and also surprisingly takes on the mantle of the suffering servant.[59]

Revelation 4 also utilizes Isaiah 6 to help the church understand their God and his plans. In Revelation 4, John sees a throne in heaven with one sitting upon it (4:2), with six-winged creatures around the throne proclaiming, 'Holy, holy, holy is the Lord God Almighty' (4:8). As Mathewson notes, by alluding to Isaiah 6, Revelation 4 'portray[s] God as the holy, eschatological judge who will come in the future'.[60] In this sense, Isaiah's vision of a king who reigns during the eighth century BC and who will bring judgment upon his people at that time is the same holy Lord who will bring eschatological judgment in the end times. This must be understood, however, in the light of the slain lamb in Revelation 5, whose blood provides atonement for the sins of the world, in a way symbolized in Isaiah's experience of atonement in Isaiah 6.

These two examples do not exhaust how Isaiah 6 may bear witness to Christ and address his church.[61] Instead, they are samples of the way in which the NT drew upon the OT as normative Scripture for understanding God's nature and plans for the world.

The king in Isaiah 24:21–23 and 25:6–8

With Isaiah 1 – 12 primarily focusing on Judah and Israel's judgment through Assyria, though having hints of hope for a great future after Assyria falls, Isaiah 13 – 23 has an international emphasis upon how God will judge the nations, including Israel, with an eye particularly upon the Babylonian era (chs. 13–14; 21; 612–539 BC).[62] These particularized oracles of judgment extend and culminate in Isaiah 24 – 27, where the book's message reaches its height through eschatological

---

[59] For more on analogy as a way of linking the OT to the NT, see Greidanus 1999: 220–222.

[60] Mathewson 2005: 190–191.

[61] There are, of course, other quotations of Isa. 6 in the NT (e.g. Matt. 13:14–15; Acts 28:26–27).

[62] By framing the oracles against the nations with oracles against pride, Isa. 13 – 23 relates to similar reasons for the judgment of Israel in Isa. 1 – 12. See Hamborg 1981: 156; Seitz 1993: 118; Jenkins 1989: 250; Johnson 1988: 27.

language and a cosmic scope.[63] According to Beuken, the central message of Isaiah 24 – 27 is 'the break-through of YHWH's kingship on Mount Zion (24:21–23) and its inauguration by the returning exiles at that very place (27:13)'.[64] Isaiah 24 – 27 looks to an eschatological time when the heavenly king establishes his rule in Zion. This brings to the fore the 'already but not-yet' tension of YHWH's kingship that was already surfacing in Isaiah 1 – 12. YHWH rules right now (Isa. 6), but we await the full realization of his reign (24 – 27). Two passages will receive our attention (24:21–23; 25:6–8).

Isaiah 24:21–23

Isaiah 24 reads like a war scene of unfathomable proportions.[65] The earth will be 'laid waste' (*bqq*; 24:1, 3; Jer. 19:7; 51:2; Nah. 2:3, 11) and 'destroyed' (*blq*; Isa. 24:1; cf. Nah. 2:11). Its inhabitants (Isa. 24:1, 5, 6, 17) will be scattered (24:1), even consumed by fire (24:6), with just a small remnant remaining (24:6). Wine, joy, and song will evaporate (24:7–11). The city will be in shambles (24:10, 12). Why such far-reaching destruction? God's instruction has been transgressed, the everlasting covenant broken (24:5; cf. 24:20).[66] When the portrait of destruction in Isaiah 24 seems to reach its height in the announcement that the earth will never again arise following flood and quake (24:18–20), the imagery climbs to even greater heights in 24:21–23:

> On that day the LORD will punish
> the host [*ṣābā'*] of heaven, in heaven,
> and the kings of the earth, on the earth.
> They will be gathered together
> as prisoners in a pit;

---

[63] Blenkinsopp 2000: 346–348; Oswalt 2005: 79; Sweeney 1987; 1988; 1996: 320–324. For a survey of approaches on the date of Isa. 24 – 27, see C. B. Hays (2013), who argues against the predominant post-exilic view for a pre-exilic date on linguistic grounds.

[64] Beuken 2010: 25. See also Cunha 2013.

[65] On military destruction in Isa. 24, see K. M. Hayes 2002: 141–149.

[66] There are various interpretations concerning the identity of the broken 'everlasting covenant' (24:5): expectations between creator and creature from the beginning (Oswalt 1986: 446); the Mosaic covenant (Johnson 1988: 27); all covenants and their cosmic implications (G. V. Smith 2007: 417). The strongest background is the Noahic covenant (Seitz 1993: 181–182) due to shared emphases on the earth (24:5–6; Gen. 6:11), the eternal covenant (24:5; Gen. 9:16), and the flood from windows in heaven (24:18; Gen. 7:11). Though some argue that the Noahic covenant is unconditional and cannot be broken, Mason (2007) examines how expectations, such as not murdering, are evident in 9:1–17.

they will be shut up in a prison,
  and after many days they will be punished.
Then the moon will be confounded
  and the sun ashamed,
[23b] for the LORD of hosts [*yhwh ṣĕbā'ôt*] reigns
  on Mount Zion and in Jerusalem,
and his glory will be before his elders.

(Isa. 24:21–23)

Line 23b provides an explanation ('for' [*kî*]) for what comes before it. YHWH's reign on Zion and the presence of his glory there before his elders is the reason for the far-reaching judgment that will occur 'on that day' (24:21).

Several observations will illumine the force behind the claim concerning YHWH's reign in 24:23.

First, it is not incidental that YHWH is referred to as 'LORD of hosts' (*yhwh ṣĕbā'ôt*) in 24:23. This royal title (cf. 6:3) resonates with 24:21, where it is declared that 'the LORD will punish the host [*ṣābā'*] of heaven'. Debate surrounds the identity of the *host*, with some thinking they are deities and others arguing that they are 'astral angels of the nations' (Dan. 8:3; 10:13, 20).[67] Though conclusive evidence is not forthcoming, we can still detect the *sense* being conveyed. The term modifying 'host', *mārôm*, is often translated 'heaven' (LXX) but can also convey the idea of 'height'.[68] Why use *mārôm* instead of the typical term for 'heaven', *šāmayim*? Within Isaiah 24 – 27 *mārôm* applies to the 'exalted [*mārôm*] people of the earth [who] will languish' in judgment (24:4) or to the 'inhabitants of the height [*mārôm*], the lofty city' who will be laid low (26:5).[69] Since *mārôm* calls to mind haughty powers that set themselves against God in this context, a wooden translation of 24:21 could read, 'YHWH will judge the host of the height in the height' (24:21). By using *mārôm* Isaiah 24:21 announces 'God's implacable enmity against all which raises itself

---

[67] As deities, see Millar 1976: 66; Cunha 2013: 67–68. As angels, see Kaiser 1974: 194–195, along with G. V. Smith 2007: 424; Blenkinsopp 2000: 356. Many suggest that the moon and sun are not judged in 24:23a, but instead there is a comparison between God's glory and the light of the sun and moon to highlight God's greatness, as in Isa. 60:19–20 (Cunha 2013: 65; J. Gray 1979: 206; Kaiser 1974: 195; Oswalt 1986: 455). With Johnson (1988: 55) and Wildberger (1997: 510), I agree that using terms for shame to describe the sun and the moon has a polemical sense.

[68] For an overview on this noun, see Firmage, Milgrom and Dahmen 2004: 402–409, esp. 408.

[69] Translations throughout this paragraph are my own.

against him, whether a star in heaven or a king on earth (cf. 34:4, 5).'[70] This host of *mārôm* signifies the greatest conceivable powers that are set against God; such will be put in their place. This is because 'the LORD of hosts' will reign on Zion.

Second, the declaration that 'the LORD of hosts will reign' (24:23) relates to the other realm of God's judgment. The 'kings' (*mĕlākîm*) of the earth (24:21) will experience judgment because the 'LORD of hosts reigns [*mālak*]' (24:23).

Third, the location of YHWH's rule on Mount Zion is significant amid this schema of all-encompassing judgment. Since the pre-eminent powers of heaven and earth will experience his judgment (24:21), the mountain is a fitting middle point, ideal for a king who is heavenly, yet desires to establish his kingdom upon earth. The highest powers above (the host) and below (kings) will have their day of judgment when the Lord of hosts reigns on his mountain.

Fourth, as in Isaiah 6:3, YHWH's reign in 24:23 results in a display of his 'glory' before his elders. As a common attribute of a king,[71] the presence of his 'glory' (*kābôd*) heightens the recognition of YHWH's kingly presence. Additionally, this calls to mind God's glorious presence on Mount Sinai (Exod. 24:16; cf. Isa. 4:5).[72] While a case could be made that the elders here are members of the divine council,[73] it seems most likely that these elders are like those who gazed upon the Lord in his glory at Sinai, as representatives of the people.[74] Just as God's people experienced his royal presence at Sinai, so they look forward to the establishment of his glory and reign on Zion.[75] This future perspective is a counterpart to the vision of God in Isaiah 6. The holy king who reigns in heaven and whose glory fills the earth now (Isa. 6) will establish his reign eschatologically in Zion as he judges heaven and earth, with his glory being manifest on his mountain (24:21–23).

Fifth, and finally, the expectation that 'the LORD will punish [*pqd*]' in 24:21–23 forges associations with Isaiah 13 – 23.[76] Local warnings

---

[70] Oswalt 1986: 455. In 24:18 the windows of *mārôm* will open and from there God will bring judgment.

[71] See the discussion above on Isa. 6.

[72] Cunha 2013: 65; Johnson 1988: 56–57.

[73] See Willis 1991: 75–85.

[74] This could signal an end to the era of God's judgment against his elders announced earlier in the book (Isa. 3:14; cf. 66:18–22; Exod. 24:1–11).

[75] Debate arises concerning whether to translate 24:23 as 'YHWH has become king' (Cunha 2013: 63–65) or 'YHWH will reign' (Wildberger 1997: 510–511). The temporal phrase 'In that day' (24:21, NIV84) favours a future sense.

[76] For more on how Isa. 24 – 27 extends the notions of judgment from Isa. 1 to 23 and 28 to 33, see Kim 2013.

of judgment against nations (*pqd*; 13:11; 23:17; cf. 10:12) in chapters 13–23 extend to a cosmic, even mythic, scale in chapter 24, as they culminate in YHWH's rule on Zion. This presents God's future rule on Zion as a central way for conceptualizing judgment, not only in chapter 24, but also in chapters 13–23. All nations and powers for all time – not just those within the eighth and seventh centuries BC – will come to nothing if they stand opposed to God. The holy king who reigns currently and gloriously in heaven in Isaiah 6 is the one who will establish his reign on Zion through cataclysmic judgment of all 'hosts' and 'kings' who stand against him (24:21–23).

Isaiah 25:6–8

The gloom and doom associated with YHWH's reign on Zion in Isaiah 24 has a bright and cheerful side in Isaiah 25. Judgment gives way to an eruption of praise in 25:1–5 (cf. 25:9–12; 26:1–6), for the faithful will find tyrannical powers overthrown by YHWH. As the supposedly strong city falls (24:10; 25:2–3, 5), Zion emerges as a glorious alternative under God's reign.[77] This is portrayed chiefly through a feast:

> On this mountain the LORD of hosts will make for all peoples
>   a feast of rich food, a feast of well-aged wine,
>   of rich food full of marrow, of aged wine well refined.
> And he will swallow up on this mountain
>   the covering that is cast over all peoples,
>   the veil that is spread over all nations.
>   He will swallow up death for ever;
> and the Lord GOD will wipe away tears from all faces,
>   and the reproach of his people he will take away from
>   all the earth,
>   for the LORD has spoken.
>
>   (Isa. 25:6–8)

At the very location of YHWH's rule in 24:23 a feast will occur, for it will be 'on this mountain' (25:6).[78] The host of this feast will be the 'LORD of hosts', which is a title that occurs only in 24:23 and 25:6 within Isaiah 24 – 27. This feast on Zion, then, is set within the context of YHWH's reign on Mount Zion that is referred to in 24:21–23.

---

[77] On the contrast between these two cities in Isa. 24 – 27, see Bürki 2013.
[78] MacDonald 2008: 193–194.

Why envisage the positive side of God's reign through a feast? In the ancient world, kings often held feasts to display the extent of their power.[79] When King Belshazzar hosts a feast, he invites a thousand lords from the provinces and shows off his goods (Dan. 5:1–10). When King Ahasuerus puts on a feast, he invites dignitaries from many provinces and uses the opportunity to display his abundance (Esth. 1:1–8). This motif occurs throughout the ANE. One of the most well-known examples comes from Ashurnasirpal II (883–859 BC), king of Assyria, who claims to have held a banquet for more than 69,000 men and woman, including 5,000 international dignitaries.[80] In these three examples the number of participants and their international composition are noted, while also highlighting displays of wealth and power that took place at the banquet. Isaiah 25:6–8 shares these interests. Though the number of attendees is not specified, this is a feast for 'all peoples' (25:6) – a group of participants vast in number and international in scope. The menu at this feast also points to YHWH's greatness. The richest of fare is offered:

> a feast of rich food, a feast of well-aged wine,
>   of rich food full of marrow, of aged wine well refined.
>
> (25:6)

He also uses the setting of the feast to display his power by swallowing Death (*mwt*), described here as the cover that looms over all nations. Though an ancient myth of that time portrays Death (Mot) as swallowing the god Ba'al, the swallowing of Death by YHWH proclaims his power over all other deities and over the dreadful reality of death itself.[81]

While the feast certainly promotes King YHWH's power, feasts also shape the identity of the people around him. An invitation to partake in the king's feast was a badge of honour; in fact, people not attending feasts in the ANE would fight over the privilege of having the king's leftover food designated to them.[82] A place at the king's table was a great privilege. When David invites Mephibosheth to eat

---

[79] For more on feasts and politics in the ANE and OT, see Altmann 2011: 78–98; Cho and Fu 2013: 133–136; MacDonald 2012; J. L. Wright 2010a; 2010b.

[80] See in Grayson 1996: A.0.101.30 102–154; cf. A.0.101.1 iii 77b–84a; Cho and Fu 2013: 135.

[81] Kim 2013: 31.

[82] Parpola 2004.

at the king's table, Mephibosheth is astounded (2 Sam. 9:7–11). Haman is thrilled at feeling like an insider when Esther invites him to a feast (Esth. 5:12). 2 Kings ends with Jehoiachin receiving the privileged opportunity to dine at the table of Evil-merodach, the king of Babylon, a sign of favour (25:27–29). Since joining in a meal, especially a banquet at the king's table, was a sign of relational and social standing, the prospect of attending a feast conveys far more than the chance to ingest food to meet one's daily nutritional requirements. An invitation to a feast means that the king *wants* you at the feast; it is a sign of honour to be in his presence and solidifies your identity as one of his people.[83]

Chapters 24 and 25 work together to depict two destinies, with YHWH's reign on Mount Zion as the fulcrum. YHWH will destroy those setting themselves against God, whether in the heavens or upon the earth, when his reign is established on Zion (24:23). Those awaiting God's salvation will rejoice in YHWH's judgment of evil (25:1–5) and will have the privilege of participating in the king's feast where they will be in awe of his great power as he devours death (25:6–8). The significance of this within the unfolding message of Isaiah should not be overlooked. Since Isaiah 24 – 27 extends and universalizes expectations of judgment and salvation within the eighth and seventh centuries BC that are found in Isaiah 1 – 23, a declaration of YHWH's future reign on Zion reveals that these cycles of judgment and restoration point to the end towards which history is moving. Judgment and salvation will reach their culmination when YHWH's reign is fully established in the eschatological future (24 – 27).

It is not by chance that the motif of YHWH's kingship appears at this crucial juncture of Isaiah, as once again our minds are directed through the organization of the book to God as king. Isaiah 24 and 25 serve as counterparts to Isaiah 6. Whereas YHWH's present reign in heaven explains why he must purge his people during the eighth century in Isaiah 6 amid the Assyrian era, the anticipation of YHWH's future reign entails a more ultimate time of judgment and salvation for heaven and earth, even for all nations. For this reason, during all eras, readers are to be aware of God's near and future judgment and salvation. God reigns now and will come as king, so all powers set against him will ultimately fail, though all who hope in the king will delight in his salvation as they partake in his feast.

[83] J. L. Wright 2010a: 213–217.

Isaiah 24 and 25 and canon

Unlike Isaiah 6, Isaiah 24:21–23 is not directly quoted in the NT. Can we legitimately enquire into how this passage bears witness to Christ? Some, such as Richard Longenecker, argue that Christians are permitted to apply a literal hermeneutic to OT passages, but not to utilize other interpretative methods found in the NT, particularly *pesher*, which would include typology and allegory.[84] Others, such as Richard Hays, argue that the canonical reality of Scripture legitimates intertextual readings of all Scripture, thereby justifying an attempt to read Isaiah 24:21–23 in the light of any NT passage one wishes, particularly with a Pauline hermeneutic.[85] While Hays helpfully corrects Longenecker's lack of factoring in literary and canonical realities, the problem with Hays's proposal, as Seitz points out,[86] is that it misconstrues how to relate the Old and New Testaments in this process. Instead of reading the OT in the light of the NT and with Paul's hermeneutic, which would subsume all of the OT's message under what one finds in the NT (making the OT unnecessary), it is more appropriate to read the OT and NT in association with one another in the light of how each testament bears its own discrete witness to Christ. Prior to the formation of the NT, the OT was the church's scripture, was read publically (1 Tim. 4:13) and preached (2 Tim. 4:2), led people to salvation in Christ (2 Tim. 3:15) and built up God's people in the faith (2 Tim. 3:16; Rom. 15:4). The assumption was and remains that the OT can teach the church about Christ and his ways, even without recourse to the NT canon. Though we now live after the formation of the NT canon, this does not mean that the OT's discrete witness to Christ is now eclipsed or that the NT has exhaustively treated every OT passage that pertains to Christ. What this means, instead, is that we now have two mature witnesses bearing witness to Christ that should be read in correspondence with one another, while allowing each to have its voice.[87]

---

[84] Longenecker (1975) limits *pesher* interpretation to the apostles because it requires an authoritative revelation from Jesus, which the apostles received. The idea is that an authoritative interpreter has the spiritual ability to explain and clarify the 'fuller meaning' of a passage. This is akin to the high priest at Qumran, who revealed the mysteries in the OT for that community. According to Longenecker, without access to Jesus, the revealer of mysteries, the post-apostolic church cannot utilize a *pesher* method.

[85] R. B. Hays 1989: 178–192.

[86] Seitz 2011.

[87] A representative quote from Seitz (2011: 139) captures this well: 'What is at issue is a discrete voice that acknowledges as crucial the claims of the NT about the witness of the Old, but that does not believe the New's material use of the Old can be the primary or comprehensive means to think about its theological witness as Christian

So how does one undertake a canonical reading of Isaiah 24:21–23? We begin by reiterating that this vision of God's eschatological judgment of all powers – heavenly and earthly – corresponds within Isaiah to the judgment of nations from the eighth to the sixth centuries BC (chs. 13–23), resulting in a canonical sense that God's judgment will recur throughout history until it culminates 'in that day' when God's reign is fully established upon Zion (24:21–23). Since the God of Isaiah 24:21–23 is one with Christ, a canonical reading would invite us to consider how judgment has been ushered in by Christ's glorious first coming and will be more fully established by his second coming. As professed in the Apostles' Creed, Christ has ascended into heaven, is seated at the right hand of the Father and will one day come to judge the living and the dead. With Christ already reigning as king – 'son of God, our Lord' – and coming again in judgment, we read this passage as already being inaugurated though awaiting its culmination. As one looks at how this corresponds with the NT witness to Jesus, we see that the NT testifies that Christ's earthly reign issued a blow to Satan (Luke 10:18),[88] that the cross is a triumph over 'rulers and authorities' (Col. 2:15), and that Christ's second coming will climactically defeat all kings (Rev. 19:18–19), Satan (20:10) and death itself (20:14; cf. Isa. 25:8).

God's reign as king does not only entail judgment. Isaiah 25:6–8 uses the motif of a feast to depict the blessed hope of salvation for those waiting on YHWH when he comes as king. As we consider this canonically, it is important not simply to view this passage as one 'on its way' to its real meaning in the Lord's Supper or a similar developmental argument, although it is reasonable to posit that Jesus and the NT writers would expect readers to understand the Lord's Supper and Christ's anticipation of future feasts (cf. Matt. 26:29; Mark 14:25; Luke 22:18) in the light of Isaiah 25:6–8. Instead, we must allow this passage to speak as an authoritative revelation of God in itself. This feast points us to the king's inclusivity ('for all peoples'), lavish generosity ('of rich food'), power over death ('swallow up death for ever') and commitment to remove 'the reproach of his people'. In this passage we see Christ's international supremacy, one seated at the

---

(*Footnote 87 cont.*) Scripture . . . *any proper biblical theology would of necessity be about letting each mature witness do its specific work as Scripture, in that completed form, and then as a coordinated witness of both Testaments together*' (emphasis original).

[88] Green 1997: 419.

right hand of the Father having dominion over all now and more fully when he comes again, who invites all people to live as his people – the holy catholic church, a communion of saints. We see that God is one who generously holds nothing back from his people, a Father sending his Son and a Son lavishing on his people the richest of blessings. In particular, he defeats death through the cross and resurrection, offering the blessed hope of the 'life everlasting'. A peculiar challenge occurs, however, in Isaiah 25:8. While all peoples will come to the feast and benefit from the death of death, pointing to inclusivism, the promise to 'remove the reproach of his people' refers to Israel (particularism). While some Reformed readers may quickly set 'Israel' aside as a 'type' of the church, this passage reminds non-Jewish readers that amid the incorporation of Gentiles into the king's people, his commitment to remove the shame of Israel continues and will come about in due course.[89] Albeit in its own idiom, the NT also points to a similar inclusivity (John 10:16; Eph. 2:11–22), generosity (Eph. 1:3; 4:7), present and future victory over death (Acts 2:24; 1 Cor. 15:26, 54–55; 2 Tim. 1:10; Rev. 21:4), and commitment to Israel (Rom. 11:25–27). As a canonical witness, Isaiah 24:21–23 and 25:6–8 testify concerning a king whose reign entails the judgment of all powers – in heaven and on earth – and, through the imagery of a feast, the generous salvation of all nations, though retaining Israel's particularity.

God as king in Isaiah 33

From the cosmic and eschatological heights of Isaiah 24 – 27 the book of Isaiah shifts back to the particularities of the eighth-century BC context in Isaiah 28 – 33.[90] The recurrence of the term 'woe' (*hôy*; 28:1; 29:1, 15; 30:1; 31:1; 33:1, NIV) throughout these chapters conveys a sense of condemnation structurally, as pride (28:1), drunkenness (28:3), resistance to God's word (29:15–16), foreign alliances (30:1; 31:1) and faithless behaviour (33:1) are confronted with warnings of coming destruction. While judgment is prominent in Isaiah 28 – 33,

[89] With R. B. Hays (1989: 184) I agree that the unbelief of Jews is only 'a temporary complication of the plot' and '[God] will not permit this anomalous situation of division and unbelief to terminate the story of election'.

[90] Some date the woe oracles to the pre-exilic prophet, with other texts from pre-exilic, exilic and post-exilic times interspersed (Laberge 1982). As for Isa. 33, many place it in post-exilic times (Sweeney 1996: 429; J. D. W. Watts 2005: 499), but others (Roberts 1983b: 16–25; Blenkinsopp 2000: 445) opt for Isaianic authorship.

hope is important too, as Stansell observes how messages of hope follow these woes (28:5–6, 23–29; 29:5–8, 17–24; 30:18–26; 31:5–8; 32:1–8, 15–20; 33:2–24).[91] Furthermore, as Sweeney points out, the prospect of human (32:1) and divine kingship (33:17, 22) frames the final two chapters of this part of Isaiah to grant perspective on how the era of hope will be established following judgment.[92] Of most significance to us, assertions of God's kingship bring Isaiah 28 – 33 to a close, crystallizing this message of judgment and hope in the coming reign of God in chapter 33. Isaiah 33 has two slopes (1 – 6, 7 – 24) that begin in the valleys of judgment (Isa. 33:1, 7–14a) and then climb to the heights of hope (33:2–6, 14b–22). At the pinnacles of hope are declarations of YHWH's exaltation as king; these will occupy our attention (33:5–6, 17, 22).

The first part of Isaiah 33 (vv. 1–6) opens by announcing that the treacherous will be destroyed (33:1). In the light of this announcement the faithful call on God to be gracious and bring salvation (33:2–4), presumably involving the judgment of the tyrants from verse 1. This hopeful prayer culminates in a declaration of hope about YHWH:

> The LORD is exalted, for he dwells on high;
> he will fill Zion with justice and righteousness,
> and he will be the stability [*'ĕmûnâ*] of your times,
> abundance of salvation, wisdom, and knowledge;
> the fear of the LORD is Zion's treasure.
>
> (Isa. 33:5–6)

This expression of confidence is part of Isaiah's recurring message that YHWH alone will be exalted as he humbles all other human powers.[93] Kingship comes to mind in several ways in these verses.

First, as Balogh notes, the word pair of justice and righteousness in 33:5 'has clear juridical connotations and is often mentioned in connection with the activity of the king as the representative of jurisdiction'.[94] For example, in 2 Samuel 8:15 we read, 'So David reigned over all Israel; and David administered justice and righteousness for

[91] Stansell 1996: 71.
[92] Sweeney 1996: 354.
[93] On exaltation in Isa. 28 – 33, see Stansell 1996: 73–74. YHWH's exaltation frames (28:1–6; 33:5–6) and is central (30:18) to this section of the book (cf. 2:11, 17; 5:16; 12:4).
[94] Balogh 2008: 481.

all his people' (NASB).[95] YHWH will fill Zion with justice and right-eousness, for he is its king.[96]

Second, as Beuken observes, Isaiah 33:5–6 shares a number of terms with Isaiah 11:1–9.[97] Isaiah 11:1–9 looks forward to a Davidic king, who will have 'wisdom' (*ḥokmâ*) and 'fear the Lord' (*yir'at yhwh*; 11:2–3), who will bring about 'justice' (*mišpāṭ*) and 'righteousness' (*ṣedeq/ṣĕdāqâ*; 11:4, NIV) and will be marked by 'faithfulness' (*'ĕmûnâ*; 11:5), which is the same term translated as 'stability' in 33:6. This will result in God's 'knowledge' (*da'at*) filling the earth (11:9). Just as a human king may be expected to have these characteristics according to Isaiah 11:1–9, YHWH will bring about justice and righteousness and will himself be their faithfulness, salvation, wisdom and knowledge in 33:5–6.[98] Thus, in the first section of Isaiah 33, the hope for the faithful as they await the judgment of their enemies is that YHWH will reign as the exalted king who will establish justice, wisdom and security for his people.

From the heights of expectation concerning YHWH's future glory and Zion's well-being in 33:5–6, verse 7 initiates a transition that plunges into deep despair, as warriors threaten, highways are desolate, humans have no regard for one another and the earth is withering (33:7–9). The mood shifts in 33:10, where YHWH declares: 'Now I will arise . . . now I will be exalted.' Not only does this continue the theme of YHWH's exaltation from 33:5 but it also echoes the description of YHWH's throne as high and exalted in Isaiah 6:1.[99] This is not good news, however, for many, for YHWH's rising in 33:10 gives way to a dramatic vision of his fiery judgment (33:11–14a). Who is able to dwell in the presence of such consuming fire? In language similar to Psalms 15 and 24, those who have the same character as God from verse 5 can survive – they must live righteously (33:15). The reward for such faithfulness is a scenario similar to YHWH's in verse 5,[100] as is illustrated by noting similar roots.

> The LORD is exalted [*śgb*], he dwells [*škn*] on high [*mārôm*] . . .
>
> (33:5, NRSV)

---

[95] Balogh (ibid. 481–482) also notes 1 Kgs 10:9; Ps. 72:1; Jer. 22:15; 23:5; 33:15.

[96] Leclerc (2001: 84–85) thinks there is a transition from Isaiah's hope in human governors (1:21–26) to YHWH (33:5–6). This causes him to date this passage to the post-exilic era.

[97] Beuken 1991: 16–17.

[98] Though the emphasis is upon God as the king, the divine king could utilize a human king (32:1) to promote these ideals.

[99] Beuken 1991: 20.

[100] Balogh 2008: 487.

> [The faithful] will dwell [*škn*] on the heights [*mrm*];
> his place of defence [*mśgb*] will be the fortresses
> of rocks . . .
>
> (33:16)

Just as YHWH is exalted and secure on high (33:5), so are the faithful who will dwell securely with the consuming fire.

With Isaiah 33 climbing the slope towards hope in this second section of the chapter, the vision culminates with two statements concerning God's kingship (33:17, 22). In 33:17 we read:

> Your eyes will see the king in his beauty . . .
>
> (33:17, NRSV)

There is debate concerning whether 33:17 refers to a Davidic king or to God as king. Balogh offers the strongest support for the former.[101] To begin, since 'YHWH's kingship does not exclude the coexistence of a subordinate human king',[102] an appeal to YHWH as king in verse 22 does not conclusively mean that the king in 33:17 is divine too. Additionally, there is no article with 'king' in 33:17 (*melek*, not *hammelek*; 'a king' not 'the king'), when one might expect one when it is applied to YHWH (6:5). Furthermore, the notion of 'seeing' God is problematic in OT thought, making it unlikely that 33:17 refers to seeing God as king. Finally, YHWH is never described as beautiful elsewhere in the OT, while the term more readily applies to a human king (Ps. 45:3; 1 Sam. 16:12; 17:42; Ezek. 28:12). For these reasons,[103] Balogh and others argue that 33:17 speaks of seeing a human king.

Against Balogh, it seems more plausible to view the referent in 33:17 as God. First, the flow of thought within Isaiah 33 is pointing in this direction. The major question prior to 33:17 concerns who is able to dwell with God (33:14b). This interest is evident in 33:16, where we read that the faithful will dwell in circumstances similar to YHWH's own situation from 33:5 (see above). Amid a focus upon dwelling with God in 33:14b–16, it seems logical to continue this line of thought by declaring that God's people will see God, the king in

---

[101] Ibid. 489–490. See also Young (1965: 421), Blenkinsopp (2000: 445) and Childs (2001: 248), who think a human king is in view in v. 17.

[102] Balogh 2008: 489–490.

[103] Balogh (ibid. 490) offers several other less convincing reasons, such as a focus on 'land' or putting the 'king' in the first position.

33:17.[104] Second, a lack of a definite article with 'king' is not surprising here because it is common for Hebrew poetry to omit definite articles where we could expect them. Wildberger suggests that a lack of article conveys the sense that there will be no rivals, so there is no need to specify definiteness in terms of who is king.[105] Third, since Isaiah 'sees' (*r'h*) God in 6:1 (cf. 6:5), there is not a problem with 'seeing' (*ḥzh*) God as king in 33:17. Fourth, even though the term 'beautiful' (*yāpeh*) regularly applies to humans, this does not mean that it cannot refer to God in 33:17. The nature of metaphorical language is to apply language from one domain to another domain; the more unexpected the connection, the more potent. By applying a characteristic typically attached to a human being, the portrayal of YHWH as a beautiful king metaphorically conveys God's great splendour, which they will see in due course. Finally, in the light of these other lines of evidence, the specification of God as king in Isaiah 33:22 confirms that the referent of 33:17 is God.[106]

The promise that 'your eyes will behold the king in his beauty' (33:17) is stirring when read in the light of Isaiah 6. In Isaiah 6 the narrator opens by stating that Isaiah 'saw' (*r'h*) the Lord (6:1). In 6:5 Isaiah also declares that 'my eyes have seen the King'. The associations between 6:5 and 33:17 are particularly strong with the terms 'eyes' (*'ayin*) and 'king' (*melek*), along with the concept of 'seeing' (*r'h/ḥzh*),[107] being similar. There are, however, two unique developments from Isaiah 6 to Isaiah 33:17. First, there is a transition from 'my eyes' (6:5) to 'your eyes' seeing (33:17; cf. 33:20). Seeing YHWH is not just the privileged one-time experience of the prophet in Isaiah 6.[108] 'You' – the faithful (33:14b–16) – will be able to see YHWH as king in the future.[109] Second, there is a shift in the connotations associated with seeing God. In Isaiah 6 seeing the holy king is a dangerous and fearful

[104] Leclerc (2001: 86) appeals to form criticism to make a similar point. Since 33:14–16 is a temple entrance liturgy, the focus in 33:17 is upon approaching God.
[105] Wildberger 2002: 301.
[106] Some argue that this is a post-exilic text because a human king is not in view (Leclerc 2001: 86; Sweeney 1996: 429), but post-exilic prophets continue to hope for a Davidic king (cf. Hag. 2:21–23; Zech. 13:1) as does the Chronicler. See Childs 2001: 248.
[107] The choice of *ḥzh* (to see) in 33:17 may be due to a connection with 26:11 (Beuken 1991: 24).
[108] Waschke 2004: 528.
[109] Wildberger 2002: 301. 'Your' is singular in 33:17–24, though first common plural suffixes also appear throughout ('our'). Since 33:14b–16 uses the singular to refer to the one who can dwell with God, 33:17 takes up the singular and personalizes it for the audience by shifting to the second person.

experience, as is evident by the seraphim covering their eyes (6:2) and Isaiah declaring that he is undone (6:5). In Isaiah 33:17 looking upon God becomes highly desirable, not dreadful.[110] It is a pleasant prospect to see the king in his beauty in 33:17. For a people who will be safe from fiery judgment (33:14), the anticipation of seeing God, the king, in his beauty is a beam of light as they wait for God to act (33:2).

As Isaiah 33 continues to build this vision of hope, the culminating reason for Zion's blessed future is as follows:

> For the LORD is our judge, the LORD is our ruler,
> the LORD is our king; he will save us.
>
> (33:22, NRSV)

In this one verse, three titles from ancient leadership traditions are applied to YHWH.[111] He is 'judge', taking on the significant leadership role from Israel's early days in Canaan. He is 'ruler' (*mhqq*), absorbing an important leadership title from among the tribes (Deut. 33:21; Judg. 5:14). He is their 'king', as was proclaimed at the exodus from Egypt (Exod. 15:18). Not only do these titles call to mind ancient traditions, but the titles 'judge' and 'king' are also not unexpected within the context of Isaiah. With the first movement of Isaiah 33 (vv. 1–6) declaring that God will fill Zion with justice (*mišpāṭ*) and righteousness (33:5), it is fitting for the second movement (33:7–24) to crown God with the title of 'judge' (*špṭ*). Also, Isaiah 33 coordinates with God's role as judge in 2:2–4 and 66:16 to anchor Zion's hope in their God who brings justice to Zion.[112] God's role as judge, however, is not to be disassociated from his role as king. When the people requested a king in 1 Samuel 8, they wanted a king who would 'judge' (*špṭ*) them (8:5–6, 20). During Solomon's reign, the people were in awe of his insight as judge (1 Kgs 3:28; cf. 2 Kgs 15:5 // 2 Chr. 26:21). This combination is even apparent in proverbial wisdom (Prov. 29:14). Leclerc captures the essence of 33:22 when he says, 'The king is the particular guarantor of justice. Because of the failure of the king to effect justice in the social realm, the prophet looks forward to an ideal king who will rule in justice and righteousness.'[113] Zion's destiny is secure, for God is its king and judge.

---

[110] Wildberger 2002: 301.
[111] Blenkinsopp 2000: 447.
[112] Beuken 1991: 25; Leclerc 2001: 166.
[113] Leclerc 2001: 160. See also G. V. Smith 2007: 563.

Another aspect of God's kingship is noted at the end of 33:22: 'he will save us'. In Hosea 13:10 the prophet taunts the people, saying, 'Where now is your king, to save you in all your cities?' In Zechariah 9:9 the coming king is depicted as one who has salvation. In Isaiah 25, within a context highlighting God's future reign as king (24:23; see above), the people celebrate this king since they have waited for him to save them (25:9; cf. 12:2). Similarly, in 33:22, God's kingship and his salvation intertwine. What have the people been saved from? Within Isaiah 33 referents are vague, though realities of tyranny (33:1), disregard from fellow humans (33:8), desolate landscapes and roadways (33:8–9), and a city occupied by foreign powers (33:19) hint at both external threats and internal troubles (33:14a; cf. 33:15–16). The opaqueness of the precise referent (no nation is specified) enables Isaiah 33 to speak a word of challenge to the faithless and a word of hope to the faithful throughout various eras of Israel's history.[114] God will come as king to set his city right, throwing off all enemies from within and without with his burning fire. God the king will save his faithful people (33:14b–16, 22).

In summary, Isaiah 33 crystallizes Zion's hope in the exaltation and reign of YHWH as king. While YHWH's reign implies dreadful judgment, the positive aspects of this reign for the faithful are in view in Isaiah 33:17 and 22. God's people will have the privilege of gazing on the king in his beauty, and Zion's hope has a sure anchor in God's being a king who will bring justice and salvation to his city. Within the book of Isaiah, Isaiah 33 plays a significant role. While some treat it as the conclusion to the first half of Isaiah,[115] it is best to interpret Isaiah 33 as concluding Isaiah 28 – 33 and also as co-ordinating with Isaiah 34 – 35 and 36 – 39 as a 'triptych' of transitional chapters between Isaiah 1 – 32 and 40 – 66.[116] For our purposes, it is significant to note that, just as Isaiah 6 and 24 – 25 focus attention upon God as king at critical junctures within the structure of Isaiah, so Isaiah 33 does the same, though with its own unique purpose of

---

[114] Sweeney 1996: 432–433.
[115] Brownlee 1964: 47–59; Sweeney 1996: 430–431. Evans (1988: 129–147) hesitantly endorses the structural division of Isa. 1 – 33 and 34 – 66, though acknowledges that this does not undermine other structural possibilities. In my view connections between Isa. 1 and 36 – 39 and the gap between Isa. 39 and 40 are too strong to warrant dividing the book after Isa. 33.
[116] Thompson 2002: 331. For connections between Isa. 33 and other parts of the book, see Beuken 1991 and Stansell 1996.

highlighting how beautiful this prospect will be for the king's faithful people in Zion.[117]

Isaiah 33 and canon

Since methodological reflections introduce our canonical considerations of Isaiah 6 and 24 – 25, we can dive right into how Isaiah 33:5–6 and 17 and 22 bear their own unique witness to Christ. To begin, the culminating hope of Isaiah 28 – 33 resides in God's exaltation as king. This creates a perspective of hope in the tumultuous eighth-century context of 'woe'. The exalted king in Isaiah 33 will bring about justice and salvation (33:5–6, 22) and will allow himself to be 'seen' by his faithful (33:17). Where else can one look for injustice to be set right in this world other than to God? Has anyone donning flesh ever exhibited such justice and righteousness in his treatment of others as Christ did? Has God's justice that leads to salvation ever been on greater display than at the cross of Christ and in the hope that he will come again? Is not Christ's incarnation a beautiful demonstration of God, the king, allowing himself to be seen (33:17)? While couched in differing language, the NT witness corresponds with the similar wonder concerning a God who makes himself 'seen' in Christ (John 1:14; Hebrews 1:1–3; 1 John 1:1) and who has come and will come as saviour (1 Thess. 1:10; 1 Peter 1:8–9; Rev. 19:1) and judge (Rom. 3:25–26; 2 Thess. 1:6–10; Rev. 20). Thus Isaiah 33 bears witness to God's coming as a just and saving king, whom the faithful can gaze upon, with the NT bearing witness to this same God from its own vantage point and concerns.

God the king in Isaiah 36 – 37

Isaiah 36 – 37 provides us with our final snapshot of God as king in Isaiah 1 – 39.[118] Whereas portrayals of God as king in Isaiah 6 and Isaiah 24 – 25 and 33 are in a vision report and poetry respectively, Isaiah 36 – 37 presents God's kingship in a historical narrative, showing how God can overcome the mighty Assyrian King

---

[117] See Waschke (2004), who argues from a redaction-critical perspective that Isa. 33 was composed to bring about a focus on Zion and YHWH as king within the entire book in connection with Isa. 1 and 6.

[118] I will deal with Isa. 34 – 35 in chapters 2 and 3 as they relate to God's coming as a saving king (40:9–11; 52:7) and as a warrior king (59:15–20; 63:1–6).

Sennacherib during the crisis in 701 BC.[119] While many scholars focus on how Isaiah 36 – 37 portrays Zion's salvation or depicts Hezekiah as a model king, there is a more overarching purpose in these chapters: to declare that God is an unrivalled king.[120] We will consider several features from this narrative that emphasize YHWH's kingship.[121]

There is an overt emphasis upon Sennacherib as king in these chapters. From the opening verse, the narrator puts a spotlight on 'Sennacherib king of Assyria', who has taken possession of all of the cities of Judah apart from Jerusalem (36:1; 701 BC). Throughout the rest of the narrative the narrator always refers to Sennacherib as 'king of Assyria' (36:2; 37:8, 37) and the Rabshakeh, Sennacherib's spokesperson, always speaks of him as 'the great king, the king of Assyria' (36:4, 13; cf. Hos. 5:13; 10:6),[122] 'king' (Isa. 36:8, 14, 15, 16), or 'Lord' (36:8, 9, 12), never on a first-name basis.[123] In addition to the constant use of royal titles, the rhetoric of the Rabshakeh's speech (36:4–10, 13–20) targets the futility of trusting in other human kings, such as Egypt's pharaoh (36:4–6, 9) or Hezekiah (36:15), and Sennacherib's letter (37:9–13) reminds Hezekiah that 'the king of Hamath, the king of Arpad, the king of the city of Sepharvaim, the king of Hena, or the king of Ivvah' (37:13) have had no success standing against King Sennacherib. The argument is that no king is worthy of trust other than the king of Assyria, for no king can stand against him. What is more, the gods of the nations (36:18–19; 37:12) could not protect their people, so Hezekiah's God YHWH (36:7, 15; 37:10) will be unable to deliver Zion, as well. Thus a prominent

---

[119] Debate concerning the date of Isa. 36 – 37 and whether it was written initially for 2 Kings or Isaiah is abundant. Many argue that 2 Kgs 18:13–16 was the original core text (account A) with 2 Kgs 18:17 – 19:9a, 36 – 37 (account B1 // Isa. 36:2 – 37:9a, 37 – 38) and 2 Kgs 19:9b–35 (account B2 // Isa. 37:9b–36) later emerging as legendary accounts of Jerusalem's preservation. For an overview, see Seitz 1991: 47–118; Williamson 1994: 189–211. All agree that the accounts come after Sennacherib's death in 681 BC (Isa. 37:38). The time of Manasseh (Seitz 1991: 100–102, 116), Josiah (Sweeney 1996: 484–485), Zedekiah (Smelik 1986: 86) and after the exile (Clements 1980: 60–62) are suggested as possibilities. While most believe that it was initially written for its context in 2 Kings, though mindful of Isaianic traditions, Ackroyd (1987: 105–120), Smelik (1986) and Conrad (1991: 34–51) have raised the possibility that it was written for its place in Isaiah.

[120] Beuken (2000: 339), Clements (1994: 239), Oswalt (1986: 629–689), Sweeney (1996: 465) and Brueggemann (2008: 34–37) acknowledge that the tension here is between YHWH and Sennacherib, though their insights are underdeveloped.

[121] I assume that Isa. 36 – 37 can be read as a coherent literary whole. See Smelik 1986 and Abernethy 2014a: 94–113.

[122] This title applies to God in Ps. 48:2 (cf. Matt. 5:35). For Assyrian texts where this title is used, see Wildberger 2002: 391.

[123] See also Isa. 37:10–11.

dynamic within the narrative is that King Sennacherib is claiming that other kings or their gods cannot stop the Assyrian king and the spread of his empire.

Who is King Sennacherib having a showdown with? Is it merely with Hezekiah? The real battle is between Sennacherib and YHWH. Though Sennacherib threatens Hezekiah, Judah's king turns to God for help on two occasions. First, he sends word to Isaiah to appeal to God, for he hopes that '[YHWH] your God will hear the words of the Rabshakeh, whom his master the king of Assyria has sent to mock the living God' (37:4).The threat of the Rabshakeh is not simply an assault against Hezekiah's status as king but also an assault against the living God. God must act on behalf of his own name.[124] Second, in response to Sennacherib's letter (37:9–13), Hezekiah turns directly to God in prayer saying:

> O LORD of hosts, God of Israel, enthroned above the cherubim, you are the God, you alone, of all the kingdoms of the earth; you have made heaven and earth. (37:16)

The opening words of this prayer place an emphasis on God's cosmic kingship. The language is similar to 2 Samuel 6:2 ('the ark of God, which is called by the name of the LORD of hosts who is enthroned on the cherubim' [NRSV; cf. 1 Sam. 4:4]), when David brings the ark into Jerusalem as a symbol of God's kingship. Addressing God as the 'LORD of hosts' evokes God's status as king. As the one who sits between the cherubim, Hezekiah calls upon the king who is surrounded by seraphim in Isaiah 6.[125] What is more, Hezekiah declares that YHWH alone is God of the 'kingdoms of the earth'. This assertion of God's international sovereignty raises tension regarding whether YHWH will out duel Sennacherib, the supposed 'great king'. By acting on behalf of Zion, 'all the kingdoms of the earth may know that you alone are the LORD' (37:20). The role of Hezekiah in this narrative is apparent. He can do very little other than look to God as the supreme king who will be able to stand against the threats of King Sennacherib.

The parallels between Sennacherib and YHWH in Table 1.2 further display how the focus of these chapters is upon the identity of the supreme king.[126]

---

[124] Oswalt 1986: 626.
[125] On divine kingship and enthronement amid cherubim, see Brettler 1989: 83.
[126] For a similar table, see Abernethy 2014a: 112.

Table 1.2 Parallels between Sennacherib and YHWH

Sennacherib	YHWH
Messenger (the Rabshakeh) delivers the words of Sennacherib (36:4, 14, 16; *kōh 'mr hammelek*)	Messenger (Isaiah) delivers the words of YHWH (37:6, 10, 21, 33; *kōh 'mr yhwh*)
Initial words try to sway the trust of the audience (36:4–10; 37:10; *bṭḥ* [eight times])	Initial words try to sway the trust of the audience (37:6; *'al-tîrā'*)
Claim of supremacy over all enemies – nations, kings and gods (36:14–20; 37:11–13)	Claim of supremacy over the enemy – Assyria and Sennacherib (37:6–8, 22–29, 33–35)
Believes 'the city' (*h'îr*) will be under his control (36:15; 37:10)	Believes 'the city' (*h'îr*) will be under his control (37:33–34)
Promises 'eating' (*'kl*) and cultivable land (incl. *kĕrāmîm*) for the submissive (36:17)	Promises 'eating' (*'kl*) and cultivable land (incl. *kĕrāmîm*) for his people (37:30)

The evidence presented in Table 1.2 indicates that the real tension within these chapters centres upon whether Sennacherib or YHWH will be victorious. Unlike Sennacherib's words that fall flat, YHWH's words are fulfilled. Just as God promises (37:7), a distraction lures Sennacherib's attention away from Jerusalem (37:8–9). Just as God promises (37:29, 33–35), God intervenes through his angel to deliver his city dramatically and wipe out the encamped Assyrian army (37:36). The story, however, does not end with Zion's deliverance. It ends with King Sennacherib being murdered in the house of his own god (37:38), just as God promised (37:7). The narrative declares that YHWH is the real sovereign and that Sennacherib and his gods are no match for the God of all the kingdoms of the earth (37:16–17).

The great king, the king of Assyria, Sennacherib, was an unstoppable force during the late eighth century BC. At the culmination of a devastating campaign through Judah the odds for Jerusalem did not look good. Though the prophet Isaiah makes it clear that Sennacherib's success is divinely sanctioned as punishment for God's people (e.g. Isa. 3:1 – 4:1; 7:17, 20; 8:4, 7; 10:5–6), a different perspective emerges in Isaiah 36 – 37. The unstoppable force is stopped; God graciously and powerfully intervenes, showing that he, not Sennacherib or any other power after him, is the king of all the kingdoms on earth. And though Isaiah 39 reveals that God would allow another foreign nation, Babylon, to capture his city, there is no question about who holds all of the power after Isaiah 36 – 37. Come what may, YHWH is the supreme king as evidenced in real time and space in the narrative of YHWH's overcoming King Sennacherib to save his city. This provides a historical basis to hope for reversal amid the bleak exile that looms in the backdrop of Isaiah 40 and beyond.

Isaiah 36 – 37 and canon

The narrative in Isaiah 36 – 37 displays how King YHWH is supreme over King Sennacherib of Assyria. Placing this narrative within Isaiah helps God's people to hold on to hope in God's sovereignty in the aftermath of exile, when many would question whether God remains supreme (ch. 39). Would God's people dare to believe that he is an unrivalled king, even when other kings are having their way? Isaiah 36 – 37 aims to stoke the embers of faith among the people of God; God is unrivalled even when evidence is pointing in the other direction. Fundamental to belief in Christ is the conviction that no earthly king or power is his rival. Though Jesus was born during the time of King Herod and suffered under Pontius Pilate, Jesus' resurrection and ascension to heaven, where he is seated at God's right hand, show that Christ's reign is unstoppable. For this reason Christians refer to Jesus as 'our Lord', an eminently political and theological title. Just as God is a supreme king over Sennacherib in Isaiah 36 – 37, so Christ had no rivals during his time on earth and will continue to have no rivals throughout the history of the world. The NT, which was also written during a time of empire, offers a corresponding witness to Jesus' supremacy over other kings, with Jesus being contrasted with Herod in Matthew 2 and with kingdom rhetoric interlacing the interactions between Pilate and Jesus and his subsequent crucifixion (cf. Matt. 27:11, 29, 37, 42). The humble, crucified king is the Lord of all. Thus the narration of YHWH's supremacy over King Sennacherib bears witness, at least indirectly, throughout all time that no human king can stand against Christ, our king.

Conclusion

We have considered four passages, Isaiah 6, 24 – 25, 33 and 36 – 37, from Isaiah 1 – 39 that assert God's kingship. All of these come at crucial junctures within the argument of Isaiah 1 – 39, forcing readers of Isaiah constantly to orient their thoughts around God as king. These passages, however, are not monolithic. They each contribute something unique concerning God's kingship and in their own particular style. Set within an eighth-century context in Judah where injustice was rampant and where Israel, Aram and Assyria were threats, the vision of God reigning as the holy king in Isaiah 6 provides a basis for his executing purging judgment upon Judah with the lingering hope of a holy seed. Set within an eschatological setting, Isaiah 24 – 25 poetically presents the future reign of God on Zion as the basis for cosmic judgment – everything must be levelled – and for a glorious salvation. In historical eschatology (possibly linked to the eighth-century context) the prospect of gazing upon God as king in his beauty and the declaration that God is judge, ruler, saviour and king in 33:17 and 22 provide delightful rays of hope for those worthy of ascending the hill of the Lord amid internal and external threats. Set during Sennacherib's invasion of Judah (701 BC), Isaiah 36 – 37 recounts in narrative form how God is the all-powerful king of the entire world as he defeats Sennacherib. These passages operate from a variety of angles at programmatic places within Isaiah 1 – 39 to leave us with a wide-ranging impression of God's kingship. God is king already (6:1–5), but his reign is not yet fully realized (24:23; 33:17, 22). God is a king who must judge both now (6:1–13; 37:36 [cf. 10:33–34]) and more extensively later (24:21–23; 33:5–6). God is a king who is dreadful to gaze upon (6:1–5), yet gazing upon him is a beautiful prospect for the faithful (33:17). God's kingship is seen through temple (6:1–5), military (24:21–23; 36 – 37), judicial (33:22) and feasting (25:6–8) imagery.

While these passages are closely tied to the historical circumstances of Judah, particularly in the eighth century, they have been preserved for future generations of God's people who would continue living amid this tension between the already and the not yet of God's reign. Through Isaiah 6 God's people experience the healthy dread and glimmer of hope that comes from seeing that God reigns right now as the holy king who is willing to forgive Isaiah. Through Isaiah 24 – 25 God's people look to the future when God's reign will be eschatologically realized upon Zion, with judgment meted out on a cosmic scale and with salvation experienced as God's people dine with their king. Through Isaiah 33 God's people find further encouragement from knowing that they will see God as king in his beauty, far removed from the terror of the judgment Isaiah witnessed in Isaiah 6. Finally, through historical narrative God's people see a historical example of how God manifested his kingship by defeating Sennacherib, which is a token of hope for greater works of salvation to come (25:9; 33:22). These passages all work together to call for God's people to turn their eyes away from the competing gods and powers of this world and live under and in anticipation of God's reign.

Chapter Two

God, the only saving king in Isaiah 40 – 55

A dark, Babylonian abyss resides between Isaiah 39 and 40. Isaiah 39 anticipates Babylonian captivity, and while the details of the exile are not spelled out in Isaiah, as they are in Jeremiah and Lamentations, the experience of trauma looms behind Isaiah 40 – 55. Something devastating will or has transpired between Isaiah 39 and 40. Surely, the loss of land, temple and king stemming from Babylonian captivity would lead many to question God's status as the only 'God . . . of all the kingdoms of the earth' (Isa. 37:16). The people feel like their way is hidden from God and that he is not treating them fairly (40:27). Is Babylon with its king and its gods more powerful than YHWH? If YHWH is the true king, why does he not act on behalf of Israel? Has God abandoned his people and his promises? While the historically narrated announcement of exile in Isaiah 39 effectively initiates a transition to God's message for those who will or have experienced exile in chapters 40–55, it is not the only bridging chapter between Isaiah 1 – 39 and 40 – 55. Prior to Isaiah 39, a vision of transformation – the return of God and exiles to Zion – in chapter 35 lurks as a bright light behind the dark cloud of anticipated exile in chapter 39.[1]

> The wilderness and the dry land shall be glad . . .
> They shall see the glory of the LORD,
>   the majesty of our God.
> Strengthen the weak hands,
>   and make firm the feeble knees.
> Say to those who have an anxious heart,
>   'Be strong; fear not!
>   Behold, your God
>   will come with vengeance,

---

[1] Some critical scholars hold that 'Deutero-Isaiah' wrote Isa. 35 (Scott 1936), while most understand it as a post-exilic addition that bridges with other parts of the book (Williamson 1994: 211–221).

> with the recompense of God.
> He will come and save you.'
>
> . . .
>
> And a highway shall be there,
>   and it shall be called the Way of Holiness . . .
> And the ransomed of the LORD shall return
>   and come to Zion with singing;
> everlasting joy shall be upon their heads;
>   they shall obtain gladness and joy,
>   and sorrow and sighing shall flee away.
>
> (Isa. 35:1–4, 8, 10)

Though exile to Babylon was coming (Isa. 39), the eye of faith, through the lens of Isaiah 35, sees beyond it to the time of redemption. This vision of hope is a frame of reference for the comforting message in Isaiah 40 – 55, and even some parts of Isaiah 56 – 66. In the face of despair and the temptation to trust in foreign gods, Isaiah 40 – 55, like Isaiah 35, declares that God will come in his glory, as king. This is the 'gospel' for the wounded, torn and tempted in Isaiah 40 – 55. By examining how Isaiah 40:1–11 and 52:7–10, in conjunction with chapter 35, establish an arc within Isaiah 40 – 55, it will be evident that the coming of God as king is the anchor of these chapters. We will then reflect upon a few themes in Isaiah 40 – 55 as they relate to God's kingship.[2]

The king will come in Isaiah 40:1–11 and 52:7–10

There is a type-scene within modern movies that involves playing opera amid bleak circumstances. In *Life Is Beautiful* Guido plays La Barcarolle by Offenbach on a record player in a Nazi concentration camp with the hope that his wife will hear it as a love song from him. In *The Shawshank Redemption* Andy broadcasts *Figaro* to the sweet delight of his fellow prisoners. In Isaiah 'Comfort, comfort my people says your God' (40:1) are operatic words sung into despairing ears

---

[2] The claim here is not that Isa. 40 – 55 was an independent book, but the text as we have it clearly invites us to read chapters 40 – 55 as addressing an exilic setting, for the chasm between Isa. 39 and 40 is clear, as are the references to Babylon (e.g. 43:14; 48:20), as Calvin observes (1979b: 197). Debate also concerns whether 40 – 55 is a literary unit. Correspondence between Isa. 40 and 55 through the motif of fulfilling God's word (40:6–8; 55:10–11) frames this section. The inclusio between 56:1–8 and 66:18–24 frames 56 – 66 to set it apart from 40 – 55, although numerous motifs occur across these sections.

and hearts. Dismantling any doubt that the covenant formula 'I will be your God, and you will be my people' has come to nothing,[3] Isaiah 40:1 assures exiles that 'your God' – the God of the covenant – desires comfort for his people. These words bring light into a deep, dark cave, where there is no obvious exit. The chosen city, Jerusalem, is in shambles. There is no Davidic king on the throne. For the exiles, the Promised Land is no longer home. For those left in the land, taxation, decentralization, foreign dominion and traumatic memories make life unsettling. They are saying:

> My way is hidden from the LORD,
> my cause [*mišpāṭ*] is disregarded by my God.
>
> (40:27, NIV84)

God seems to have forgotten them. The words of Isaiah 40 aim to break this tide of doubt and replace it with hope in and allegiance to God. What is the 'comfort' that these verses offer? What is its 'gospel'? A closer look at Isaiah 40:1–11 will specify that their hope resides in God's glorious coming as king. As we will see, these verses correspond with Isaiah 52:7–10 to anchor the message of chapters 40–55 around this prospect.

The tender king is coming in Isaiah 40:1–11

Throughout the subunits (1–2; 3–5; 6–8; 9–11) of Isaiah 40:1–11 there is an emphasis on proclamation.[4] The audience is to 'comfort, comfort . . . speak tenderly' to Zion by announcing that judgment has passed (40:1–2).[5] Next 'a voice cries' out to summon preparation for

---

[3] G. V. Smith 2009: 93; Baltzer and Machinist 2001: 49.

[4] See Carr (1995) for an overview of the various divisions of this chapter. While the relationship between vv. 1–8 and 9–11 is difficult to decipher (Blenkinsopp 2002: 185), the shared notion of the coming of God in 3–5 and 9–11 unites them. Sacon (1974: 113) notes syntactical parallels (imperatives followed by content clauses) in 1–2 and 9–11.

[5] It is difficult to identify the audience and speakers in these verses. Some (Cross 1953; Motyer 1993: 299) argue that God is addressing his heavenly council, as in Isa. 6:8, with a heavenly being serving as the voice of the individual in 40:3 and 40:6. It is rare, however, for heavenly beings to receive the task of addressing God's people as a whole (R. J. Clifford 1984). Others believe that God is addressing a group of prophets (Blenkinsopp 2002: 179–183) or 'lookouts' (cf. 52:7; Goldingay and Payne 2006a: 63, 73, 79; Berges 2012: 357), but there are no other mentions of a group of prophets in 40 – 55 and the need to retain ambiguity until 52:7 ('lookouts') seems unlikely. It may be, as some argue (G. V. Smith 2009: 90–93; Oswalt 1998: 50–51), that the ambiguity here is intentional, enabling anyone who hears this message to receive it as a call to join in the task of proclaiming comfort to God's people.

God's return (40:3–5). Then the voice commands the prophet to 'cry (out)', though the prophet views this as futile in the light of the frailty and faithlessness of humanity (40:6–8). The surety of God's word, though, counters the prophet's concerns. Finally, Zion is fearlessly to 'lift up [its] voice' and declare to those all around that God is coming as a tender king (40:9–11). These verses are all about trumpeting good tidings, so we must consider the content of the message. Of particular interest to us is the central hope that God will come in 40:3–5 and 9–11.

Preparing for the glorious king in Isaiah 40:3–5
Following the comforting news of forgiveness and that judgment has come to an end (40:1–2), an anonymous voice cries out:

> In the wilderness prepare the way of the LORD;
>> make straight in the desert a highway for our God.
> Every valley shall be lifted up,
>> and every mountain and hill be made low;
> the uneven ground shall become level,
>> and the rough places a plain.
>
> (Isa. 40:3–4)

The scene is that of ensuring a smooth journey by clearing and straightening paths and highways in desolate regions and by levelling high and low terrain to make passage easy.[6] How are we to understand this scene? Some argue that road preparation here pertains to enabling exiles to return smoothly from Babylon. As S. Paul puts it, 'Just as God led Israel through the desert after their exodus from Egypt, He will now lead them through yet another desert, from Babylonia to Israel.'[7] This view, however, is unsatisfactory. Though 'way' can refer to the return of exiles elsewhere in Isaiah (42:16; 43:19; 49:11; 51:10), those instances envisage God's making a way for them, whereas in 40:3 others are preparing a way for God.[8] The focus here is upon preparing for God's return.[9]

---

[6] The scene may reflect preparations for processions of Babylonian gods or for a returning king (Goldingay and Payne 2006a: 74). Westermann (1969: 38) notes a parallel in a Babylonian hymn: 'Hasten to go out, (Nabu), son of Bel, you who know the ways and the customs. Make his way good, renew his road, make his path strength, hew him out a trail.'

[7] Paul 2011: 130.

[8] For a critique of interpreting 40:3 as a return of exiles, see Koole 1997: 58–60.

[9] Baltzer and Machinist (2001: 53) think the scene parallels a king who commissions the building of roads.

In what sense can someone 'prepare the way of the LORD'? Since 'no one would have thought God's way could be hindered by physical obstacles',[10] the command to prepare the way in the wilderness is non-literal. The 'wilderness' (*midbār*) can be symbolic in Isaiah for Zion's great desolation (32:15; 35:1 with *'ărābâ* [desert]; 51:3 with *'ărābâ* [desert]). The wilderness, then, symbolizes Zion's desolation. The concept of preparing a way is akin to its use in Malachi 3:1 when read in conjunction with Malachi 4:5, where God's messenger prepares the way for God's coming by turning the hearts of the people to where they should be.[11] Since God's way here is 'first and foremost Yahweh's way, his manifestation of glory', the people must prepare their hearts to meet their God.[12] In Isaiah 40:3–4, amid Zion's desolation, despair and doubt, the voice is calling for the audience to be spiritually ready for the coming of God.[13]

While Isaiah 40 – 55 is certainly a book of comfort, this call to prepare spiritually reveals how the audience is struggling in their faith, as they are following foreign gods (e.g. 40:18–20; 44:9–20; 46:1–7), doubting God's trustworthiness (40:27) and needing to be commanded to heed God's word (55:1–3a, 6–7). Additionally, as Koole notes, since being in God's presence requires righteous and faithful living (cf. Ps. 24:3), hearers would receive the metaphorical command to prepare the way of the Lord as 'a call for faith and repentance' in the light of God's coming.[14] The despondent audience – the 'wilderness', those living in the aftermath of judgment and God's apparent absence – are to awaken their faith, turn away from foreign gods, and wait in hope (40:31) for the coming of God. In this sense, they are to prepare for God's return.

Following upon the call to prepare for God's coming (40:3–4) we gain a further sense of what God's coming will entail in 40:5.

---

[10] G. V. Smith 2009: 96.

[11] The only other combinations of 'to prepare' (*pnh*) and 'way' (*derek*) aside from 40:3 and Mal. 3:1 occur in Isa. 57:14 and 62:10. Those verses symbolically express God's desire for his people to be with him. Just as going to great measures to clear a road shows how important a person's arrival is, so God's call for the preparation of a way displays how dear his faithful people are to him.

[12] Lim 2010: 61–68, esp. 62. Lim argues that God's way is both eschatological, as it pertains to God's coming, and ethical, as it relates to the need for God's people to align their lives with God. Lund (2007: 85–95, esp. 95) interprets YHWH's way both as metaphorical for YHWH's powerful actions and as applying to a literal situation where God's people can 'reestablish Jerusalem as the city where YHWH's presence is to be found'.

[13] G. V. Smith 2009: 96.

[14] Koole 1997: 60.

> And the glory of the LORD shall be revealed,
> and all flesh shall see it together,
> for the mouth of the LORD has spoken.
>
> (Isa. 40:5)

The concept of God's 'glory' (*kābôd*) invites us into the realm of God's kingship in the light of ancient traditions. Within Isaiah glory often is a part of kingship, whether it refers to foreign kings (8:7; 14:18) or to God as king in 6:3 or 24:23, as we have seen.[15] One also recalls how in Psalm 24:7–10 YHWH is called the 'king of glory' five times as he enters Zion. Thus the anticipation of God's glory being revealed would call to mind God's return as king.

The revelation of YHWH in the full weight of his kingship, in his glory, intertwines with traditions in Israel's history where God manifests his presence at the completion of the tabernacle (Exod. 40:34–35) and temple (1 Kgs 8:11; cf. Isa. 4:5).[16]

> Then the cloud covered the tent of meeting, and the glory of the LORD filled the tabernacle. And Moses was not able to enter the tent of meeting because the cloud settled on it, and the *glory of the LORD* filled the tabernacle. (Exod. 40:34–35)

> so that the priests could not stand to minister because of the cloud, for *the glory of the LORD* filled the house of the LORD. (1 Kgs 8:11)

Part of Judah and Israel's self-understanding was that the very glory of God, the covenant king who resided upon the throne (ark) in the midst of the tabernacle and temple, had chosen to reside in the midst of his people. One can only imagine the trauma experienced by those who witnessed the fall of the temple, which symbolized the departure of God's glory from his chosen city. Not only was God's presence lost, but the very identity of the people would have been shaken. These were a people whom God chose to dwell among – but no more. Ezekiel dramatically envisages the glory of YHWH departing from the temple and his city (10:4, 18; 11:23) during initial phases of Babylonian exile. Despite the devastating news that God's glory is departing from his people, Ezekiel holds out hope that the Lord's

---

[15] On God's glory in Isaiah, see Wagner 2012: 123–237. He regularly observes how 'glory' pertains to rhetoric involving kingship. Cf. G. V. Smith 2009: 96–97.

[16] Blenkinsopp 2002: 183.

glory will again fill a new, cosmic temple (43:4–5; 44:4). The language of Isaiah 40:5, then, would have resonated with exiles: with those who had a history full of stories concerning God's glorious, manifest royal presence, but who saw no evidence of it at the time. Isaiah 40:5 lifts the eyes, indeed the hearts of his people, by declaring that God's glory will be revealed. The glorious God will return to his forsaken city as king.

At the revelation of God's glorious return as king 'all flesh shall see it together' (40:5b). This is a development in a motif that we saw unfolding in Isaiah 1 – 39. In Isaiah 6:1 it was the prophet who 'saw' the holy king. In Isaiah 33:17 the eyes of the faithful will 'see' the king in his beauty. In Isaiah 35:2, a passage very similar to Isaiah 40:1–11, those who experience transformation ('the wilderness') will

> see the glory of the LORD,
> the majesty of our God.
> (35:2)

Now, in Isaiah 40:5, it will be 'all flesh' who see the glory of the Lord as he returns as king to Zion.[17] Thus Isaiah 40:3–5 develops a message that extends beyond the announcement in 40:1–2 that judgment is in the past. Judgment is not simply over, but preparations need to take place for the dramatic revelation of God's glory when he comes as king. When he comes, all nations – even those oppressing Israel[18] – will see God's glory manifest as he returns to his people and his city as king. The mouth of the Lord confirms that this will be (40:5c).

The good news of the tender king in 40:9–11
Isaiah 40:9–11 invites Zion to join in the mix of declaring the coming of God. While it shares with 40:3–5 the hope that God will come, these verses depict his coming with their own set of imagery that balances the king's transcendence with his tenderness. Verse 9 begins with a command to 'go on up' a high mountain. While the reason for this is not clear initially, the subject of the command is the herald

---

[17] Wagner 2012: 174. Isa. 52:10 shares a similar focus on the universal revelation of God's glory (cf. 41:5, 20; 49:7; 62:2). See also Pao 2002: 47–48, who notes the universal interest in Isa. 40:3–5 in the light of Isa. 52:10. On 'all flesh', see in 49:26 and 66:16, 23 (Oswalt 1998: 52).

[18] Blenkinsopp 2002: 183.

of good news, Zion,[19] so this clarifies the reason for ascending the mountain: Zion has a message to proclaim. In the second half of verse 9 the notion of ascent continues through the command to 'lift up your voice'. The content of Zion's proclamation stretches from the end of verse 9 to verse 11:

> 'Behold your God!'
> Behold, the Lord GOD comes with might,
>   and his arm rules for him;
> behold, his reward is with him,
>   and his recompense before him.
> He will tend his flock like a shepherd;
>   he will gather the lambs in his arms;
> he will carry them in his bosom,
>   and gently lead those that are with young.
>   (Isa. 40:9b–11)

There is a dual focus on his 'arm' (*zĕrô'a*) in verses 10–11 that balances God's coming between his power and his tenderness.[20] On the one hand, in verse 10, his arm is 'ruling' for him. The verb 'to rule' (*māšal*) conveys the general idea of 'having control or dominion', such as the sun and moon ruling over day and night (Gen. 1:18) or God's having dominion over the raging sea (Ps. 89:9).[21] Throughout Israel's history God's 'arm' symbolizes his acting in power to save his people, especially from Egypt (Exod. 15:16; Deut. 4:34; Pss 44:3; 77:15; 89:11). Elsewhere in Isaiah, especially in Isaiah 40 – 66, God's 'arm' symbolizes God's acting on behalf of his people to save them (33:2; 48:14; 52:10; 53:1; 59:16; 63:5, 12). This is especially noteworthy in 52:10, where the revelation of God's arm corresponds to the good news of God's reign. The vision of God's arm ruling, then, conveys the hope of his coming to save his people in an expression of great power in 40:10, akin to God's mighty acts in the exodus event (cf. Isa. 63:12). He is coming in saving dominion. While God's coming with a ruling arm may be bad news for some, the descriptors of having 'his reward'

---

[19] Debate surrounds whether Zion is the bearer ('Zion, herald of good news'; AV; NASB; NRSV) or the recipient ('You who bring good tidings to Zion', NIV; JPS). The feminine imperatives ('Go on up . . . lift up . . . lift up . . . say'), feminine pronouns ('your voice') and feminine participles ('herald of good news') are best explained as modifying Zion, making it most likely that Zion is the bearer rather than the recipient of the good news. See Koole 1997: 71–72; Oswalt 1998: 52, n. 28.

[20] See Motyer 1993: 302 and Oswalt 1998: 55, who note the balancing use of 'arm'.

[21] Nel 1997: 1136–1137.

and 'his recompense' with him convey positive connotations of rightful payment (cf. 2 Chr. 15:7; Isa. 62:11; Jer. 31:16).[22] As God's arm comes in power, his people will receive what they are waiting for: his salvation.[23]

While the power of God's ruling 'arm' (*zĕrô'a*) is emphasized in verse 10, the caring, shepherding nature of God's 'arm' (*zĕrô'a*) is in view in verse 11: 'he will gather the lambs in his arms'. '[V]irtually everyone was at least indirectly acquainted with shepherds' work' in the ANE,[24] so the imagery of God's 'shepherding' (*r'h*) and 'gathering' (*qbṣ*) his flock would resonate with the audience.[25] The primary tasks of shepherds were to help sheep find pasture and 'food' (*r'h*) and to gather them when they would 'scatter' (*qbṣ*). This is precisely what God is doing in 40:11. Due to the potency of this imagery, gods and rulers were called shepherds throughout the ancient world. For example, in the Enuma Elish we have a scene where Marduk is declared to be king, and as this takes place, he is called a shepherd:

> His lordship shall be supreme, he shall have no rival,
> He shall be the shepherd of the black-headed folk,
> his creatures.
>
> (VI: 106–107)[26]

The poem goes on to describe how Marduk had the job of providing for the other gods as the king, sovereign over all others. As another example, King Hammurabi calls himself a 'beneficent shepherd whose scepter is righteousness'.[27] Within Scripture shepherd-boy David is called by God to take on the role of shepherding God's people as king (Ps. 78:70–72; cf. Ps. 2:9).[28] This shepherding motif emphasizes how the ruler is to care for those under his dominion.

In the context of Isaiah 40, where devastation and scattering in exile looms in the background, the vision of God as shepherd certainly

[22] See Childs 2001: 302 as he discusses how these terms positively focus on God's salvation, in contrast to 35:4, where God is coming both in 'vengeance' (*nāqām*) and salvation.

[23] On God's reward as salvation, see G. V. Smith 2009: 100.

[24] Laniak 2006: 46.

[25] In Jer. 31:10, Ezek. 34:13 and Nah. 3:18 these same verbs ('to graze' and 'to gather') occur in contexts where shepherding imagery is utilized, revealing how such actions were often associated with a shepherd.

[26] All translations of the Enuma Elish derive from Foster 1997. Citations indicate the tablet and line numbers.

[27] Laniak 2006: 61.

[28] Ibid. 107–108.

addresses their circumstances. God will 'tend' (*r'h*) his flock in the sense of meeting all their needs, initially the grave challenges of renewing life in a war-torn land. With his sheep scattered in exile, he will also gather them. With his sheep wounded and weak, he will carry them in his chest. He will lead the young ones as they go. Their God, who will come as king, will be tender, shepherding his flock. Thus when verses 10 and 11 are read together, Zion's gospel in verses 9–11 is that God is coming as king, both in saving power (40:10) and in tender care (40:11).[29]

In summary, from several angles, the message of comfort in Isaiah 40:1–11 centres upon the hope of God's coming as king. With judgment past, preparations need to be made because the glorious king is coming (40:3–5)! Zion should declare to those all around that the king is coming in great power and great tenderness (40:9–11). The hope of God's coming as king sits strategically at the start of Isaiah 40 – 55. If God desires to comfort his people and to win them away from despair and other deities, he must rekindle embers of hope with the truth that God's story with his people is not over. A new chapter in God's plan is about to unfold: God's glorious, kingly presence of ages past will manifest itself again, in a universal fashion, and he will save his flock as a mighty, tender king.

The victorious, saving king is coming in Isaiah 52:7–10

The primary focus of Isaiah 41 – 48 is that God will use Cyrus to rebuild Jerusalem (44:24 – 45:7) and that Babylon and other gods are futile (44:9–20; 46:1–4; 47:1–3). It becomes apparent, however, that God has a greater work of salvation in store beyond the rebuilding of Jerusalem through Cyrus after Babylon's fall. The return of God from Isaiah 40:1–11 emerges again in Isaiah 49 – 55, amid an alternation between passages depicting God's redemption of Zion (49:14–26; 50:1–3;51:1 – 52:12; 54) and God's use of his servant (49:1–13; 50:4–9 [10–11?]; 52:13 – 53:12).[30] While we will return to how God's servant coordinates with God's redemption of Zion in a later chapter, here we will consider how Zion's salvation must be understood in the light of YHWH's kingship.

While Isaiah 49 – 55 initiates a new phase of argument, there is obvious correspondence between 40:1–11 and 52:7–10 that gives

---

[29] Though Childs (2001: 302) conjoins the two realities by stating, '[God's] strength is manifest as he leads his flock like a shepherd, carrying in his arms the weak', the distinctness of both his power and care should be maintained.

[30] G. V. Smith 2009: 337.

Isaiah 40 – 55 a sort of coherence around the prospect of YHWH's reign as king.[31] Table 2.1 displays the similarities between 52:7–10 and 40:1–11.[32]

Table 2.1 The similarities between Isaiah 52:7–10 and 40:1–11

Isaiah 52:7–10	Corresponding texts from 40:1–11
How beautiful upon the *mountains*	40:9 Go on up to a high *mountain*,
are the feet of him who brings *good news*,	O Zion, herald of *good news*;
who publishes peace, who brings *good news*	lift up your voice with strength,
of happiness,	O Jerusalem, herald of *good news*;
who publishes salvation,	lift it up, fear not;
who **says** to Zion,	**say** to the cities of Judah,
'Your God reigns.'	'Behold your God!'
[8] The voice of your watchmen – they lift up	
their voice;	40:5 and all flesh shall see it together
together they sing for joy;	[cf. 52:10]
for eye to eye they see	
the return of the LORD to Zion.	40:1 **Comfort, comfort my people**
[9] Break forth together into singing,	
you waste places of Jerusalem,	40:10–11 . . . and his *arm* rules for
for the LORD has **comforted** his **people**;	him . . .
he has redeemed Jerusalem.	he will gather the lambs in his
[10] The LORD has bared his holy *arm*	*arms* . . .
before the eyes of all the nations,	
and all the ends of the earth shall see	40:5 and all flesh shall see it together
the salvation of our God.	[cf. 52:8]

While Isaiah 40:1–11 and 52:7–10 develop their messages in differing ways according to the needs of their respective literary contexts, the conceptual and terminological overlap between these passages is striking, as some scholars note.[33] Both passages envisage the declaration of good news and comfort, centre this good news on the coming

---

[31] Wagner (2012: 168–170), adopting the view of Berges, argues that Isa. 40:1–5 was initially the opening of Deutero-Isaiah that coordinated with 52:7–10, which was the conclusion to an initial phase of the corpus's formation. He posits that 40:6–8 was added later to extend its introductory role to relate to Isa. 55. Isa. 40:9–11 was later added to associate with ch. 61. A problem with this is that 40:9–11 corresponds with 52:7–10 as well. For this reason Ehring (2007: 90–95) argues that 40:1–5, 9–11 belong together as an initial prologue to a section that concluded with 52:7–10 as an epilogue. Tiemeyer (2012: 234) also believes 40:9–11 belongs with 40:1–5, though she thinks 52:7–10 was written first, with 40:1–11 written later to allude to it.

[32] See Beuken (2009: 100–101) for a similar collection of shared terms. Tiemeyer (2012: 236–244) uncovers eight similarities between the terms found in 40:1–11; 52:7–10; 62:11; 63:1–6; and 59:15 – 20:1: (1) God's arm/strength, (2) justice and righteousness, (3) God as coming victor, (5) seeing, (6) glory and honour, (7) watchmen and messengers, (8) missing people.

[33] See Ehring 2007: 90–93.

of God as king and share the concern that all nations see this revelation. One might be tempted to be content with a brief statement that Isaiah 52:7–10 declares, like Isaiah 40:1–11, that Zion's great comfort resides in the coming of God as king. This is true, but we would miss out on the unique texture of 52:7–10 within the logic of Isaiah 51:1 – 52:12 if we conflated these passages too quickly.

Three prominent connections between 51:1–11 and 52:7–10 bind these chapters together: (1) comforting wastelands (51:3; 52:9; cf. 51:12), (2) God's saving arm (51:5, 9–11; 52:10), (3) God's salvation (51:6, 8; 52:7, 10). Isaiah 51:1–3 opens this section with an analogy: just as God brought life out of barren Abraham and Sarah (51:2), so God will 'comfort' (*nhm*) Zion and all of its 'waste places' (*ḥārĕbôt*; 51:3) by making it lush like Eden and full of joy. This corresponds with 52:9, where the 'waste places' (*ḥārĕbôt*) of Jerusalem are to rejoice because of YHWH's 'comfort' (*nhm*) for his people when he comes as king. Next the motif of God's 'arm' (*zĕrô'a*) surfaces, with God declaring that his arms – the hope of the nations – will act in saving justice (51:5). This leads the prophet to call upon God to awaken his arm, which previously acted so mightily in defeating Israel's ancient, mythic foes to act now against Babylon (51:9–11). God's holy arm answers this wake-up call in 52:10 with the prophet declaring that YHWH has laid bare his holy 'arm' (*zĕrô'a*), in parallel with 'salvation' (*yĕšû'â*), before all peoples. Furthermore, the eternal 'salvation' (*yĕšû'â*) that God contrasts with the ephemerality of threatening humans and even creation in Isaiah 51:6, 8 is declared by the lovely feet of the gospel messenger 'who publishes salvation [*yĕšû'â*]' in 52:7. What does the one publishing salvation make known (52:7)? In what way has God laid bare his arm (52:10)? What is the comfort for Zion's waste places (52:9)? The answer is found at the end of 52:7 and develops into verse 8:

> 'Your God reigns' . . .
> for eye to eye they see
>   the return of the LORD to Zion.

Just as ancient gods such as Ba'al and Marduk are recognized as king upon victory and then establish their palace, so Yahweh's great victory over Israel's foes (51:9–11, 21–23; 52:3–4) leads to the declaration that Yahweh reigns as king as he restores and returns to Zion.[34] By utilizing

---

[34] On the mythic backdrop, see Mettinger 1997 and Blenkinsopp 2000: 343.

the concepts of comforting waste places (51:3), God's arm (51:5, 9–11) and God's salvation (51:6, 8) from 51:1–11, Isaiah 52:7–10 provides a frame of reference for these hopes. God's comfort for the waste places (52:9), his action in salvation (52:7) and the revelation of his arm (52:10) will come to pass when God's triumph results in his reign as king upon return to Zion.

The scene of the lovely feet trotting through the mountains to bring the report that God reigns and is returning to Zion is a fitting high point, not simply in chapters 51–52 but also within Isaiah 40 – 55. While we will see that the reign of God as king interrelates with his use of a suffering servant (52:13 – 53:12) and the need for God's people to respond to this message in trusting obedience (55:1–3, 6–7), the force of the connections between 40:1–11 and 52:7–10 (see Table 2.1) remind us that Isaiah 40 – 55 is about comfort for the afflicted, about a God worthy of unwavering allegiance, about a king who will come to save his people in a mighty display of power that will be apparent to all nations. In this way, these verses frame Isaiah 40 – 55 in the light of a motif already introduced in Isaiah 35. Amid the wilderness of Zion's desolation, Isaiah 40:1–11 and 52:7–10, in continuation from Isaiah 35, offer announcements of comfort that God is coming as king to renew Zion. These passages, however, are not monolithic in how they depict God's coming. In 40:3–5 the Lord will come with his royal glory (cf. 35:2) – that glory which once inhabited the temple – manifesting itself in theophany. In 40:9–11 YHWH comes as king with a powerful arm to save, yet also with a tender arm like a shepherd. In Isaiah 52:7–10 God's arm again appears, this time amid a scene where YHWH returns to reign on Zion following a victory where his salvation is revealed throughout the entire world.

As we will see in the next chapter, this is not the last we hear of God's coming in the book of Isaiah. But for now, within chapters 40–55, we would do well to allow Isaiah 40:1–11 and 52:7–10 to reorient our hopes, our desires for comfort, our longings for vindication around the prophetic declarations that God himself is promising to come as king in all of its various nuances (glory, might, tenderness, saving power). Just as the current threat to the very existence of Christian presence in Christianity's most ancient church locations in Syria and Iraq prompts great despair and doubt, Isaiah 40 – 55 is balm in similar circumstances when Israel's existence had unravelled. Isaiah 40:1–11 and 52:7–10 provide an arch within the message of Isaiah 40 – 55 that aims to help the despairing endure in the light of the hope that the powerful, saving, tender, victorious king of the universe is coming.

Isaiah 40:1–11 and 52:7–10 in canonical context

The canonical force of Isaiah 40:1–11 and 52:7–10 cannot be under-estimated. Through coordination with chapter 35, along with 60 – 62, in addition to their strategic placement within the structure of Isaiah, Isaiah 40:1–11 and 52:7–10 emboss the hope of God's coming as king and the need to prepare for it at the core of Isaiah's message. Though there is a return from exile during the Persian era, the hope of God's comforting return does not fully materialize. For this reason Zechariah, a post-exilic prophet, reframes the timing of Zion's comfort to being beyond the initial return from exile (1:17). Zechariah waits for the time when God's glory will be in the midst of Jerusalem (2:5), where God will again dwell (2:10–11) and when he will come (14:5) and reign as king over the entire earth (14:9).[35]

These hopes for the glorious return of God as the tender and saving king have very strong layers of correspondence to Jesus. It is in Jesus that God's glory is manifest. John's Gospel suggests something similar: 'And the Word became flesh and dwelt among us, and we have seen his glory' (1:14). Throughout the Gospel of John Jesus manifests this glory in a number of ways, whether through providing wine at a wedding to protect a family's shame (2:11) or through Lazarus' revivification (11:4, 40). As the manifestation of God's glory, Jesus is the one for whom the way of the Lord was prepared. In the Gospels John the Baptist takes on the role of the voice in Isaiah 40:3, calling those who will listen to make straight the way of the Lord (John 1:23). The coming of Jesus is not a generic notion of God's coming; instead, Jesus' coming is the manifestation of God's royal presence. This is why Matthew can coordinate John the Baptist's message that the 'kingdom of heaven has come near' with his role as the voice calling for preparations to be made (Matt. 3:2–3). Indeed, the very good news of Jesus in Mark's Gospel (1:1–3) is initiated with the words of Isaiah 40:3 and conjoined with Malachi 3:1 to anchor Jesus' coming in the light of the grand hope of the coming of God from Isaiah. In Luke, in the reign of Tiberius Caesar (3:1), John the Baptist is again portrayed as the voice preparing the way for the Lord (3:3–4). The discreet witness of Isaiah 40:3–5 to God who will come in great glory, whom people are to prepare for, accords with the God who has come near in Jesus Christ the king.

---

[35] The Qumran community prepared for the Lord's return by moving to the wilderness. On Isa. 40:3–5 in Judaism, see R. E. Watts 1997: 82–84.

What is more, the character of Christ's coming certainly accords with the witness of 40:9–11 that God will come as a powerful and tender king. Through many miracles, defeating demons and by conquering death in Christ, God's saving power is on full display. What is more, the tenderness of our God is fully evident as Jesus loves outcasts, shows compassion for a people who are like sheep without a shepherd (Mark 6:34), is a champion for mercy, and dies for sinners. Indeed, John's Gospel depicts Jesus as a shepherd who cares so dearly for his people that he lays down his life for his flock (10:11).

Isaiah 52:7–10 also bears witness in conjunction with 40:1–11 to Christ. In Mark's Gospel John the Baptist's message draws upon the kingdom and good news language from 52:7: 'the kingdom of God has come near. Repent and believe the good news' (Mark 1:15, NIV).[36] What is more, Paul draws upon 52:7 ('How beautiful are the feet of those who bring good news!'; Rom. 10:15, NIV84) in Romans 10:15 to make the case that the good news of Christ must be preached to Jew and Gentile if there is any hope for belief. It is in Christ that God's arm has been laid bare, that God's saving reign as king has been initiated. This is why Mary can sing, 'He has performed mighty deeds with his arm' (Luke 1:51, NIV84).

While we can certainly profess that Isaiah's gospel, the good news that God will come, is made true in Jesus, the complete manifestation of God's glorious presence awaits its full realization when Christ comes again (Rev. 21:23). In the meantime, however, the church may be said through the Spirit to be partakers of 'the glory that is to be revealed' (1 Peter 5:1, NASB; cf. 4:13; Col. 1:27) in Christ the king, as we wait for the appearing of the Chief Shepherd (1 Peter 5:4).

God's kingship in other motifs in Isaiah 40 – 55

Amid the opening anticipation that YHWH will come as the saving king (40:1–11) and its development into a scene where YHWH is returning as a victorious king to Zion (52:7–10), there are two motifs worth considering that further impress upon us a sense of God's kingship in Isaiah 40 – 55: (1) kingship and righteousness, (2) YHWH's supremacy over other gods.

---

[36] Blenkinsopp 2002: 344.

Kingship and righteousness

The concept of righteousness in Isaiah is worthy of an entire monograph and is the source of many debates with regard to how it informs the NT use of the concept,[37] so I must limit myself to several reflections on righteousness in Isaiah 40 – 55 in the light of our study on God as king. As many scholars point out, there is a shift that occurs from Isaiah 1 – 39, where *righteousness* primarily refers to ethical human behaviour often in parallel with justice,[38] to Isaiah 40 – 55, where *righteousness* primarily refers to the divine action of setting things right often in parallel with salvation.[39] These two realms then intertwine in 56:1, enabling the book to close in a dialectic between the need for ethical human righteousness and God's commitment to establish righteousness within the world.[40] Amid this recognition that God's righteousness in Isaiah 40 – 55 often pertains to his saving action, I would like to suggest that we should think of God as the unrivalled king as we intertwine his saving action with his righteousness.

Righteousness is a regular characteristic of the rule of kings in the OT,[41] as we will see further in chapter 4.[42] These same ideals are applied to God as king, as we see in Psalms 97 and 98. In Psalm 97:1

[37] For an overview, see Scullion 1992; Seifrid 2001; Reumann 1992; Reimer 1997. Brunner's (1987: 210–225) understanding of righteousness as 'a comprehensive order that corresponds to God's will which pertains to the entire world, natural and human' may be broad enough to capture many uses of the term, though I agree with most scholars that each occurrence of *ṣedeq* and *ṣĕdāqâ* should receive its own consideration in context.

[38] *ṣedeq* with *mišpāṭ* in 1:21; 16:5; 26:9; 32:1; *ṣĕdāqâ* with *mišpāṭ* in 1:27; 5:7, 16; 9:7; 28:17; 32:16; 33:5. In Isa. 1 – 39 these nouns also parallel terms like 'faithful' ('*mn* in 1:21, 26; 11:5), 'equity' (11:4), 'steadfast love' (16:5) and 'peace' (32:17), but the regular use of the hendiadys in Isa. 1 – 39 is telling. On several occasions, there is ambiguity as to whether human ethical behaviour or God's actions are called to mind (cf. 1:27; 5:16).

[39] *ṣedeq* with a term for 'salvation' (*yš'*; 45:8; 51:5); *ṣĕdāqâ* with a term for 'salvation' (*yš'*; 45:18; 46:13; 52:6, 8). These all refer to God's action. 'Righteousness' also refers to ethical human action in 48:1, 18 and possibly in 42:6; 45:13; and 51:7. These terms also occur in parallel to 'torah' (51:7), 'faithfulness' (48:1) and 'peace' (48:18). Importantly, however, it never occurs in parallel with *mišpāṭ* in Isa. 40 – 55. Additionally, as de Jong (2011) argues, the word *bĕṣedeq* in 42:6 and 45:13 should be translated as 'legitimately', not with a salvific sense.

[40] For the clearest articulations of this argument, see Rendtorff 1993c; Oswalt 1997; Goldingay 2013.

[41] E.g. 2 Sam. 8:15; 1 Kgs 10:9; Ps. 72:1–2; Isa. 9.7[6]; 11:4; 16:5; 32:1; Jer. 22:15; 23:5.

[42] On the intersection between righteousness and human kingship, see Brunner 1987: 213, Scullion 1992: 727 and von Rad 2005: 370–383.

we see many of the characteristics of human kings noted above being applied to God:

> The LORD reigns, let the earth rejoice;
> let the many coastlands be glad!
> Clouds and thick darkness are all round him;
> righteousness and justice are the foundation of his throne.
>
> (Ps. 97:1–2)

In Psalm 98 we see similar features, but of particular importance is the coordination of God's righteousness as king with the notion of salvation. Psalm 98 opens with these statements about God:

> The LORD has made known his salvation;
> he has revealed his righteousness in the sight of the nations.
> He has remembered his steadfast love and faithfulness
> to the house of Israel.
> All the ends of the earth have seen
> the salvation of our God.
>
> (Ps. 98:2–3)

Here God's salvation for and faithfulness to his people, Israel, are wrapped up in God's righteousness that will become known throughout the world. God is both setting things right through salvation and maintaining right treatment of his people in the process. In response to God's saving and faithful action, verses 3–6 call for all the earth to join in jubilant song with wide-ranging instruments 'before the King, the LORD' (98:6). By referring to God as king in 98:6 the assumption is that his acts of saving righteousness (98:2–3) relate to his status as king (cf. Ps 145:7),[43] for praise is a fitting response to the king's salvation and righteousness.

The concept of God as the king who acts in righteousness and salvation to set things right in Psalms 97 and 98 may be similar to what we find in several verses in Isaiah 40 – 55. As was argued above, Isaiah 51 – 52 is arranged in such a way that the hopes for comfort, salvation and God's arm in the first part of chapter 51 culminate in the vision of God's reigning as king in 52:7–10. Since YHWH's kingship is the primary paradigm for conceptualizing the realization

---

[43] On divine kingship and righteousness/justice, see Scullion 1992: 732; Seifrid 2001: 425–428.

of these hopes, it is also probable that the repeated mention of God's righteousness in Isaiah 51 would be understood in the light of God's kingship in 52:7–10 too. Isaiah 51:1 opens with the statement

> Listen to me, you who pursue righteousness,
>   you who seek the LORD . . .
>
> (Isa. 51:1a)

On its own, a reader might interpret 'righteousness' (*ṣedeq*) with an ethical sense, meaning that people are pursuing God's ethical standards of righteousness. This seems unlikely, however, since verses 1b–3 go on to emphasize how God will restore and comfort Zion. God's people are pursuing righteousness in the sense of hoping to experience God's salvation that is near (51:5).[44] To those pursuing God's saving righteousness (51:1), God goes on to say:

> My righteousness draws near,
>   my salvation has gone out,
>   and my arms will judge the peoples;
> the coastlands hope for me,
>   and for my arm they wait.
>
> (Isa. 51:5)

In 51:5 the scope of God's righteousness expands to the entire world. What is more, God's righteousness and salvation are not disassociated from his international judicial action. While Isaiah 33:22 looks to God as the judge, lawgiver, saviour and king in Zion primarily for Israel, Isaiah 51:5 declares that God is going to set things right, not merely for Israel, but indeed for all nations. The long-lasting, definitive nature of God's righteousness appears in 51:6, 8:

> my salvation will be for ever,
>   and my righteousness will never be dismayed.
>
> (Isa. 51:6)

> but my righteousness will be for ever,
>   and my salvation to all generations.
>
> (Isa. 51:8)

---

[44] For an overview of positions, see Koole (1998: 138–139), who opts for a blending of the ethical and salvific senses.

God is assuring his people that the expression of his righteousness and salvation will be unending. Since God's reign in Zion (52:7–10) is the culmination of the hopes in Isaiah 51, particularly the hope for salvation (51:5–6, 8; 52:7, 10) which often parallels righteousness, it is reasonable to understand the anticipation of God's righteousness in the light of his coming rule in Zion that extends throughout the entire world.

If God's expressions of saving righteousness in chapter 51 should be understood in the light of his reign as king (52:7–10), it is at least possible to suggest that other uses of the concept of righteousness in 40 – 55 also may call to mind God as king:

> I bring near my righteousness; it is not far off,
>   and my salvation will not delay;
> I will put salvation in Zion,
>   for Israel my glory.
>
>   (Isa. 46:13)

> Shower, O heavens, from above,
>   and let the clouds rain down righteousness;
> let the earth open, that salvation and righteousness
>   may bear fruit;
> let the earth cause them both to sprout;
> I the LORD have created it.
>
>   (Isa. 45:8)

By way of summary, righteousness is often the responsibility of a king. Within the logic of Isaiah 51 – 52, where God's rule as king is prominent, promises of God's saving righteousness find their realization in God as the king who will set all things right not just for Israel but for the entire world. All things will be 'righted' when God rules as king from Zion.

Righteousness and kingship in canonical context
Throughout the OT the righteous and saving actions of God in Israel's history (cf. Judg. 5:11; 1 Sam. 12:7; Mic. 6:5) fill the testimonies of the people of faith.[45] In the light of this history the book of Isaiah envisages an act of saving righteousness by God as king that sets things right for ever (51:6, 8). The New Testament declares that it is

[45] Von Rad 2005: 372, n. 7.

in Jesus Christ that we see God's act of saving righteousness on display. For those hungering and thirsting for righteousness (Matt. 5:6) – for God to set things right – Jesus assures them that they will become 'full' in God's kingdom: the reign of Jesus will set everything right, not just for Israel but for the entire world. As Paul puts it,

> For I am not ashamed of the gospel . . . that brings salvation to everyone who believes: first to the Jew, then to the Gentile. For in the gospel the righteousness of God is revealed – a righteousness that is by faith from first to last. (Rom. 1:16–17, NIV; cf. Rom. 3:22)

While we can certainly profess that Christ's first coming reveals God's righteousness, there is a sense that it has only been inaugurated. Much in the world remains to be set right, so we await the second coming of Christ (cf. Rev. 19:11) when the king will come to bring to completion his work of making all things new. As we will see in a later chapter, God's servants are to be avenues for righteousness in this world in the meantime.

YHWH as supreme over other 'gods'

As noted above, Isaiah 40 – 55 addresses an audience tempted to turn to other gods. It is no surprise, then, that these chapters aim to dismantle any inkling the people may have of turning anywhere else but to YHWH. A memorable instance of this is found in 44:6–20, where the prophet satirically confronts the folly of following after a god made of wood when the rest of the wood is burnt in fire to cook food (cf. 40:19–20). One also thinks of direct statements like the following:

> Bel bows down, Nebo stoops low;
>   their idols are borne by beasts of burden.
> The images that are carried about are burdensome,
>   a burden for the weary.
>
> (46:1, NIV84)

Along with these kinds of statements, Isaiah 40 – 55 seems to be aware of competing mythic ideas that endorse the kingship and supremacy of other gods. Isaiah 40 – 55 seems to be tailored to declare that YHWH is the supreme king, a status that belongs to no other god.[46]

---

[46] On the complexities and rhetoric surrounding the notion of monotheism in Isa. 40 – 55, see MacDonald 2009; H. Clifford 2010.

72

The Enuma Elish is a Babylonian myth that recounts how Marduk became king of heaven and earth. Here is its basic storyline: with Tiamat, the matrix who birthed the gods, rallying a faction of the gods to destroy those gods who were aligned with Anshar – the grandfather of Ea, the one who killed Tiamat's husband Apsu – and promoting her son Kingu to be king, Marduk the son of Ea steps forward on behalf of Anshar's cohort to battle Tiamat. Upon victory over Tiamat and Kingu, Marduk is proclaimed king by Anshar and the allied gods, creates heaven and earth, and establishes his royal sanctuary in Babylon. This myth probably dates to the thirteenth or twelfth centuries BC,[47] and the myth was widely adopted, even by Assyria by the time of Sennacherib.[48] Those reading Isaiah would certainly have been familiar with the traditions in Enuma Elish concerning Marduk as the supreme god and probably would have picked up on the ways that Isaiah 40 – 55 makes the case for YHWH's supremacy as king in the light of those traditions. I will limit myself to four main ideas as they impinge upon understanding God as king in Isaiah 40 – 55: kingly saviour, kingly creator, commander of destinies and temple/city builder.

YHWH as the kingly saviour
Marduk's role as saviour of the gods is fundamental to his status as king. If Marduk had not dared to face Tiamat and been victorious, he would not have been king. In fact, Marduk knows that saving the gods from Tiamat will show that he is worthy of supreme kingship, so he makes a deal with Anshar prior to facing Tiamat that he will become king if he is victorious (II: 158–159; III: 58–60, 118–119). After he defeats Tiamat and saves the gods, they declare:

> Formerly [we called you] 'The Lord, [our beloved] son,'
> Now 'Our King' . . . [shall be your name],
> He whose [sacral] sp[ell] saved our lives.
>
> (V: 151–153)

Fundamental to the gods' declaration that Marduk was king is the recognition that he had the power to save them from their fearsome enemy.

---

[47] On the origins of Enuma Elish, see Flynn 2014: 104–118. Many date the myth to the time of Kassite rule over Babylonia (1125–1104 BC), but Flynn points out that this was a time of peaceful occupation, which mitigates the conditions necessary for the production of this myth. It was perhaps around the time that Tukulti-Ninurta I of Assyria captured Babylon in 1215 BC when it was written.

[48] Ibid. 97–98.

Isaiah 40 – 55 asserts that it is YHWH who is the God with supreme saving power. In fact, proclamations that YHWH is the saviour often occur in contexts of polemic towards other 'gods'. Here is an example:

> Assemble yourselves and come;
>> draw near together,
>> you survivors of the nations!
> They have no knowledge
>> who carry about their wooden idols,
> and keep on praying to a god
>> that cannot save. . . .
> And there is no other god besides me,
> a righteous God and a Saviour;
>> there is none besides me.
> Turn to me and be saved,
>> all the ends of the earth!
> For I am God, and there is no other.
>> (Isa. 45:20–22)

Though there may be a temptation to turn to other 'gods', there is no other saviour for the entire earth than YHWH (cf. 43:11–13). Similarly, Isaiah 51:9–10 points to God's saving power, though with clear allusions to mythic traditions. After an appeal for the ancient, mighty arm of God to awaken and act in ways akin to past events, verses 9b–10 envisage the previous acts of God in mythic language:

> Was it not you who cut Rahab in pieces,
>> who pierced the dragon?
> Was it not you who dried up the sea,
>> the waters of the great deep,
> who made the depths of the sea a way
>> for the redeemed to pass over?
>> (51:9b–10)

Rahab is often a mythic code word for Egypt (Isa. 30:7; cf. Ps. 87:4), though it is often associated with the sea in some sort of mythic victory of YHWH over Rahab, perhaps at creation (Job 26:12; cf. Ps. 89:10–11).[49] While it is difficult to discern the referent of Rahab

---

[49] Janzen (1994: 458–478, esp. 474–476) argues that the theology in 51:9–11 is critiqued by the fourth servant song (different view of power / the arm of the Lord). God's arm, however, could act both in violent power and in redeeming suffering.

in ancient myths, the 'dragon' in Isaiah 51:9 finds a parallel with the Ba'al myth from Ugarit. What is more, by speaking of God as drying up the 'great deep' (*tĕhôm*), we find a possible allusion to Marduk's defeat of Tiamat. By alluding to mythic traditions that assert the supreme kingship of Ba'al and Marduk, Isaiah 51:9–10 makes a powerful point that Lessing captures well:

> The Babylonians think Marduk defeated Tiamat and is the true god who maintains the cosmos as its king. But look, Yahweh's arm shattered his enemies then (Egypt) and will do so again now (Babylon). Then who do you suppose will be shown to be the real king, the creator of the heavens and the earth?[50]

An eschatological glimpse of God's answering this request to lay bare his arm from 51:9 in 52:7–10 anchors God's salvation in his status as saving king.

> How beautiful upon the mountains
>   are the feet of him who brings good news,
> who publishes peace, who brings good news
>   of happiness,
>   who publishes salvation,
>   who says to Zion, 'Your God reigns.' . . .
> The LORD has bared his holy arm
>   before the eyes of all the nations,
> and all the ends of the earth shall see
>   the salvation of our God.
>
> (Isa. 52:7, 10)

When considering this scene in the light of the mythic backdrops reflected above, the proclamation that 'your God reigns' goes hand in hand with YHWH's being mighty in salvation; so mighty, in fact, that all the ends of the earth will see the saving power of our God, the rightful king who reigns on Zion. Thus with mythic traditions campaigning for allegiance to a particular deity in the light of saving power, Isaiah 40 – 55 counters these by declaring that it is YHWH who is the mighty saviour who has saved in the past and will save yet again – he is the king.

---

[50] Lessing 2010: 240.

YHWH as the kingly creator

It was not just Marduk's victory over Tiamat that proved that he was worthy to be king; his power as creator further fuelled the gods' acknowledgment of his supremacy and the expanse of his dominion. Marduk was not finished with Tiamat when he defeated her. He took her corpse and fashioned it into the sky (IV: 138), created a heavenly sanctuary upon it (IV: 144–145) and placed stars, the sun and the moon in it, which served to establish time and seasons and weather patterns (V: 1–50). It is after Marduk's dramatic acts of creation that Anshar declares him 'king' (V: 79). The Igigi gods then fall prostrate and declare, 'This is the king!' (V: 88). What is more, they proceed to declare, 'Lugaldimmerankia is his name, trust in him!' (V: 112). Lugaldimmerankia means 'king of the gods of heaven and earth',[51] which directly relates to Marduk's acts of creating heaven and earth prior to this. These instances and others (cf. V: 133–135, 150–153; VI: 99–100) throughout Enuma Elish demonstrate how Marduk's supremacy as king is interrelated to being the creator of heaven and earth.

Aside from Genesis 1 – 2, there is perhaps no other corpus in the OT that depicts God's power as creator as much as Isaiah 40 – 55.[52] Of utmost significance for Isaiah 40 – 55, as H. Clifford puts it, Yahweh's act in creating the cosmos and his people 'is the foundational belief that guides the monotheistic theology of Deutero-Isaiah'.[53] Isaiah 40 opens this corpus through a vast vision of God, before whom the nations (40:15, 17), their idols (40:18–20) and their rulers (40:23) are nothing in comparison to him. Fundamental to God's incomparability is his status as creator:

> 'To whom will you compare me?
> Or who is my equal?' says the Holy One.
> Lift up your eyes and look to the heavens:
> who created all these?
> He who brings out the starry host one by one
> and calls forth each of them by name.

---

[51] Seri 2006.

[52] On creation in Isa. 40 – 55 in the light of Marduk traditions, see Lessing 2010. Debate often revolves around how creation and salvation relate, with some making creation subservient to salvation (Stuhlmueller 1959). Lee (1995) is correct to situate both creation and redemption under the larger rubric of God's sovereign power. On creation throughout the entire book of Isaiah, see Ollenburger 1987a; R. J. Clifford 1993.

[53] H. Clifford 2010: 268.

Because of his great power and mighty strength,
　　not one of them is missing.
Why do you complain, Jacob?
　　Why do you say, Israel,
'My way is hidden from the LORD;
　　my cause is disregarded by my God'?
Do you not know?
　　Have you not heard?
The LORD is the everlasting God,
　　the Creator of the ends of the earth.
He will not grow tired or weary,
　　and his understanding no one can fathom.
　　　　　　　　　　　　　　(40:25–28, NIV)

References to God as the creator of heaven and earth appear time
and time again throughout Isaiah 40 – 55 (42:5; 44:24; 45:12). When
one looks at these portrayals of God as creator in their literary
contexts, they almost always occur in contexts that are asserting
YHWH's exclusivity, often to assure Israel that they can trust him to
redeem. As Lessing puts it, 'Isaiah argues that Yahweh's creational
wisdom and strength are vastly superior to that of Marduk's. . . . The
prophet's soaring creational theology . . . does not take place in a
vacuum. He employs it to convince Babylonian exiles that Yahweh is
the king and creator.'[54]

Isaiah's creation theology is not limited to God's creation of the
cosmos. God is also the one who has created Israel (43:1, 7). This goes
hand in hand with God's kingship:

> I am the LORD, your Holy One,
> 　　the Creator of Israel, your King.
> 　　　　　　　　(Isa. 43:15; cf. 44:6)

During a time where Israel's faith was under serious threat, Isaiah
40 – 55 boldly assures them that their God, YHWH, who is the
Holy One enthroned in Isaiah 6, is the creator of Israel, their
king. The one who created Israel in the first place, who is the all-
powerful creator of heaven and earth, will certainly act on behalf
of his people to save them. While Babylon may embrace Marduk as
the creator-king, Isaiah 40 – 55 begs to differ. 'Bel [Marduk] bows

---

[54] Lessing 2010: 235.

down',[55] according to Isaiah 46:1. A manufactured god that depends upon humanity is surely not to be depended upon. Instead, it is YHWH who made his people (46:4), and as we have seen above, it is YHWH who is the creator of the entire universe. This establishes YHWH as the sovereign one with all-encompassing power, the king of Israel and all nations. So, as Israel looked around in nature and even to their own existence, they were to see a world and a people deriving from the powerful hands of their God, who alone is God and king.

YHWH as commander of destinies

A significant feature of a divine king in the ANE is the ability to control destiny and to have those who can influence destiny acting favourably on your behalf. When Kingu is made king by Tiamat, he is given the tablet of destinies (cf. I: 157, 160; II: 40–45). As Marduk steps forward to face Tiamat and Kingu, he is given the status of supreme destiny by his cohort of gods who direct their influence of destiny in Marduk's favour (II: 159, 161; III: 60, 63, 65, 118, 120, 139; IV: 33). With destinies handed over to Marduk, he is able to bring about all that he decrees and commands (IV: 1–8, 20–24), which culminates when he uses words to cast a spell that results in the capture of Tiamat, rival gods and Kingu. Marduk then confiscates Kingu's tablet of destinies (IV: 121) and delivers it to Anu (V: 70). As the god with control over destiny and with destiny in his favour, Marduk is then declared to be king.

As Israel and Judah crumbled and as God's people found themselves in the aftermath of destruction and exile, they might have been tempted to believe that other gods, particularly Marduk and his pantheon, had more power than YHWH in controlling the outworking of history. To counter this, YHWH declares his mastery over past, present and future. He is the one who brings about what he intends. One way of conveying this is through declaring that God's word will accomplish what it sets out to achieve, as we see in the following verses that frame Isaiah 40 – 55:

> The grass withers and the flowers fall,
> but the word of our God endures for ever.
> (40:8, NIV84)

---

[55] Bel is often a name for Marduk. 'Bel' means 'lord' and is a title applied to Marduk (Koole 1997: 496; cf. Jer. 50:2; 51:44).

As the rain and the snow
   come down from heaven,
and do not return to it
   without watering the earth
and making it bud and flourish,
      so that it yields seed for the sower and bread for the eater,
so is my word that goes out from my mouth:
      It will not return to me empty,
but will accomplish what I desire
      and achieve the purpose for which I sent it.
                                                    (55:10, NIV84)

In a way similar to how the gods praise Marduk as the supreme king in the light of his power to utter unalterable decrees (IV: 1–15), so Isaiah 40 – 55 proclaims that it is YHWH whose word will not fail.

Yahweh is also the one who can declare the former and the latter things. No other god can do this:

I foretold the former things long ago,
   my mouth announced them and I made them known;
      then suddenly I acted, and they came to pass.
For I knew how stubborn you were;
   the sinews of your neck were iron,
   your forehead was bronze.
Therefore I told you these things long ago;
   before they happened I announced them to you
so that you could not say,
   'My idols did them;
   my wooden image and metal god ordained them.'
            (Isa. 48:3–5, NIV84; cf. 41:21–29; 42:9)

In an apologetic move, God argues that he made known what would come to pass so that his people would not be tempted to think that other gods have brought about the realities of the exodus, the exile, and ultimately the return from exile through Cyrus. Israel is to serve as witnesses to the fact that:

'I have revealed and saved and proclaimed –
   I, and not some foreign god among you.
You are my witnesses,' declares the LORD, 'that I am God.
   Yes, and from ancient days I am he.

79

No one can deliver out of my hand.
When I act, who can reverse it?'
(43:12–13, NIV84)

It is indeed God who brings about all things, whether 'light' or 'darkness', 'well-being' or 'calamity' (45:7). By repeatedly asserting that God knows, declares and brings about the former and the latter things, the prophet is not merely providing ammunition for comfortable theologians to construct doctrines concerning God's sovereignty; he is trying to direct those wandering and wondering hearts, dismayed in the aftermath of exile and pondering whether other gods are in control of history, to YHWH as the true king of time and history.

YHWH as temple/city builder

After victory over Tiamat and creating the heavens with a sanctuary there, Marduk declares that he will build a house for himself, where 'I shall establish my kingship' (V: 124). As the myth progresses, Marduk chooses Babylon as the location for this sanctuary, which the Annuna gods construct. Upon completion of this shrine, the gods hold a banquet and again assign their destinies to Marduk and declare him to be king. The pattern here is noteworthy. Upon becoming king following victory, as Mettinger notes, 'The subsequent building of a Temple provides the visible symbol of the royal status of the victorious god.'[56] Within a context where the temple and its city are destroyed (51:3) the absence of these symbols of God's supremacy would surely have led Israel to doubt God's supremacy. While we will pursue the concept of Zion later in the book, it is sufficient for now to point to the rebuilding of the temple by Cyrus (44:28) and the Lord's return to Zion (52:8) in Isaiah 40 – 55 as indicators that the story of God as king has not evaporated because these symbols are in shambles; there will be new chapters in the story of Israel and the nations where Yahweh's sovereign kingship will again become apparent when Zion is again established with God's royal presence in its midst.

YHWH as supreme king in canonical context

As we have seen above, the claim that God is king cannot be limited to statements that have the term 'king' in it. One angle on God's kingship given in Isaiah 40 – 55 is the recognition of Yahweh's supremacy as saviour, creator, commander of destiny and temple

[56] Mettinger 1997: 144.

builder in contrast to wannabes. If he is supreme in all of these areas, he is the rightful king of everything, according to ANE logic. As we step into the wider canonical context, we find many of these same realities in the person of Jesus Christ. John's Gospel affirms that it was through Jesus that all things were made (John 1:3). Or, as Paul puts it, 'For in him all things were created: things in heaven and on earth, visible and invisible, whether thrones or powers or rulers or authorities; all things have been created through him and for him' (Col. 1:16, NIV).

Not only is Jesus supreme in his role in creation, but we also see his power in salvation. On earth, Jesus cast out demons, calmed storms and overcame illness. In his death and resurrection Jesus broke 'the power of him who holds the power of death' (Heb. 2:14, NIV), overcame death, attained forgiveness of sins through cancelling our debts and condemnation at the cross (Col. 2:14), and triumphed over all powers and authorities (Col. 2:15). What is more, Jesus is the sovereign one who holds the destinies of his churches in his hands (Rev. 1:20), who can unleash the seals of the scroll of destiny (Rev. 6), and who has all authority in heaven and earth (Matt. 28:18) to build his church (Matt. 16:18). When read in this canonical context, the rhetorical argument asserting that YHWH is the supreme king as creator, saviour, commander of destiny and temple builder in Isaiah 40 – 55 bears witness to the church's profession that Jesus Christ is Lord, for he is one with the God spoken of in Isaiah.

Conclusion

When a nation loses nearly every sign that God is with them, where do they turn? Do they give up? Do they see if the gods of their captors will give them a new lease on life? To the despairing, Isaiah 40 – 55 speaks words of comforting light into disheartening darkness. This corpus is designed with an arch of comfort and good news from 40:1–11 to 52:7–10 that offers a hopeful lens for the people of faith, a gospel that God will come in power and tenderness to rule as king upon Zion. When this king comes, he will set things right: all will be as it should be. To the doubting and straying, Isaiah 40 – 55 counters other traditions of divine supremacy with its own assertions; it is YHWH who is saviour, creator, commander of destiny and temple builder. He is the supreme king over Israel and all the earth; no other god compares to him.

Chapter Three

God, the warrior, international and compassionate king in Isaiah 56 – 66

The presentation of God as king in Isaiah 56 – 66 develops in very close connection to Isaiah 40 – 55 (and even the entire book). While Isaiah 40 – 55 emphasizes the positive side of YHWH's kingship, showing that YHWH alone is God and the king who is coming to save, the motif of kingship in chapters 56–66 has several distinct emphases, with eschatological judgment as a corollary to salvation, an international emphasis and the utilization of YHWH's kingship to motivate repentance. In this chapter I will focus on three major vantage points as they relate to God's kingship in Isaiah 56 – 66: (1) the warrior king, (2) the glorious international king, (3) the cosmic and compassionate king. I will conclude with some reflections that synthesize the various portraits of God's kingship through-out Isaiah that were examined in the first two chapters above, and in this one.

Before diving into specific vantage points on kingship within Isaiah 56 – 66, a few comments on the chiastic structure of Isaiah 56 – 66 will clarify the function of God's kingship there within (see Table 3.1 overleaf).[1]

While I am typically sceptical of chiastic structures, this one has strong textual merit and explanatory power. We can begin with levels A, B and C. Level A opens and closes these chapters with a shocking revelation that those foreigners (56:3, 6–7) who celebrate the 'Sabbath' (*šabbāt*; 56:2, 4, 6; 66:23) will 'gather' (*qbṣ*; 56:8; 66:18) at YHWH's 'holy mountain' (*har qodšî*; 56:7; 66:20) in YHWH's 'house' (*bayit*; 56:5, 7; 66:20) during the era of eschatological salvation. Next to these

---

[1] The outline has been adapted and reworded from Goldingay 2013: 152. While Goldingay subdivides Isa. 60 – 62 to place 61:1–4 at the centre, this division is not clear to me, for the messenger in 61:1–4 speaks again in ch. 62.

Table 3.1

A. Faithful outsiders to be in God's service upon salvation (56:1–8)
  B. Confronting the faithless insiders with judgment and assuring the
     faithful with salvation (56:9 – 59:8)
    C. Prayer for forgiveness and restoration (59:9–15a)
      D. The warrior king judges the wicked and redeems the repentant
         (59:15b–21)
        E. Zion's international renown amid King YHWH's glory and
           his messenger (60 – 62)
      D'. The warrior king judges and saves the nations (63:1–6)
    C'. Prayer for forgiveness and restoration
        (63:7 – 64:12[11])
  B'. Confronting the faithless insiders with judgment and assuring the
      faithful with salvation (65:1 – 66:17)
A'. Faithful outsiders to be in God's service upon salvation and judgment
    (66:18–24)

framing passages (level B), one enters into historical realities where apostate Judahites, who think they are in right standing with God, are confronted concerning their idolatry (56:9 – ch. 57; 65:1–7, 11–12; 66:3, 17) and injustice (58 – 59:8); judgment will fall upon them, though God will forgive and save those who turn to him in repentance (57:1–2, 13b–19; 65:8–10; 66:2, 5–14). The prayers (level C) in 59:9–15a and 63:7 – 64:12[11] are repentant pleas for God's mercy. What do levels A, B and C accomplish? By juxtaposing the visions of the un-expected having a place in God's service (level A) with indictments against insiders (level B) it is apparent that one of the major aims of Isaiah 56 – 66 is to force a reader to reckon with who will be part of God's community in the future; the faithful, even if a foreigner, will be 'in', while the unfaithful, even if a supposed 'insider' through ethnicity, nationality, or prestige, will be 'out'. This juxtaposition aims to prompt the presumptuous to repentance, with prayers of repent-ance (level C) being provided for them to take upon their own lips, while also assuring faithful outsiders that there will be a home for them in God's kingdom.

Near the middle of the chiasm there are two stirring depictions of YHWH coming as a warrior king (level D) who will enact inter-national judgment and establish salvation through his mighty arm (59:15b–21; 63:1–6). These passages surround an extended depiction of Zion's future glory within which a messenger is announcing the good news (60 – 62). What this shows is that Zion's glory (level E) can only be understood in the light of its connection with YHWH, the warrior king (level D).[2] The very core of the structure of Isaiah 56 – 66 impresses upon us that King YHWH will act in eschatological judgment and salvation with the result being Zion's transformation into the capital and crown jewel of the entire world, which only the repentant and faithful will enjoy.[3] As we will see, while the concept of God's kingship radiates most brightly at the centre of the chiasm (59:15b – 63:6), its rays of light infuse the rest of Isaiah 56 – 66 to make it unmistakeable that YHWH's kingship is a central component in this final section of the book. Below, we will begin by examining the warrior king in level D, then the international king of glory in level E, and then return to portrayals of God as a compassionate king amid the calls for repentance in level B.

The warrior king and his saving righteousness

'Righteousness' and 'salvation' are common terms in Christian lingo. If a poll were taken of what comes to mind when hearing the terms 'righteousness' and 'salvation', few today would mention 'kingship', let alone divine kingship. In the ancient world, however, setting things right – which is one way the Hebrew term often translated as 'righteousness' is used – and bringing salvation were the prerogatives of gods and their kings. It is for this reason that a king – whether human or divine – is often spoken of as a warrior. M. Brettler is correct when he states, '[O]ne of the main functions of the human king was as warrior, and thus the metaphor "YHWH is warrior" is often invoked as a submetaphor of "YHWH is king".'[4] The foundational example of this appears in the song that Moses and Israel sang after YHWH delivered them from Egypt through the Sea of Reeds in Exodus 15. In its opening verses we read:

---

[2] On the cohesion between 59:15b–21 and 63:1–6 and chs. 60–62, see Lynch 2008.

[3] Schemes for dating the materials in Isa. 56 – 66 impact its interpretation. A prominent explanation comes from P. A. Smith 1995. Treating 63:7 – 64:12 as an already existing exilic lament concerning Zion's misfortunes, he sees Isa. 60:1 – 63:6 as a response to this. With Zion's glory not being realized as the post-exilic era unfolded, Isa. 56:1 – 59:21 and 65:1 – 66:17 were written to explain why Zion's glory was delayed: it was due to their rebellion but would come later. Isa. 66:18–24 was then written as a conclusion. For other explanations that prioritize how Isa. 56 – 66 was written in the light of the rest of Isaiah, see Stromberg 2011a: 41–54.

[4] Brettler's statement (1993: 135–165, esp. 146) stems specifically from reflection upon Pss 46:10[11] and 47, where God, the king, causes wars to cease.

> I will sing to the LORD, for he has triumphed gloriously;
>   the horse and his rider he has thrown into the sea.
> The LORD is my strength and my song,
>   and he has become my salvation . . .
> The LORD is a man of war;
>   the LORD is his name.
>
> (Exod. 15:1–3)

Israel is praising YHWH for being a warrior ('man of war'; cf. Isa. 42:13) in the light of how he has so powerfully defeated Egypt, even its king, Pharaoh. 'Salvation' (Exod. 15:2) depends upon YHWH's intervention as a warrior. The reason God acted as a warrior on Israel's behalf was to fulfil part of YHWH's grander mission of reigning as king upon establishing his people in the land. It is fitting, then, for the song to close with the declaration 'The LORD will reign for ever and ever' (Exod. 15:18).

This close relationship between God's role as warrior and reign as king in Exodus 15 and other passages (Deut. 33:5; Pss 24:9; 29:10; 68:21[22]–24[25]) leads P. D. Miller to conclude his study on the divine warrior concept in the OT by stating, 'It is impossible to talk of God as king without talking of God as warrior.'[5] A king is one who fights for his people against their enemies and saves them.[6]

YHWH's role as a warrior is on full display throughout Israel's history.[7] The narratives about Israel's deliverance from Egypt, its victories against enemies while en route to the Promised Land, its partial conquest of the Promised Land, and even Zion's deliverance from Assyria during the time of Hezekiah are crafted to display how Israel's very existence depends upon YHWH's fighting on behalf of his people, as their king. It is not surprising, then, that Psalms, Israel's grammar of faith, contains many declarations that intertwine God's kingship with his role as saviour and warrior. Here are a few examples (cf. 72:12; 98:1–2, 6):

---

[5] Miller 1973: 174. See also Lind 1980.

[6] J. L. Wright (2008: 37) points out that from the earliest civilizations the king is understood as a warrior, as is evident in the Victory Stela of Naram-Sin of Mesopotamia (twenty-third century BC). Wright's study helpfully explores the intersection between YHWH as king and human agents who develop from Judges to 1–2 Samuel.

[7] For an overview of research on warfare, including the divine warrior, in the OT, see Trimm 2012.

> Who is this King of glory?
> The LORD, strong and mighty,
> the LORD, mighty in battle!
> (Ps. 24:8[9])

> You are my King, O God;
> ordain salvation for Jacob!
> (Ps. 44:4[5])

Thus, in the OT mindset, salvation and righteousness were not abstracted from the person or office that could bring such about: people looked to a king, whether human or divine, to save and set things right, often as a warrior.[8]

Though passages earlier in Isaiah intertwine YHWH's kingship with his role as saviour and judge (24:21–23; 33:22; 52:7),[9] Isaiah 56 – 66 offers the most fully developed portrayal of YHWH as a warrior king who will save his people and judge his enemies. It is particularly striking how the anticipations of God's coming 'righteousness' and 'salvation' from Isaiah 40 to 55 (cf. 45:8; 46:13; 51:6–8; 52:7–10) find graphic and vivid expression in God's coming as a warrior in Isaiah 56 – 66. While level D of the chiasm (59:15–20; 63:1–6) will receive priority below, it will be evident that the frame of Isaiah 56 – 66 in 56:1 and 66:18–24 (level A) relates to these depictions of YHWH's coming as a warrior king.

Isaiah 56:1

Isaiah 56:1 opens the final section of the book on an ethical and eschatological note:

This is what the LORD says:

> 'Maintain justice [mišpaṭ]
> and do what is right [ṣĕdāqâ],
> for my salvation is close at hand
> and my righteousness [ṣĕdāqâ] will soon be revealed.'
> (56:1, NIV)

This is a stirring call to carry out social justice through the use of the terms mišpāṭ (justice) and ṣĕdāqâ (what is right), which were major

---

[8] On God as a king and warrior in Zech. 14, see Longman III and Reid 1995: 69–71.
[9] See also Isa. 31:4, 8 (von Rad 1991: 104–105).

concerns throughout Isaiah 1 – 39 (e.g. 1:27; 5:7; 9:7[6]; 32:16) and develop further in Isaiah 58 – 59. This ethical command is motivated by God's nearing intervention: the 'salvation' (*yěšû'â*) and 'righteousness' (*şědāqâ*) of God that were longed for in Isaiah 40 – 55 (cf. 51:6, 8) are about to break in. With God about to fulfil his promise to save and set things right, the audience should repent. By fusing the socially concerned use of 'righteousness' (*şědāqâ*) from Isaiah 1 – 39 with the hopes for salvific righteousness from Isaiah 40 – 55, Isaiah 56:1 draws the entire book together. God's coming eschatological intervention demands a human response.[10] What is important to observe here is that the notions of God's 'salvation' and 'righteousness' are kingly notions. Just prior to this, in Isaiah 51 – 52, hopes for God's righteousness and salvation (51:6, 8) through God's mighty arm (51:9) culminate with the announcement that 'Your God reigns' in 52:7, as the entire world will see the 'salvation' (*yěšû'â*) of God (52:10). This language corresponds with Exodus 15, where Israel praises YHWH for acting as a warrior to 'save' them (*yěšû'â*; 15:2) and declares him king (15:18) in the light of his strong arm (15:16). It is likely, then, that Isaiah 56:1 opens the final phase of the book with the anticipation that the king will soon manifest his salvation and righteousness.

How will the coming 'salvation' (*yěšû'â*) and 'righteousness' (*şědāqâ*) of God be manifest? Due to injustice committed by God's people (58:2; 59:9, 14), God's 'righteousness' (*şědāqâ*) is delayed. YHWH will not tarry for long, however, for YHWH's astonishment at their injustice will reach a tipping point when he takes over the task of implementing 'righteousness' (*şědāqâ*) by coming as a dreadful and redeeming warrior to 'save' (*yš'*) and set things right through judgment (59:15b–20 and 63:1–6).[11]

Isaiah 59:15b–20

Isaiah 59:15b–16a sets the scene into which YHWH enters as the warrior king:

> The LORD saw it, and it displeased him
> that there was no justice.

---

[10] Rendtorff (1993c: 181–189) was one of the first to recognize the structural importance of Isa. 56:1. See also Oswalt 1997 and Goldingay 2013. On the complex relationship between human response and divine action, along with reflections on how 56:1 opens chs. 56–66 with an eschatological vision, see Oh 2014: 54–63.

[11] Ortlund (2010: 179–180) also notes how the notions of salvation and righteousness in 56:1 manifest themselves in 59:15–20.

He saw that there was no man,
and wondered that there was no one to intercede . . .

Sin had driven a wedge between God and the people (59:2). Falsehood, unjust gain, pursuing worthless things, violence, shedding innocent blood, wicked thoughts, oppression, injustice and no concern for peace characterize the community in Isaiah 59. Though some may be wondering whether God's hand is too short to save (59:1), Isaiah is making it increasingly clear that any supposed delay in God's intervention is because his very own people are unjust and he is tarrying due to his own mercy (59:2–8). Since God deeply desires justice and detests oppression, the Lord 'sees' the situation. As is common in the OT, the statement that God 'sees' indicates that he is aware and about to take action (Exod. 3:7).[12] Through an ironic play on sounds, we are told (Isa. 59:15b–16a) that upon 'seeing' (*wayyarě'*) it was 'displeasing' (*wayyēra'*) to YHWH. What was the reason for such displeasure? There was no justice. From the opening chapter of the book (1:16–17, 23, 27) through to Isaiah 59 (cf. 5:7; 56:1; chs. 58–59) God calls for justice from among his people, and he looks but sees no justice. There is no one championing the need for justice (59:16a). While God is delaying his intervention with the hope that the community may right the ship, God is pushed to the brink in 59:15b–16a: the continual lack of injustice is so displeasing that he will take matters into his own hands.

The tension emerging in 59:15–16 draws us back to Isaiah 56:1. In 56:1 God would soon be coming to save and set things right, so the audience would be wise to carry out justice and righteousness. Now, with no one having responded and God's displeasure reaching its boiling point, God's 'salvation' (*yěšû'â*) and 'righteousness' (*ṣědāqâ*) manifest themselves through his coming as a warrior:

> then his own arm brought him salvation [verb *yš'*],
> and his righteousness [*ṣědāqâ*] upheld him.
> He put on righteousness [*ṣědāqâ*] as a breastplate,
> and a helmet of salvation [*yěšû'â*] on his head;
> he put on garments of vengeance for clothing,
> and wrapped himself in zeal as a cloak.
>
> (59:16–17)

---

[12] Koole 2001: 198.

God's 'arm' is a common metaphor for conveying his powerful action in human history (cf. Ps. 98:1), particularly in the exodus event (Exod. 6:6; 15:16; Deut. 4:34; 5:15; 7:19; 9:29; 11:2; 26:8; Ps. 77:15). Earlier in Isaiah there was anticipation that God's arm would devastate the Assyrians (30:30), and there was a yearning that God's arm would act to bring an even greater salvation when he took up his reign on Zion (33:2; 51:5, 9; 52:10; 53:1). What is more, in Isaiah 52:7–10, God's reign as king in Zion (52:7) was directly related to YHWH's laying bare his holy 'arm' as an act of salvation seen throughout the entire world. In the coordination of 'arm' with 'salvation' in 59:16 there is a development in how God, the king, will bring salvation through his arm. While he might initially have expressed his arm through his servant in 53:1, there will also be a time when God's arm will establish salvation through his coming as a warrior, according to 59:16. God will take matters into his own 'arm', bringing salvation from oppression and being sustained by his desire to set things right.

Verse 17 specifies how God will take up his concerns for salvation and righteousness: it will be through arming himself as he enters the fray. The 'breastplate' (*širyôn*) and 'helmet' (*kôbaʻ*) were common features of protective battle attire, as we see Goliath's donning these (1 Sam. 17:5) and Saul's trying to get David to wear them (17:38). These items protect against blunt force, arrows and spears. Along with protective armour, we are also told that the warrior will wear 'garments of vengeance for clothing' and a 'cloak of zeal'. A 'cloak' (*mĕʻîl*) is often a garment that is uniquely tailored to distinguish a person, say worn by priests (e.g. Exod. 28:4; Lev. 8:7), a prophet (1 Sam. 15:27; Ezra 9:3, 5) or even royalty (1 Sam. 18:4; 24:5, 11; Ezek. 26:16), or perhaps given as a special gift (1 Sam. 2:19).

What is striking about YHWH's array for battle is that there is no mention of offensive weapons, as the passage merely describes what he is wearing.[13] In ancient literature, garments can signify something about the nature or condition of the person wearing them. Outside the Bible, in the Enuma Elish, when Marduk prepares to battle Tiamat we read about Marduk:

---

[13] Koole (ibid. 201) is at a loss for how to interpret the passive nature of this attire, so he suggests that this is 'because God's first concern is to defend his people, with whom he shows solidarity'. A better answer is to emphasize how the attire highlights YHWH's character.

He was garbed in a ghastly armored garment,
On his head he was covered with terrifying auras.
(IV: 57–58)

By describing Marduk's armour as ghastly and head coverings as terrifying we gain a particular impression about Marduk: he is one to be greatly dreaded in battle.[14] Within the Bible too clothing and attire can symbolize the character and quality of a particular person. When Job is defending his own uprightness, he states:

I put on righteousness, and it clothed me;
my justice was like a robe and a turban.
(Job 29:14)

While garments can symbolize positive character traits, they can also signify negative ones. So, in Psalm 109:29, we read:

May my accusers be clothed with dishonour;
may they be wrapped in their own shame as in a cloak!

We also find qualities clothing the Davidic king in Isaiah 11:[15]

Righteousness shall be the belt of his waist,
and faithfulness the belt of his loins.
(11:5)

While it is unlikely that Isaiah 59:17 has a Davidic king in mind, for the emphasis in this passage is that no human is found to intervene, Isaiah 11:5, along with Job 29:14 and Psalm 109:29, illustrates how attire can be a means of symbolically conveying something about the person wearing it.

While Isaiah places offensive weapons, such as the sword or fire, in the hands or nostrils of YHWH elsewhere (cf. 10:17; 27:1; 31:8; 34; 66:15–16, 24), the main concern in Isaiah 59 is to portray the essence and motivation of the warrior who is coming in judgment. As Motyer puts it, 'When the Lord dons this clothing he is publicly revealing what he is. But he is also declaring what he intends to do and that he is able to do it.'[16] YHWH is a warrior who exudes righteousness and salvation and is zealously coming in vengeance (1:24; 34:8; 35:4; 47:3;

---

[14] Neufeld (1997: 28–29) points to Enuma Elish too.
[15] Ibid. 27–28.
[16] Motyer 1993: 491.

61:2; 63:4). Presumably, God's 'righteousness' includes righting the crooked social order in Isaiah 59:1–8 that has astonished him to the point of action.[17] YHWH can no longer sit back idly as injustice spawns in his world; with passion and a quest for vengeance against the unjust, YHWH is coming as a warrior to set things right ('righteousness') and to save. YHWH's breastplate and helmet emphasize his qualities and ambitions – his commitment to righteousness and his mission to save.

Verse 18 specifies the objects of God's wrath and the principle undergirding it:

> According to their deeds, so will he repay,
>   wrath to his adversaries, repayment to his enemies;
>   to the coastlands he will render repayment.
>
> (Isa. 59:18)

The principle at work here is retribution. While some Christians and modern society often bristle at the notion of God's repaying sin with judgment, it is important to remember that retribution has an element of hope to it, especially for those being oppressed. Blenkinsopp captures this well: 'the basic idea seems to be a setting right of what has been skewed and distorted by sin, an affirmation that injustice will not ultimately prevail'.[18] So who are YHWH's adversaries and enemies? Mention of the 'coastlands' at the end of this verse makes it clear that YHWH is coming to bring judgment upon the nations. This, however, is not the entire story. Earlier in Isaiah YHWH's 'adversaries' and 'enemies' are his very own people who are engulfed by sin (1:24). Additionally, since God's coming as a warrior stems in part from observing injustice among his own people (59:1–8), there are grounds for understanding apostate Judahites as being among the enemies who will receive God's wrath.[19] God's judgment will be against all who sin against him, whether at home or abroad.[20]

---

[17] Though Neufeld's argument that 'righteousness' and 'justice' are personified characters is not convincing, he is correct that YHWH's coming in 'righteousness' does not merely entail salvation but also the establishment of a social order where justice and righteousness are the norm (1997: 32–33).

[18] Blenkinsopp 2003: 198–199.

[19] Oswalt (1998: 527) takes things one step further by identifying sin as the true enemy: 'God comes to destroy the final enemy of what he has created: not the monster Chaos, but the monster Sin.'

[20] Koole (2001: 205) captures this well: 'It is against this injustice, which prevails in Israel (as in chap. 1) and against Israel (as in chap. 34), that the avenging God of justice acts.'

The judgment that YHWH will render as a coming warrior will be so dramatic that

> they shall fear the name of the LORD from the west,
>   and his glory from the rising of the sun;
> for he will come like a rushing stream,
>   which the wind of the LORD drives.
>
> (Isa. 59:19)

YHWH's judgment will sweep through like a rushing river to such an extent that the entire world will be a witness to it.[21] Importantly, God's glory will be recognized. As was discussed in the previous chapter, the revelation of God's glory as king is a great hope throughout Isaiah (e.g. 6:3; 24:23; 40:5). Here God's glory is revealed in association with his coming as a warrior in judgment. Since 'name' and 'glory' often appear in connection 'with Yhwh's royal heavenly throne',[22] there seems to be recognition that YHWH the warrior is also YHWH the king. This has implications for understanding the notion of glory that continues in Isaiah 60 – 62, as we will explore below. As Ortlund observes, '[O]ne after-effect attending YHWH's theophany in 59:19 of universal fear before divine glory' is that 'Zion shines with YHWH's own glory' when he comes as 'Warrior and King'.[23] The renown ('name') and royal esteem ('glory') of YHWH will solicit reverence from the west and east as he comes to set things right as the warrior king.

Are sinners without hope when YHWH comes as a warrior? Verse 20 offers a more positive outlook:

> And a Redeemer will come to Zion,
>   to those in Jacob who turn from transgression . . .
>
> (59:20)

The warrior, YHWH, will not merely come in judgment to punish sin: 'God assumes the warrior stance so that he may fill the role of redeemer.'[24] YHWH's redemption will be for those who repent (cf. 1:27) from their transgression in Jacob. Despite YHWH's disappointment at

---

[21] I am employing the standard interpretation of 'like a rushing stream' instead of emending 'rushing' (ṣar) to 'envoy' (ṣîr). Oh (2014: 115–118) emends the text to mean 'envoy' to endorse a messianic reading of this passage, which I believe is unlikely.

[22] Lynch 2008: 252.

[23] Ortlund 2010: 181.

[24] Oswalt 1997: 530, emphasis original.

the lack of justice that he sees, there is hope for those who genuinely turn to God in faith-filled repentance, looking to YHWH alone for mercy as they are warned of his coming as a warrior. The repentant ones are those who can utter the prayer just before this passage (59:9–14), a prayer that resonates with the term 'transgression' (*pešaʿ*) in verse 20. Here is a sampling from that confession:

> we hope for justice, but there is none;
>> for salvation, but it is far from us.
> For our *transgressions* are multiplied before you,
>> and our sins testify against us;
> for our *transgressions* are with us,
>> and we know our iniquities:
> *transgressing*, and denying the LORD,
>> and turning back from following our God . . .
>> (59:11–13)

For those who repent, the coming of the warrior king will be an occasion of redemption.

In summary, Isaiah 56:1, and before that Isaiah 40 – 55, anticipates the coming of God's salvation and righteousness. This finds expression in YHWH as a warrior king in 59:15b–20. As injustice reigns, YHWH sees it, is displeased and takes it upon himself to set right all that is corrupt and to save those who repent. There is good reason to view this warrior as a king. For one, a king was often the lead warrior who was responsible to save and set things right. Additionally, since glory is often attached to the notion of kingship, the international reverence for 'his glory' (59:19) that stems from YHWH's coming as a warrior suggests that he is esteemed as king. Finally, Isaiah 59:15b–20 prepares for YHWH's taking up his reign in Zion in Isaiah 60 – 62. YHWH's coming as warrior intersects with the establishment of his rule in Zion.

Isaiah 63:1–6

As noted before, Isaiah 59:15b–20 and 63:1–6, level D of the chiasm, frame the vision of the glory of Zion in 60 – 62 (level E) with messages regarding YHWH's coming as a divine warrior. There are many linguistic parallels between these two passages,[25] such as 'there was no' (59:16; 63:5), 'astonished' (59:16; 63:5), 'supporting' (59:16; 63:5), 'right-eousness' (59:16, 17; 63:1), '[His/my] arm saved for [him/myself]' (59:16;

---

[25] Lynch 2008: 242.

63:5), 'garments' (59:17; 63:1), 'vengeance' (59:17; 63:4), 'wrath' (59:18; 63:3, 5) and 'redeem' (59:20; 63:4). This creates a tight connection between these passages, though Isaiah 63:1-6 develops its message in a different fashion and with explicit connections with Isaiah 34 and 35.

Isaiah 63:1-6 unfolds as a dialogue between an observer and YHWH. The observer opens the dialogue by asking:

> Who is this who comes from Edom,
>   in crimsoned garments from Bozrah,
> he who is splendid in his apparel,
>   marching in the greatness of his strength?
>   (Isa. 63:1a)

Someone catches the observer's attention. He is dressed in bright red garments,[26] with a level of splendour to his apparel and a great degree of power (Pss 33:16[15]; 147:5). While there is a level of ambiguity concerning this figure, it is apparent that this is a warrior, YHWH, for in Isaiah 34 – another gruesome passage depicting YHWH's bringing judgment as a warrior – YHWH's sword is said to descend upon Edom (34:5) and Bozrah (34:6) who are the recipients of judgment in 63:1. Just as Isaiah 35 anticipated YHWH coming as the saving king to Zion, a motif developed particularly in Isaiah 40 – 55, so Isaiah 34 prepares for the coming of YHWH as a warrior in judgment that develops in this final part of the book. Why is Edom the object of judgment here? Smith offers several reasons that I will summarize.[27] For one, Edom came to symbolize Israel's enemies because they were a regular source of hostility (cf. Ps. 137:7; Isa. 34:1–6; Amos 9:12; Obadiah; Mal. 1:2–4). Additionally, 'Edom' (*'ĕdôm*) lends itself to wordplay with 'humankind' (*'ādām*) and 'red' (*'ādōm*), which are both suitable in this context. YHWH's judgment will be bloody and against all humanity. The observer, then, sees a warrior coming up in might out of Edom, which is symbolic of the nations in general, and clothed in bright red garments.[28]

---

[26] See Koole (2001: 332), who interprets 'red' (*ḥāmûṣ*) as 'a bright, intense colour' due to its connection with a verb and noun that refer to sour wine.

[27] G. V. Smith 2009: 657.

[28] Debate surrounds the term translated as 'marching' here, for it often means 'to stoop'. Carvalho (2010: 142–143) argues that the scene is of YHWH as a 'spent warrior' who is returning home, exhausted after battle with garments covered in blood. This, she suggests, may be evoking sympathy towards this warrior who has battled alone and come out victorious, though exhausted. This interpretation is difficult to reconcile with the description of the warrior coming in the 'greatness of his strength'.

The warrior responds to the questions from the observer by identifying himself in the second half of verse 1:

> It is I, speaking in righteousness,
> mighty to save.
>
> (Isa. 63:1b)

Significantly, the concepts of 'righteousness' and 'salvation' from 56:1
and 59:15–20 occur here. In a way similar to when YHWH put on the
breastplate of righteousness and the helmet of salvation as a means
of expressing his nature in 59:17, so now he identifies himself by these
same concepts. He is righteous and a saviour. Since 'righteousness'
can refer to righteous deeds performed by YHWH in victory (cf. Judg.
5:11), particularly saving action in Isaiah 56 – 66 (56:1; 59:16–17),[29]
YHWH's claim to be speaking in 'righteousness' may connote speech
in the aftermath of victory.[30] While the onlooker described this warrior
as marching in the 'greatness' (*rab*) of strength in 1a, this warrior in
1b affirms his 'greatness' (*rab*), while specifying that his greatness is
to save. This initial self-revelation is important here, for amid the
gruesome discussion that follows, we are to interpret the implied
bloodbath as this warrior understands it: YHWH's mighty work of
salvation.

While the warrior has responded in part to the observer's initial
ponderings, the warrior has bypassed an element that the observer is
particularly keen to understand more fully. Verse 1 opened with an
interest in the 'crimson' garments of the one coming from Edom, so
the observer follows with a direct question concerning his garments:

> Why is your apparel red,
> and your garments like his who treads in the wine press?
>
> (Isa. 63:2)

In this verse it becomes apparent that the warrior's clothing is not
simply red, like a fabric dyed red entirely; instead, the red upon his
clothing is more like a red that splatters upon a different coloured
cloth, leaving an obvious stain. In Israel the wine press was a regular
fixture in society, for once the precious grapes were gathered, they had

---

[29] Miller 1973: 173.
[30] I follow the JPS ('I that speak in victory') here. See, however, Oswalt 1998: 596;
G. V. Smith 2009: 658; Blenkinsopp 2003: 245–246, who interpret this as YHWH's
speaking what is right in contrast to deceptive speech.

to be trampled upon in a press in order for the grape juice to separate from the skins and filter into a vat. The red in YHWH's garments appears like those who have deeply stained their garments by treading upon grapes. Since 'red' symbolizes both death and possible danger,[31] the enquirer rightly probes further concerning these stained garments. The warrior answers this second question directly:

> I have trodden the winepress alone,
>> and from the peoples no one was with me;
> I trod them in my anger
>> and trampled them in my wrath;
> their lifeblood spattered on my garments,
>> and stained all my apparel.
>
> (Isa. 63:3)

There are several emphases in this answer. For one, the warrior alone brought about this bloodbath. No one acted with him. Just as YHWH took matters into his own hands in 59:16, we see a similar emphasis here. In ways not dissimilar from a superhero warrior (like Neo from *The Matrix* or Batman) who goes to war by himself against his enemies,[32] YHWH has gone to battle alone, slaughtering his adversaries. This is a warrior who was willing to take on the enemy alone. Additionally, he specifies that it was the lifeblood of the peoples ('them'; cf. v. 6) that stained his garments. While the warrior scene in 59:15b–20 has a particular emphasis upon the judgment of those internal to Judah, though the coastlands were also in view, the judgment of the nations is more prominent here, in a way similar to Isaiah 34. This of course does not mean apostate Israelites would be exempt from God's judgment, for Isaiah 59:15b–20 has made that point clear.[33] Finally, this is the outworking of YHWH's anger and wrath, which is a point repeated in verse 6. YHWH's 'anger' (*'āp*; 5:25; 9:12[11], 16[15], 21[20]; 10:4; 65:5; 66:15) and 'wrath' (*hēmâ*; 34:2; 59:18) are kindling throughout the book, and this is a terrifying glimpse of what YHWH's unbridled fury looks like: God's treading

---

[31] Ames 2014.

[32] Carvalho 2010 suggests *The Matrix* as an analogy, and Charlie Trimm in personal correspondence suggested Batman.

[33] Ortlund (2010: 252–253) believes that the objects of YHWH's wrath are vague here, but the mention of 'peoples' in 63:6 places more of an emphasis upon the nations. It is possible that the prime referent is the wicked nations spoken of in 60:12 (G. V. Smith 2009: 657).

in judgment upon many peoples with blood flying all over his clothes, heads and bodies bursting like grapes,[34] as he continues to tread.

What is it that leads YHWH to act in such fury? YHWH's explanation continues in 63:4–6.

> For the day of vengeance was in my heart,
>> and my year of redemption had come.
> I looked, but there was no one to help;
>> I was appalled, but there was no one to uphold;
> so my own arm brought me salvation,
>> and my wrath upheld me.
> I trampled down the peoples in my anger;
>> I made them drunk in my wrath,
>> and I poured out their lifeblood on the earth.

The opening of YHWH's justification for his bloodbath in verse 4 draws upon language similar to Isaiah 34:8:

> For the LORD has a day of vengeance,
>> a year of recompense for the cause of Zion.

Both Isaiah 34:8 and 63:4 speak of a point in time when YHWH will need to bring his vengeance (cf. 59:17; 61:2) into the world. It is striking, however, that the 'year of recompense' in 34:8 becomes the 'year of redemption' in 63:4,[35] a move that makes the positive side of YHWH's coming more explicit. This is not entirely unexpected, for this warrior identifies himself as mighty to save in verse 1, so an emphasis on redemption is fitting here, just as it was in 59:20. YHWH's quest for vengeance intertwines with his mission to bring redemption.

It is important, however, not to overlook the emphasis upon wrath in this passage, even if salvation and redemption are important. The wrath and anger noted in verse 3 arise again in verses 5 and 6. Additionally, when one compares 59:16b with 63:5b, there are a notable similarity and a difference. In both passages YHWH's arm sets out to save by himself because no one else can be found to act. A difference appears, however, when one observes that YHWH's 'righteousness' upholds him in 59:16, while it is his 'wrath' that upholds him in 63:5 (cf. 59:18 though). While there does seem to be an emphasis upon how

---

[34] Carvalho 2010.
[35] Koole 2001: 340.

God's gruesome slaughter of the nations is YHWH's act of salvation (63:1, 4b, 5b), there is also a major impression of wrath and slaughter in 63:1–6 that is not as fully developed in 59:15b–20. This is apparent when YHWH's garments in Isaiah 59:17 emphasize salvation, while in 63:1–6 they point to bloody judgment. Thus a strong taste exuding from the dregs of 63:1–6 is of bloody vengeance from YHWH, though embers of redemption and salvation intermingle, reminding us that when the warrior king comes in terrifying judgment, one of his primary goals is to redeem the repentant (cf. 63:8 – 64:12).

In summary, surrounding the heart of Isaiah 56 – 66 are two passages that speak of God as the warrior king (level D). Significantly, the anticipation of God's coming salvation and righteousness (56:1) finds expression in God's coming as the warrior king, for he will take matters into his own hands, with his own arm working salvation for him as he sets things right in the crooked, wicked world. While the emphasis in Isaiah 59:15b–20 is upon the character of God as king, made known through the nature of his attire, the garments of the warrior in Isaiah 63:1–6 show a different part of the story. In the aftermath of bloodying judgment his garments are stained red, wrath having been executed and vengeance enacted, with the warrior king's interpreting this in the light of his own self-understanding: mighty to save. By framing Isaiah 60 – 62 (level E) with these visions of God's coming as a divine warrior (level D), the restoration of Zion as the glorious habitation of the king and international capital of the world (level E) is the result of a mighty act of judgment and salvation by the warrior king (level D).

Near the conclusion of Isaiah 66 the theme of YHWH's wrath and anger comes to its culmination. While no offensive weapon is mentioned in 59:15b–20 or 63:1–6, they emerge in 66:15–17, where YHWH, as a warrior king, employs fire, chariots and the sword to slay evildoers. The recipients of this judgment are described in the final verse of the book as 'the men who have transgressed [pš'] against me' (66:24, NASB; cf. 1:2, 28), which is clearly the negative corollary to the hope in Isaiah 59:20 that the warrior king will come as a redeemer to 'those who turn from transgression [pš']' (NASB). A significant aim in Isaiah 56 – 66, then, seems to be to leave the book's readers with an unshakeable sense that God will come as a warrior king, both to save and to judge, with the hope that listeners will be stirred to repent from transgression lest they be trodden upon like grapes (63:1–6) and become corpses that memorialize what happens to those who rebel against the divine king (66:24).

Canonical reflections

Isaiah's vision of the divine warrior king coming to set things right is not new. It is a thread that weaves throughout the OT story, from God's mighty intervention in the exodus to his deliverance of Zion from Assyria. The divine warrior, however, does not only act on behalf of Israel against the nations; he also uses nations such as Assyria and Babylon to punish disobedient Israel (cf. Isa. 10:5).[36] The prophets began to expect a more climactic intervention by the divine warrior, against both the apostates in Judah and all nations (cf. Ezek. 38 – 39; Dan. 7; Zech. 14), for the purpose of saving the faithful in Judah and in all nations.[37]

As one considers how Isaiah 59:15b–20 and 63:1–6 bear canonical witness to Christ, I will offer three brief reflections.

First, in Jesus' first coming God takes matters into his own 'arm' to set things right, as in both Isaiah 59:16 and 63:5. Jesus enters the fray to set things right, to bring salvation, to do what only he can do. This is the arm of God initiating redemption (Luke 1:51). It is the fullness of time (Gal. 4:4). Neither Herod nor the religious community (Matt. 23:23) were champions for justice, so the Son of God stepped down into darkness to save and set things right as he donned the name Jesus, which contains the verbal root that means 'to save' (Matt. 1:21). With John the Baptist (Matt. 3:2), Jesus called for sinners to repent (4:17) that they might be ready for the looming fiery judgment (3:11–12), for only the repentant would be redeemed (Isa. 59:20). What is more, King Jesus saves through healing, casting out demons, advocating for the rights of the marginalized and oppressed, and ultimately through providing forgiveness of sins by dying on the cross and through conquering the power of death and the powers of evil in his resurrection. We see, then, that 59:15b–20 and 63:1–6 bear witness to God's work in Christ's first coming, as God takes the initiative to save.

Second, in Christ's second coming the divine warrior elements from Isaiah 63:1–6 reach their fullest expression. Though Christ's first coming was bloody and involved his drinking the cup of wrath on behalf of others, the second coming will be the culmination of God's judgment and salvation, where the unrepentant will be trodden in the wine press of wrath. According to Revelation 14, God's angels will

---

[36] On God's acting for Israel and against Israel, see Longman III and Reid 1995: 31–60.

[37] See ibid. 61–71.

gather the grape harvest from upon the earth – those who have followed the beast (14:9–11) – and then these 'grapes' will be thrown 'into the great wine press of the wrath of God' (14:19), where they will be trodden upon outside the city (14:20). It is Jesus who will do the treading in Revelation 19. While his army in heaven wears white linen, his robe is dipped in blood (Rev. 19:13), probably an allusion to bloodshed stemming from judgment in Isaiah 63:1–3.[38] The wine press comes into view a few verses later when we are told that from

> his mouth comes a sharp sword with which to strike down the nations, and he will rule them with a rod of iron. He will tread the wine press of the fury of the wrath of God the Almighty. On his robe and on his thigh he has a name written, King of kings and Lord of lords. (Rev. 19:15–16)

Jesus, the very lamb whose blood was shed for the sins of the world, is also the warrior king whose garments will drip with the blood of the wicked when he judges the nations in the wine press of his wrath.[39] This act of judgment is the negative counterpart to the destiny of the redeemed of the Lord who persevere until the end. The full extent of what Isaiah 59:15b–20 and 63:1–6 anticipate, when the divine warrior comes in mighty salvation and gruesome judgment, will come to fruition when Jesus, the king of kings, comes again.

Third, though Isaiah 59:15b–20 speaks of God's acting alone and exclusively to establish salvation and righteousness, the New Testament testifies that God's people can participate to a limited extent in the warrior king's mission.[40] In Ephesians 6, Paul exhorts believers to: 'take up the whole armour of God, that you may be able to withstand in the evil day, and having done all, to stand firm. Stand therefore . . . having put on the breastplate of righteousness . . . and take the helmet of salvation . . .' (Eph. 6:13–14, 17).

Just as God puts on his breastplate of righteousness and helmet of salvation in Isaiah 59:17, so the believer is to take on the very same armour as God himself. Adorned with righteousness and salvation, they do battle against the evil one, promoting righteousness in this

---

[38] Aune 1998: 1057.

[39] As Beale (1999: 963) points out, what originally applied to God in Isa. 63 is now applied to Jesus.

[40] Neufeld (1997: 124) argues that the Pauline doctrine of union with Christ serves as a basis for believers' sharing in God's battle gear.

crooked world and bearing witness to God's saving work through faith. What is more, as believers await Christ's second coming and the resurrection of the dead, they are to wear the helmet of salvation, along with the breastplate of faith and love (1 Thess. 5:8). Through wearing the triadic battle gear of faith, love and hope of salvation the weary and embattled pilgrim can persevere, ever mindful that God's destiny for him or her is not wrath but salvation through Christ (5:9).

Thus, as one considers how Isaiah 59:15b–20 and 63:1–6 bear witness canonically, they testify to God's vital and initial stage of setting things right in Christ's first coming, to the culmination of God's saving judgment in Christ, the divine warrior, in the second coming, and to how God's people can strive through the Spirit to persevere in faith and participate in the battle against evil by taking on the very armour that God himself dons as the warrior king.

The international king of glory in Zion and his tribute

When YHWH comes as the warrior king (59:15b–20; 63:1–6), this is just the start. Yes, he will certainly execute terrifying, saving judgment, but where does this lead? Isaiah 59:15b–20 provides a few hints. For one, the warrior king comes as a redeemer to Zion (59:20), which establishes a geographical focal point for the redemption of the repentant and for YHWH's reign as king. Additionally, verse 19 reports that from west to east the coastlands will fear the name of the Lord and his *glory*, emphasizing an expansive purview of YHWH's greatness. The aftermath of this international reverence plays out in chapter 60. Furthermore, if the chief reason for YHWH's coming is to address the problem of injustice (59:1–8, 15b), it is reasonable to expect that the warrior who is clothed in righteousness and salvation will establish an ordered, just society.[41] While these are just hints of the outcome of YHWH's coming as warrior king in Isaiah 59:15b–20, Isaiah 60 develops these notions into a splendid vision where the peaceful capital of YHWH's kingdom, Zion, is internationally renowned. While the realm of God's kingdom, Zion, will receive

---

[41] See Lynch (2008: 251–254), who makes similar observations concerning the relationship between 59:15b–20 and ch. 60. A number of scholars do not read Isa. 60 in the light of 59:15b–20, for many think that Isa. 60 was written first (cf. Clements 1997). This does not factor in what it means to read the final form of the book.

attention in a later chapter of this volume, we will consider here how Isaiah 60, in conjunction with 66:18–21, impresses upon us the weight, splendour and international scope of God's kingship in this final part of the book. Thus, in conjunction with the message that salvation and righteousness will come through the warrior king, Isaiah 60 portrays the positive outcome of the coming of YHWH by depicting the glory he brings to Zion and the international recognition of YHWH's supremacy.

Isaiah 60

Glory sets the stage for the message of Isaiah 60. The opening two verses say:

> Arise, shine, for your light has come,
> and the glory of the LORD has risen upon you.
> For behold, darkness shall cover the earth,
> and thick darkness the peoples;
> but the LORD will arise upon you,
> and his glory will be seen upon you.

In 59:19–20 the nations will revere YHWH's 'glory' (*kābôd*) when he comes in furious judgment and redeeming salvation to Zion. In Isaiah 60:1 Zion is exhorted to rise and shine because God's light and his 'glory' (*kābôd*) now infuse his people with brightness and splendour. The impression from verse 2 is that amid a world of darkness a bright, radiating light of glory is shining forth upon Zion. As we have seen throughout Isaiah, 'glory' (*kābôd*) often intertwines with God's kingship. In Isaiah 6:3 the seraphim declare that the holy king's 'glory' (*kābôd*) fills the earth. In Isaiah 24:23 YHWH's reign in Zion, manifesting itself in judgment against powers above and below, entails that his 'glory' (*kābôd*) resides there too. Isaiah 40:5 awaits the day when God's 'glory' (*kābôd*) will be revealed before all flesh when he comes as the shepherd king (40:9–11). In Isaiah 59 – 60 the glory of the king will manifest itself from and in Zion after the warrior king breaks forth in a judgment and salvation so dramatic that the entire earth bears witness to it. As noted previously in our discussion of Isaiah 40:5, the coming glory of God also calls to mind Israel's traditions of YHWH dwelling in their midst in the tabernacle and temple. With YHWH's glory departing from the temple in exile (Ezekiel), Isaiah 60:1–2 anticipates a time when YHWH will once again dwell among his chosen city and the redeemed.

103

While some suggest that the 'light' coming in 60:1 is the Davidic king (9:1) or the servant (42:6),[42] this is unlikely. The book of Isaiah does not present the future David or the servant as divine,[43] and it is quite clear from 60:19–20 that the light in Zion is YHWH himself:

> the LORD will be your everlasting light,
> and your God will be your glory. . . .
> for the LORD will be your everlasting light,
> and your days of mourning shall be ended.

Throughout the OT the concept of light or dawning can refer to God's presence in theophany (Deut. 33:2; Pss 27:1; 36:10; Amos 5:18; Ezek. 43:2; cf. Isa. 24:23).[44] This seems to be what is emphasized here. The days of gloom and darkness for Zion will come to an end because YHWH himself will dwell there as a bright light.

If there is any doubt as to whether YHWH's kingship is in mind in Isaiah 60, the recurring notion of nations bringing gifts and tribute to Zion makes this clear. Tribute and gift giving in ancient empires is a common way to acknowledge the supremacy of a ruler. This can be illustrated from the reigns of the Assyrian King Shalmaneser III (859–824 BC) and of King Darius of Persia (522–486 BC). In cases of annual tribute there are written records detailing the sorts of items constituents from across the empire brought to Shalmaneser III.[45] These tended to be luxury items, such as silver, gold, bronze, iron, garments, colourful wool, logs (cedar, boxwood), oxen, sheep and horses.[46] In the reliefs from Shalmaneser III, the Black Obelisk, with its five scenes, and the Calah Throne Base, with its two scenes, there are depictions of tributaries coming from around the world bearing items similar to those listed above, along with vessels (bowls, buckets), royal or martial instruments (staff, bows, helmet) and more exotic animals, such as camels, elephants, monkeys, apes, and ivory.[47] Why were tribute offerings or gifts brought to the king? Many brought tribute due to a tribute tax being imposed upon them; this was a way for Assyria to gauge the loyalty of different constituencies and for

---

[42] Oswalt 1998: 537, 557–558; Oh 2014: 139–145.

[43] Some challenge this claim, as we will see in chapter 4.

[44] Blenkinsopp 2003: 210–211.

[45] I draw upon Yamada's (2000: 236) categories of 'Spot Tribute' and 'Annual Tribute'.

[46] For an extensive list, see ibid. 241–250, with entries 1, 3, 9, 10, 12, 13, 18 and possibly 42 and 52 as occasions for annual tribute.

[47] Ibid. 250–258.

displaying Assyria's far reach. There are occasions, though, when tribute was not forced or demanded. For example, the Black Obelisk depicts Egypt, which was not under Shalmaneser III's dominion, bringing exotic gifts to him 'to show Pharaoh's friendly intentions' towards Assyria.[48]

As for the reign of King Darius of Persia, he orchestrated the building of an impressive scene of tribute bearers heading to the king and his god as he sits on a throne with troops and officials stationed behind him. These massive reliefs depict delegations from places such as Ethiopia, Cappadocia, Syria, Mesopotamia, Arabia and India offering gifts, with jewellery, camels and cattle being the most recognizable items.[49] Along with this scene, records indicate that Persia demanded tribute and gifts from the various regions of its empire.[50] The concept of 'annual tribute' is of course found in the OT – when Syria brought David tribute (2 Sam. 8:6) and when many kingdoms brought tribute to Solomon (1 Kgs 4:21). Thus the reception of tribute and gifts in the ancient world was a way of acknowledging kingship.

When we look at Isaiah 60, depictions of tribute streaming to Zion correspond with tribute scenes in the ANE. As in the examples above, the breadth of nations, including kings, who come bearing tribute, indicates YHWH's international supremacy. Nations come from the south-east, represented by Midian, Ephah, Sheba and Kedar (60:6–7); from the north, represented by Lebanon (60:13); and from the coastlands, represented by Tarshish (60:9).[51] The items these nations bring reflect the wealth of their particular region, with camels, sheep, rams, gold and spices from the south-east, with timber (cypress, pine and box) coming from Lebanon in the north, and with gold and silver coming from the wealthy coastlands.[52] While these goods will contribute to the beautification of Zion, the king is never far from view in Zion's glorification in Isaiah 60, for the nations will come praising YHWH (60:6) and bringing their goods to 'the Holy One of Israel'

---

[48] Ibid. 253. While Strawn claims that tribute in the Black Obelisk was forced (2007: 110–111) and that tribute during the Persian period was peaceful, Yamada catalogues how some tribute in the Black Obelisk was not forced. Strawn overstates the peaceful setting of Isa. 60, as he overlooks how the divine warrior comes just before this in 59:15b–20 and as he dismisses 60:12 as a late addition.

[49] Strawn (ibid. 85–116) offers a collection and explanation of images relating to the Apadana tribute scenes as they may relate to Isa. 60. On tribute in Persia after Darius, see Briant 2002: 388–441.

[50] Briant 2002: 390–394.

[51] Stansell (2009: 240) believes that the south is missing, but Sheba may be southern.

[52] For a map of economic resources by region in the light of Ezek. 27, see Rainey and Notley 2014: 28–29.

(60:9). Zion itself is spoken of as where YHWH's glory and light reside (60:1–3, 19–20), 'the place of my sanctuary', 'the place of my feet' (60:13; cf. 66:1), and is called 'the city of the LORD, the Zion of the Holy One of Israel' (60:14). In Isaiah 60, then, Zion's transformation is derivative; Zion's beautification is the by-product of all nations recognizing the great glory of YHWH, the holy king. The Holy One who was once angry with Zion has now saved and redeemed her (60:10, 15–16). The city that was once unrighteous (59:1–8; cf. 1:21–26; 5:7) now is adorned with the righteousness and salvation anticipated earlier in the book (60:17–18; cf. 51:6, 8; 56:1; 59:16–17). As the city of the king, the nations offer tribute in Zion as an acknowledgment that YHWH is the glorious king of all the earth.

In summary, in Isaiah 60, the centrepiece of Isaiah 56 – 66, there are two major dynamics that emphasize YHWH's kingship in Zion. First, Zion is the place where the very glory of God, the king, resides and shines forth. Second, because YHWH's light is so remarkable, all nations bring praise and tribute to Zion as they acknowledge YHWH as the king. YHWH is the glorious, international king in Zion.[53]

Isaiah 66:18–24

The movement from Isaiah 59:15b–20 to Isaiah 60 is that of YHWH coming as the divine warrior to judge and save, with the result being the international recognition of YHWH's great glory in Zion. This same pattern is recapitulated in the final part of Isaiah 66. Isaiah 66:15–17 depicts YHWH coming with offensive weapons to usher in judgment against all who are in rebellion (cf. 66:24). This leads to a scene where many nations come to Zion, the place of God's glory.

The scene opens in verse 18 with YHWH gathering all nations and tongues, who come and see God's 'glory' (kābôd). Those who survive – presumably the repentant ones who are not destroyed when God's glory is manifest (cf. 59:20; 66:24) – are then sent to the coastlands in the Mediterranean (Tarshish, Yavan), to northern Africa (Pul, Lud) and Anatolia (Meshech, Tubal), with one chief goal:[54] 'They shall declare my glory [kābôd] among the nations' (66:19). Isaiah 40:5 had the hope that all flesh would see God's glory, and now the book closes by sounding the same note. The glory of God will be seen and

---

[53] Blenkinsopp (2003: 212) presents YHWH's inauguration as king as the occasion for the gift giving in Zion.

[54] On place names, see Blenkinsopp 2003: 314.

proclaimed throughout the entire world, and the result is somewhat similar to Isaiah 60. These nations respond by bringing gifts of tribute, carried by horses, chariots, wagons, mules and camels to YHWH's holy mountain. While we will consider the place of the nations in God's community in a later chapter, what is important for us to recognize here is that once again there is the grand hope that in the aftermath of saving judgment (66:15–18) YHWH's glory as king will be so marvellous that all nations will acknowledge his supremacy by bringing his children back to Zion and bearing gifts.

In summary, Isaiah 60 and 66:18–24 depict the ultimate outcome of YHWH's coming as the warrior king in judgment and salvation (59:15b–20; 63:1–6; 66:15–17). God's glory as king in Zion will be so incomparable and splendid that all nations will recognize that YHWH is the supreme king of all nations.

Canonical reflections

How might the hopes of Isaiah 60 and 66:18–24 accord with what we see in Christ? While Jesus is certainly the Davidic king hoped for in other parts of Isaiah, it is important to note here that Jesus is also the divine king, the very embodiment of God's glory, who receives the international homage hoped for in Isaiah 60. The NT professes that Jesus radiates God's glory (Heb. 1:3) and it is in the face of Jesus Christ that the very glory of God is made known (2 Cor. 4:6; cf. John 1:14). As the embodiment of God's glory, it is fitting then that Magi from the east come to bring gifts to Jesus as a baby, for they saw a bright star shining its light, indicating that the king of the Jews had been born (Matt. 2:1–12). Though the glory of God manifest in Christ's first coming is splendid, this is just a pointer to a far greater manifestation of God's glory in the New Jerusalem. In fact, just as the sun and moon would no longer need to shine in Isaiah 60:19–20, so God's glory will be Jerusalem's light and the Lamb its lamp (Rev. 21:23; 22:5). The radiance of God and the Lamb in Jerusalem will result in nations bringing their glory into it (Rev. 21:24; cf. Isa. 66:12), with its gates never being shut (Rev. 21:25; cf. Isa. 60:11). There is an advance of thought in Revelation 21 – 22 from Isaiah 60. While it is God who shines brightly in glory from Zion in Isaiah 60, the Lamb appears alongside God in glory, for, as the plan of God unfolds, the Son becomes the Lamb so that through his blood people from every tribe, tongue, people and nation who believe in him (Rev. 5:9) can bask in God's glory and escape judgment when the Lamb comes as the divine warrior.

The cosmic and compassionate king

The portrayals of God as king are expansive in Isaiah 56 – 66. He is the warrior king of unfathomable proportions in 59:15b–20, 63:16 and 66:15–17, operating alone to save the repentant and destroy the godless in all nations. He is also the king of glory in Isaiah 60 and 66:18–24, whose splendour shines so brightly that all nations will acknowledge his supremacy. There is still one final way Isaiah 56 – 66 offers an expansive view of God and his kingship: in Isaiah 57:15 and 66:1 we see a king who dwells in cosmic heights, though also with the lowly in spirit. Surprisingly, both of these statements occur in the midst of confronting faithless Judahites (level B in the chiasm), as if to convey to any listening that it will be worth it to side with the supreme king, for he is compassionate too.

Isaiah 57:15 and 66:1

In Isaiah 56:9 – 57:13a God has primarily been confronting the 'insider' Judahites for unjust gain (56:11), drunkenness (56:12), sorcery (57:3) and idolatry (57:4–9). Encouragement comes in 57:13b when God commends those who take refuge in him and calls for their way to be cleared for a safe return to him (57:14).[55] What gives them confidence that God will not wipe out everyone, including the repentant? Isaiah 57:15 offers an explanation:

> For thus says the One who is high and lifted up,
>   who inhabits eternity, whose name is Holy:
> 'I dwell in the high and holy place,
>   and also with him who is of a contrite and lowly spirit,
> to revive the spirit of the lowly,
>   and to revive the heart of the contrite.'

[55] Flynn (2006: 358–370) argues that it is not the heavens but instead the temple where YHWH is said to dwell. I am not convinced, particularly because he does not factor in Isa. 24:21–23 or 37:23 and Ps. 102:19[20]. Furthermore, the close connection with 66:1 points in a cosmic direction. In favour of my position see Blenkinsopp 2003: 170–171. There is no reason why God's accessibility in v. 14 requires that his habitation in v. 15 only be in the temple, for in 66:1–6 there is a mixture of God's transcendence in the heavens (66:1), his nearness with the downcast (66:2, 5) and his place in the temple (66:6). If all three can coalesce in 66:1–6, the same can be said for 57:14–19. On Isa. 66:1–6 as a chiasm, see Webster 1986: 94–96; Beuken 1989a: 60; Tiemeyer 2006: 48–53; Stromberg 2011b: 44.

The writer's introductory depiction of YHWH as the one who is 'high and lifted up' calls to mind Isaiah 6,[56] as does the claim that his name is holy.[57] Advancing beyond Isaiah 6, YHWH's dominion is temporally unlimited. While one might expect the exalted and Holy One to utter words of judgment, as he did in Isaiah 6, the words of the king in 57:15 have a different aim in mind – to convey the delightful irony that he dwells both in unreachable heights and with lowly, broken persons. The term 'height' is the same one discussed in Isaiah 24:21, which calls to mind both a sense of exaltation and the heavens. Since the 'height' is where the Holy One dwells, the concept of holiness occurs at times when it appears elsewhere in the OT:

> he looked down from his *holy height*;
> from heaven the LORD looked at the earth.
> (Ps. 102:19[20])

> The LORD will roar from on *high*,
> and from his *holy* habitation utter his voice.
> (Jer. 25:30)

YHWH is asserting that he dwells in the most exalted (high) and exclusive (holy) realm imaginable, in the heavens far beyond earthly realms throughout eternity (cf. 2 Kgs 19:22; Isa. 37:23).

The Lord devotes just a few words in 57:15 to depict his exalted habitation, 'high and holy I dwell'. The bulk of God's words in verse 15, however, focus on the other realm of his habitation. The terms 'contrite' (*dk'*; 'crushed') and 'lowly' (*špl*; 'fallen') each occur twice, indicating that YHWH not only dwells with the contrite and lowly, but aims to revive the lowly and the contrite (cf. Ps. 34:18[19]).

Isaiah 66:1 is another passage that presents YHWH as the cosmic king.

> Thus says the LORD:
> 'Heaven is my throne,
>   and the earth is my footstool;
> what is the house that you would build for me,
>   and what is the place of my rest?'

---

[56] On how 'high' and 'lifted up' correspond with 52:13, see the discussion in chapter 4.

[57] Koole 2001: 96.

It is true that God may choose to inhabit a temple on earth, but YHWH, the cosmic king, is neither in need of nor confined to a human temple. At the dedication of the temple Solomon recognizes that even the highest heaven cannot contain God, so when they pray towards the temple he hopes that God will hear from his heavenly dwelling place (1 Kgs 8:27, 30).[58] Psalms shares a similar outlook when it professes that YHWH's throne is in heaven in several verses (Pss 11:4; 103:19). Since a 'throne' indicates the place from whence a king's authority issues forth, its location in the heavens indicates that a destroyed temple is no threat to God's rule and that YHWH's rulership extends over the entire universe.[59] In Isaiah 66:1 the apostates are to take notice that God, the king of heaven and earth, has little need for their building projects. Heaven is his royal throne and the earth is his footstool, so there is not a square inch in the cosmos where God's ruling presence is absent. Instead of looking for a constructed temple, the cosmic king desires one who is 'humble and contrite in spirit and trembles at my word' (66:2). In fact, those who tremble at God's word (66:5) have the assurance that the high king of heaven and earth will unleash judgment on those who persecute them for faithfully following God.

Isaiah 57:15 and 66:1 assert that though God is a transcendent king he is also a compassionate king who dwells with and takes notice of the lowly who are turning to him. This dual affirmation that God is transcendent and immanent aims to drive those tottering between rebellion and repentance into the gracious bosom of the cosmic king, while encouraging those who are already faithful with the delightful news that the high king of heaven is with them.

Canonical reflections

The dynamic of God's inhabiting the heavens and dwelling among the lowly in Isaiah 57:15 and 66:1 finds resonance with the life and ministry of Jesus Christ and the early church. In the incarnation the supreme God stooped in compassion by taking on flesh and dwelling on earth. The incarnate Son had a particular interest in the lowly, assuring the poor in spirit that the kingdom of heaven would be theirs (Matt. 5:3) and standing up for the lowly who would turn to him

---

[58] Blenkinsopp 2003: 294–295. For linguistic similarities between Isa. 66:1 and 1 Kgs 8:27, see Stromberg 2011b: 20. The dynamic between the heavens and the temple (city) as God's dwelling places is developed by Levenson (1984: 289, 295–296) with close connection to 1 Kgs 8 and Isa. 56 – 66.

[59] Beuken 1989a: 54–55.

(Mark 14:6). Even after his ascension into heaven, the persecuted faithful find assurance that 'the ruler of the kings of the earth' (Rev. 1:5, NIV84) is indeed dwelling in the midst of his churches (1:20). In fact, God's willingness to dwell among those who are considered to be the foolish of the world (1 Cor. 1:27; 6:19) – his church – by the Holy Spirit continues the theology attested in Isaiah 57:15 and 66:1. God, the cosmic king, is willing to reside with the lowly, his people, in Christ through the Spirit.[60]

Summary of God as king in Isaiah 56 – 66

There are three prominent aspects of God's kingship in Isaiah 56 – 66 that are strategic within the structure of this final part of Isaiah. First, the anticipation of God's coming righteousness and salvation (56:1) finds expression in YHWH's coming as the *warrior king* to set the unjust world right through the bloody judgment of the wicked and the redemption of the repentant in 59:15b–20 and 63:1–6. Second, in the aftermath of the coming of the warrior king (level D), YHWH's royal glory shines so brightly in Zion that nations come from afar bearing tribute to display their allegiance to YHWH, the *international king*, in Isaiah 60 (level E). The sequence of the warrior king's coming, which results in the king's international glory in 59:15b to chapter 60, is recapitulated in Isaiah 66:15–24, where, after the sword is unleashed in bloody judgment (66:15–17, 24), news of YHWH's glory spreads, with the result being the nations coming to him in Zion. Third, there is the ironic assertion that, though YHWH reigns in the entire cosmos, he also dwells with the lowly who take refuge in him and tremble at his word (57:15; 66:1). YHWH is also the *cosmic and compassionate king*.

These three aspects of God's kingship need to be situated within the rhetorical flow of the argument within Isaiah 56 – 66. If we start at the centre of the chiasm (level E), Isaiah 60 places the coming of God's glory as an international king in Zion at the core of the message of Isaiah 56 – 66. That this is how Isaiah 66 ends (66:18–24) is very telling structurally concerning the major interest of the final part of the book: God's international renown as king (cf. 2:2–4; 25:6–8). As one moves to the frame of the centre of the chiasm, it becomes evident that it will be through YHWH's coming as a warrior king (level D; 59:15b–20; 63:1–6; 66:15–17) that Zion will become the international

---

[60] See also Acts 7:49, where Stephen quotes Isa. 66:1 to claim that God does not dwell in houses made by human hands.

capital of the world. The reason God comes as a warrior king, though, stems from the lack of justice and wrongdoing confronted in level B of the chiasm, which would surely motivate repentance since the warrior king will redeem the repentant (59:20) who can utter the prayers found in 59:9–15a and 63:8 – 64:12 (level C). Amid the confrontations in level B, the visions of God as the cosmic king stand out, for these are contributing to the goal of promoting repentance in the light of God's supremacy and also his compassion. Thus the message seems to be that as God unfolds his plan to reign as the glorious, international king from Zion, the insiders who think they are right with God need to repent, for God is a cosmic king who is tender but also a warrior king who will purge the wicked and save the repentant as Zion is established.

God as king in all of Isaiah

Having worked through how God's kingship is portrayed in each of the major sections of the book, it is now appropriate to step back and offer a few synthetic reflections.

Divine kingship in the structure of Isaiah's sections

The *structural* prominence of God's kingship within each of the major sections of the book is undeniable. In Isaiah 1 – 39, the strategic placement of the vision of God as the holy king (Isa. 6) at the centre of Isaiah 1 – 12, the crystallization of God's judgment and salvation of the entire cosmos in the light of his reign on Zion in chapters 24–25 as part of Isaiah 13 – 27, the way God's kingship in chapter 33 grants perspective upon chapters 28–33, and how the bridging chapters of Isaiah 34 – 39 convey God's kingship through eschatological (chapters 34–35) and historical (36–37) perspectives make it unmistakeable that God's kingship manifesting itself in judgment and salvation within history to the end of times is a central aspect of the message of Isaiah 1 – 39. In Isaiah 40 – 55 there is the arc that Isaiah 40:1–11 creates with 52:7–10 around the 'gospel' of God's coming to reign as saviour in Zion. Within the chiastic structure of Isaiah 56 – 66 and the recapitulation of its core message in 66:15–24 the vision that God will reign in glory as the international king in Zion (60; 66:18–24) in the aftermath of his coming as the warrior king (59:15b–20; 63:1–6) serves to motivate the humble in the audience to take refuge in the cosmic king, for he cares for the downcast (57:15; 66:1–2). Thus the structural design of each section of Isaiah utilizes different portrayals of God's kingship to offer points of orientation for comprehending the message of the various major sections within Isaiah.

Allowing for uniqueness in each passage and section

The great temptation when doing biblical theology is to synthesize a concept to such an extent that every passage means the same thing. In God's providence he has given us passages that highlight different features of his kingship in Isaiah, which are all part of different rhetorical arguments. This diversity points to the greatness of God, the king, as well as to the many ways his kingship can relate to us today. As we have seen, God is the holy king (6:1–3; 57:15), a warrior king (59:15b–20; 63:1–6), a shepherd king (40:11), the unseeable king (6:2), the king we will see (33:17; 40:5; 52:10), the royal judge (33:22), the saviour and redeemer king (33:22; 44:6; 52:7; 59:20), the king of glory (6:3; 24:23; 40:5; 60:1–2), the king of Israel (44:6) and Jacob (41:21), the king of the nations (2:2–4; 25:6–8; 60:1–3; 66:18–24), the king of heavenly forces (24:21–23), the wise king (2:2–4), the king who inhabits the cosmos (57:15; 66:1), the king of the downtrodden (57:15; 66:1–2), the king in history (6; 36 – 37), the king at the eschaton (24:21–24; 52:7; 60), and more. The book of Isaiah does not want us to condense God, the king, into one simple idea; instead, the book invites us to allow its collage of portraits of God as king to elicit a range of responses.

Along with allowing the various portraits to shape our understanding of God, it is vital to remember too that each use of God's kingship is part of a discrete rhetorical argument. God's people need to be gripped by a vision account of Isaiah's seeing the holy king who is bringing judgment against his people within history (ch. 6); by a message of comfort that God will come as a shepherd king when losing hope (40:1–11); by an example from history where God delivers his people to reveal himself as king over the superpowers at the time (chs. 36–37); by rhetorical arguments for YHWH's supremacy as king over other gods (chs. 40–55); by terrifying depictions of God's coming as a warrior king to set an unjust world right in order to motivate repentance and to assure the repentant (59:15b–20; 63:1–6); and more. These passages individually and collectively call for awe and worship, motivate repentance, engender hope, assuage doubts and fear, provide comfort and promote courage and faithfulness – all are fitting responses to this great king.

Even within each section of the book of Isaiah, there are different emphases, so one should allow each section to perform its unique part in the symphony. In Isaiah 1 – 39 the major tenor is that God as a holy king must judge Israel, Judah and the entire world, though there is hope too for his coming salvation. In Isaiah 40 – 55 the prominent emphases are that God will come as a saviour king and that no god besides YHWH is king. In Isaiah 56 – 66 everything has a wide scope and a balance of salvation and judgment, with the warrior king's bringing eschatological and international judgment and salvation, with God's inhabiting the world and eternity as the cosmic king, and with God's rule on Zion resulting in international supremacy. Thus listening well to Scripture requires readers to allow each portrayal of God's kingship to sound its unique note as part of the rhetoric of the passage it is part of.

Recurring motifs across the book

While not leaving behind the previous point, it is also legitimate to ask if one may legitimately draw connections between motifs concerning God's kingship that unfold across the book. I would like to suggest four overarching dynamics.

Seeing the glory of the king

The notion of seeing God's glory regularly corresponds with God's kingship throughout Isaiah. In Isaiah 6 the holiness and glory of the king are so great that the seraphim declare that 'the whole earth is full of his glory' (6:3). In the process the seraphim shield their eyes from seeing him and Isaiah is in peril as a result of seeing him. Isaiah 24:23 anticipates a time when the elders will stand before God's glory as he reigns on Zion, similar to the elders doing so at Mount Sinai after the exodus (Exod. 24). In Isaiah 33:17 there is the blessed prospect of the righteous seeing the king in his beauty. The great hope that begins to arise in Isaiah 35:2 and develops in 40:5 and 52:10 is for all nations to 'see' the glory of the Lord when he comes to save and reign in Zion. This 'glory' manifests itself in God's coming as the warrior king in 59:19, resulting in fear among the nations, and who will ultimately reside in Zion like the shining of the sun and will be 'seen' by all nations (60:1–3). Indeed, the entire book ends with all nations being gathered where they will 'see' God's 'glory' and spread word about his 'glory' abroad (66:18–19). In many respects, it would be appropriate to say that the book of Isaiah is about the 'gospel' hope that the entire world will see the glory of the king when he comes to judge and save.

The international king in Zion

The 'international' nature of God's rule also is a recurring feature throughout the book. While Isaiah 6 emphasizes how the holy king will judge Israel and Judah, it becomes clear in Isaiah 13 – 27 that God too will judge all nations, which will culminate when he reigns as king in Zion (24:23). In Isaiah 59:15–20 and 63:1–6 YHWH will come as a warrior king to judge both Israel and the nations. Not only will God judge all nations as king, but there are consistent hopes that all nations will live under his rule. In Isaiah 2:2–4 the nations will stream to the king for instruction. In 25:6–8 the nations will partake in a feast hosted by the king. In Isaiah 60 and 66:18–24 all nations will come to worship YHWH and offer tribute to their king. With recurring anticipations of all nations living before God as king throughout the book, from the beginning to the end, God's kingship over all nations is a unifying theme. We will return to the topic of the nations in a later chapter.

Judgment and salvation

A third overarching dynamic for conceptualizing God's kingship across the entire book is that of judgment and salvation. As is typical in prophetic literature, judgment and salvation often intertwine, so it is not a surprise to find this duality connecting with God's kingship. In Isaiah 6 the vision of the holy king revealing his plans to judge his people, yet promising a remnant, sets the stage for the king's acting in judgment and salvation throughout the book. As for judgment, God will judge forces above and below when he reigns from Zion (24:21–23), and he will come as the warrior king to judge sinners throughout the world (59:15b–20; 63:1–6; cf. ch. 34). As for salvation, which often appears after anticipations of judgment, the king will host a feast where the nations celebrate his saving power (25:6–8); the 'gospel' is that God will come as king to save (35; 40:1–11; 52:7–10); God delivers Zion from Assyria, revealing his status as God over all the kingdoms of the earth (chs. 36–37); even when the warrior king comes, his arm is working salvation for his people as he brings judgment against his foes (56:1; 59:16–17; 63:5); as his glory resides in Zion, its saviour will be known (60:16) and its walls called salvation (60:18). Thus, as the king in Isaiah, YHWH is the one who will judge and save (33:22).

History and eschatology

The final dynamic to mention is the interplay between history and eschatology. In Isaiah 1 – 39 we receive two narratives that portray

God as king in time and space. In Isaiah 6 there is a dreadful vision of YHWH's reigning as the holy king amid the death of King Uzziah of Judah and the rise of the Assyrian Empire; the holy king must bring judgment upon his people at that time. In Isaiah 36 – 37 YHWH's supremacy as king over Assyria and Sennacherib is evident when he saves Zion from their grasp. These narratives emphasize that the holy king can both bring judgment and save his people during that particular historical era. It would be a mistake, however, to conclude that the aims of Isaiah 6 and 36 – 37 were simply to recount how God would act during that era. These historical stories that are tied to the Assyrian era establish patterns for recognizing that the same holy king will act in judgment and salvation during the Babylonian era and beyond.[61]

Along with these historical narratives, the book of Isaiah often ties poetic passages that speak of God's kingship to various historical vantage points. Whether through announcements of judgment through Assyria or Babylon or through expectations that God will come as the saving king at the end of the Babylonian exile (40:5, 9–11; 52:7–10), Isaiah's poetic visions of God's coming rule regularly associate with Israel's and Judah's experience in real time and history. As the king of history, God can and will act in judgment and salvation time and time again.

While the book of Isaiah attaches its message of God's kingship to historical eras, particularly the Assyrian, Babylonian and Persian (cf. 44:28; 45:1), there is a sense that God's ways of acting during those times will recur throughout history until their culmination in the eschaton. This is evident throughout the book. Messages of judgment within history in Isaiah 13 – 23 develop in an eschatological and cosmic direction in chapter 24, where judgment culminates when YHWH reigns as king in Zion (24:21–23). Visions of YHWH's coming as the warrior king in 59:15b–20, 63:1–6 and 66:15–17 resist historical domestication, but instead point us to a culminating intervention by God. While a reader would naturally expect God to come as the saving king upon the people's return from Babylonian exile, it becomes clear in 60:1–3 that the expectations from 35:2, 4, 40:5, 9–11, and 52:7–10 that the king of glory will come await their full realization in the eschaton.[62] In this sense, the book of Isaiah directs our attention

---

[61] See Laato 1998.

[62] Caird (1980: 256, 258) correctly observes that eschatological language is often bifocal, with an ability to speak of near historical realities in the light of eschatological language that addresses more ultimate realities.

to the eschatological future, as we await the culmination of all things when God reigns as king upon bringing judgment and salvation. Thus the people of God need to know that God rules as king right now; he has acted in judgment and salvation in the past, and he can and will do so throughout time. They also need to know that the tokens of God's rule experienced up to now are pointers to a more ultimate time when the warrior and saviour king will come to judge, save and establish his rule over the entire world.

Chapter Four
The lead agents of the king

'I was expecting more explicit messianic promises in Isaiah.' This is a typical comment that I hear from students after they read Isaiah (or any prophetic book). Especially for those nurtured within evangelical Christian churches, the impression one can have is that the chief value of prophetic literature resides in its serving as a source of texts for Advent sermons, lyrics for Handel's *Messiah* and Christmas cantatas, slogans for Christmas greeting cards, and proof texts for defending that Jesus is the sort of Messiah that the OT expected. It is surprising, then, for many to realize that only about 5% of the verses in Isaiah (63 out of 1,292 verses) speak directly about hopes for some sort of messianic figure.[1] This does not mean, however, that these promises are unimportant; instead, the small proportion of passages devoted to expressing hopes in a coming 'Messiah' reminds us that such expectations can only be understood within the larger vision of the book of Isaiah. Isaiah is chiefly concerned with offering a vision of YHWH as king and his plans for his kingdom, within which these so-called messianic texts play a part. My guess is that this chapter addresses the questions that many readers are most interested in, but one must be mindful that this topic can be grasped most fully only in the light of the focus on God's kingship that has been set forth in the previous chapters.

Our focus in this chapter is upon the 'lead agents' whom *God* will use in the establishment and maintenance of *his* kingdom. I prefer the label 'lead agents' for several reasons. To begin, 'messiah' or even 'messianic expectations' are confusing terms and debate about whether a passage qualifies as messianic can unnecessarily detract attention from what texts are trying to say.[2] Additionally, the term 'agent' describes how these figures are in the service of another,

---

[1] Defining 'messianic' and what passages qualify is elusive and debated but, for commonly cited passages, see Isa. 7:14; 9:1–7; 11:1–5[6–10]; 16:5; 32:1; 42:1–9; 49:1–6; 50:4–9; 52:13 – 53:12; 61:1–3. See also the mention of Cyrus as 'messiah'/'anointed' (44:28 – 45:4, esp. 45:1).

[2] See Heskett (2007), whose monograph is primarily a catalogue of debates regarding if and how passages in Isaiah may be understood as 'messianic'.

namely King YHWH. Furthermore, the use of 'lead' as a qualifier acknowledges that all of God's people and even foreign nations can to some extent be God's agents, though there are some select figures who rise to the fore by taking on a more prominent role of agency in God's kingdom.

A summary of the argument up front will prepare for what is to come. The claim here is that Isaiah does not envision only one lead agent; instead, there are at least three distinct lead agents whom God will use in each of the major sections of the book: (1) the Davidic ruler (1 – 39), (2) the servant of the Lord (40 – 55), and (3) God's messenger (56 – 66).[3] While Christians profess that Jesus ultimately embodies what the book of Isaiah envisions for these lead agents, I am not certain that these agents are necessarily understood to be the same individual throughout Isaiah. The book of Isaiah contains a range of expectations pertaining to the various roles God would need his lead agents to fulfil in the course of time. Instead of forcing all of these lead agents into one mould, it is better to allow the uniqueness of each figure to emerge. The common denominator, however, between these lead agents is that they are the divine king's agents and feature into his plans within his kingdom. In fact, God's Spirit empowers all three of these agents for the task assigned to them. These agents, then, are distinct, but are also united under God as king and overlap to some extent due to shared participation in God's mission. Figure 4.1 illustrates this schema.

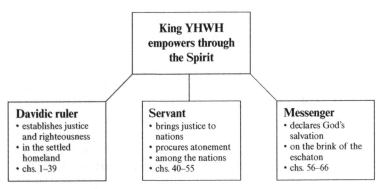

Figure 4.1 Lead agents under the kingship of God

---

[3] Whether one divides up the second section as 40 – 48 and 49 – 55 or as 40 – 48 and 49 – 57 is inconsequential for this study, though the chiastic structure of 56 – 66 will inform our treatment of 61:1–3.

As the argument unfolds below, I will consider each of these lead agents in turn, giving constant attention to their role under God as king.

The Davidic ruler in Isaiah 1 – 39

Within Isaiah 1 – 39 the Davidic ruler is a lead agent in God's kingdom. There are five passages that require attention: 7:14; 9:1–7[8:23 – 9:6]; 11:1–10; 16:5; 32:1. After examining whether or not the 'Immanuel' sign in 7:14 is anticipating a Davidic ruler, several characteristics of the Davidic ruler from the remaining texts will occupy our attention. It will become evident that the Davidic ruler is an agent whom God ordains and empowers primarily to promote justice and righteousness.

Is 'Immanuel' a Davidic ruler?

The quotation of Isaiah 7:14 in Matthew 1:23 makes the 'Immanuel' sign one of the most recognizable verses from the book of Isaiah and one quoted regularly around Christmas time. It seems almost sacrilegious, then, to question whether this sign is anticipating a Davidic ruler who will come 700 years later – that is, until one actually reads Isaiah 7:1–17. It becomes apparent, then, that this 'sign' is not necessarily a promise pertaining to the distant future. It refers, instead, to a time of crisis in the late 730s BC, when two nations have come against Jerusalem and King Ahaz. The child who will receive the name 'Immanuel' will be a young boy when the lands of the two threatening kings – King Pekah of Israel and King Rezin of Aram – will be laid waste (7:15–16). The 'Immanuel' of Isaiah 7:14, then, was a young child in the 730s BC, not necessarily a figure to arise in the distant future. While I will return later to explain how this passage can also apply to Christ, the central issue for our purposes is whether or not the 'Immanuel' child originally was a Davidic king.

A common view is to understand the 'Immanuel' child in 7:14 to be a faithful Davidic king, most likely Hezekiah. Some defend this in the light of the flow of the narrative in chapter 7.[4] Since the primary aim of King Rezin and King Pekah was to establish a new king over

---

[4] See also Blenkinsopp 2000: 232–234; G. V. Smith 2007: 206–214; Williamson 1998b: 104–109. I am blending insights from Goswell (2013: 100–105) and Laato (1988: 126–135, 154–159) in casting this narrative. Goswell is ambivalent concerning whether 'Immanuel' is a royal child, but his insights into how 7:1–17 confronts Davidic kingship feed well into Laato's explanation.

Jerusalem (7:6), God wants to assure King Ahaz of his commitment to the Davidic dynasty by offering a sign of assurance (7:10–11). Since King Ahaz shows himself to be faithless by rejecting the offer (7:12), God gives King Ahaz and his house a sign that condemns Ahaz, while also affirming his commitment to his promises to David. The 'virgin' to conceive is understood to be part of the royal family, and her child will be a faithful king after Ahaz and will receive the name 'Immanuel' (7:14). Though the house of David will experience terrible circumstances amid Assyrian threats because of Ahaz (7:17), the child 'Immanuel', who will learn right from wrong at an early age, will become a faithful Davidic king who will be a symbol of God's faithfulness to the line of David. Due to the high level of ambiguity within Isaiah 7 concerning the identity of 'Immanuel', some advocates of this view also appeal to the editorial placement of 9:1–7, with its explicit hopes for a Davidic king, in the context near Isaiah 7 as clarifying that 'Immanuel' is a Davidic king.[5] Thus the narrative flow within 7:1–17 and the surrounding literary context leads a number of scholars to argue that the sign of 'Immanuel' raises hopes for a lead agent, a Davidic ruler, who will rule faithfully in contrast to Ahaz as a pointer to God's faithfulness amid judgment.

Several challenges to interpreting this 'sign' as referring to a Davidic king lead to an alternative view that the identity of the child is unimportant. First, it is impossible to reconcile the date of this child's birth (c. 733 BC) with that of Hezekiah, who becomes king after Ahaz.[6] Second, the house of David is not the exclusive object of foreign threat and God's punishment. While King Rezin and Pekah seek to displace King Ahaz (7:6), they are also attacking Jerusalem (7:1) and desire to conquer and divide up Judah (7:6). What is more, while King Ahaz is said to be fearful (7:2) and is rebuked for faithlessly rejecting God's offer of a sign (7:12–13), 'his people' also fear (7:2) and a plurality of people are exhorted to believe in God (7:9).[7] God's judgment, then, is not simply against Ahaz and the house of David (7:13, 17), but days of calamity will also come upon 'your people', probably the nation

---

[5] Clements (1990: 230–235) is an extreme example of this. He thinks 'Immanuel' was originally a child of Isaiah but the later redactional placement of 9:1–7 shifted the referent to a Davidic king. For a critique of Clements, see Williamson (1998b: 104), who argues that 7:1–17 was already written with the question of the Davidic dynasty in mind.

[6] Chronological confusion in Kings, however, causes Blenkinsopp (2000: 234) not to allow debate surrounding Hezekiah's birth to determine one's position on Immanuel's identity.

[7] The verbs are plural in v. 9.

as a whole (7:17).[8] The sign, then, does not necessarily have to be limited to God's plans with the house of David, but instead could be focusing upon the circumstances facing the entire nation. Third, and perhaps most significant in my mind, we are told virtually nothing about who this child is or what he will do. Whether or not this child is from the line of David is not important to the inspired author; instead, the significance of this child resides in his serving as a temporal marker and having a name that points attention away from himself to God. By the time the woman gives birth, names her son 'Immanuel' and he is old enough to learn good from evil two things will take place: (1) the lands of the threatening nations will be laid waste (7:16), and (2) the child will be living in the aftermath of desolation in the land, as indicated by his eating a nomadic diet of curds and honey (7:15, 17; cf. 7:22–25).[9] *Who* this child is, then, seems to be of little importance;[10] what matters is that by the time this child is a few years old it will be evident that God is with his people both in salvation, by removing the threatening nations, and in judgment, by bringing calamity against the house of David and Judah through the king of Assyria.[11]

The hope in view, then, in Isaiah 7 does not reside in a Davidic king, at least not overtly.[12] It is the prospect of 'Immanuel' – God with us – in judgment and deliverance that is the key hope in this passage. When one reads chapters 6–7 together, the sense is that God reigns as a holy king during times when Davidic kings die (Uzziah; 6:1) and falter (Ahaz; 7:2, 12), and when foreign kings threaten (7:1). Judgment will indeed come through the initiative of this holy king, even in multiple waves from his sovereign use of Assyria and its king (6:13; 7:15–17, 25), but his people are called to keep calm (7:4) and to stand

---

[8] Goswell (2013: 100) understands 'his people' (2) and 'your people' (17) to be referring to Ahaz's entourage and royal household. While possible, the mention of 'house of David' in a list with 'your people' in v. 17 indicates a group other than Ahaz's circle. Laato (1988: 121) explains the national references in 'people' as later additions. Most, however, interpret 'people' in 7:2, 17 as referring to the nation (Williamson 1998b: 107).

[9] On 'curds' and 'honey' as negative indicators, see Abernethy 2014a: 57–58. Decisive in this decision is 7:22, where such a diet is set in the aftermath of disaster.

[10] Goldingay 2001: 64; Walton 1987: 296; R. E. Watts 2004: 96; Wegner 1992a: 127.

[11] Another prominent view is that 'Immanuel' is one of the children of the prophet (Oswalt 1986: 213; Blomberg 2002: 21; Hamilton 2008: 236–238). Williamson (1998b: 103) points out, however, that the *'almâ* is unlikely to be called such if she has already given birth (cf. Shear-Yashub). Seitz (1993: 62–63) helpfully identifies a number of crucial differences between Immanuel and Isaiah's other children.

[12] Similar sentiments are expressed by Goswell 2013.

firm in their faith (7:9) amid great threat, for it will soon be evident that God is with his people in judgment and salvation.

The same theme develops in chapter 8 where 'Immanuel' becomes a cry of hope, as the Lord uses Assyria to judge his people (8:8) and as they cling to the hope that the nations will not ultimately succeed in doing away completely with God's people (8:10).[13] It is the Lord who is the sanctuary for his people (8:14), so God's people are to revere him (8:13) and wait for him (8:17), instead of fearing what others fear (8:12). It seems then that what is most important in this context is how the name 'Immanuel' contributes to the larger aims of Isaiah 6 – 8 of showing that God, the holy king, can be trusted to be 'Immanuel' – God with us – as he brings about judgment and deliverance, initially in the context of the Assyrian crisis.[14] While I think it unlikely that the child born in Isaiah 7 is the royal king described in 9:1–7, I do believe that they belong to the same *theme* of God's being with his people. Just as God showed himself to be with his people during the crisis in the 730s BC, when Immanuel was a temporal marker that pointed to God's faithfulness, so God will show himself in 9:1–7 to be with his people by delivering them and establishing a Davidic ruler. In summary, Immanuel is a sign that points us to a theme more prominent than Davidic kingship, namely that God, the holy king from Isaiah 6, must be trusted, for he is and will be with his people in judgment and salvation.

Canonical reflections

How does the interpretation offered above on Isaiah 7:14 correspond with its use in Matthew 1:23? While some suggest a 'double-fulfillment' model,[15] 'prediction–fulfilment' does not quite capture what is happening in Isaiah and Matthew. With Wegner and Hamilton, the concept of 'patterning' best explains Matthew's use of this verse.[16] The pattern evident in Isaiah 7:14 of God's being with his people in both judgment and salvation corresponds with and escalates climactically at the incarnation of Jesus Christ.[17] It is not necessary for Isaiah

---

[13] Seitz (1993: 63) identifies 'Immanuel' in ch. 8 as Hezekiah due to the Assyrian context. It is God, however, who delivers Judah from Assyria, not Hezekiah.

[14] Walton (1987: 295) agrees that the importance of 'Immanuel' resides in his name, not in what the child does.

[15] Blomberg 2002.

[16] Wegner 1992a: 134–135; Hamilton 2008: 232–234, 239–246. Hamilton primarily uses the term 'typology', but he often coordinates this with patterning.

[17] For an emphasis upon judgment in the Immanuel sign and its outworking in Matthew, see R. E. Watts 2004.

7:14 to refer in its original context to a coming Davidic king in this understanding, for it is the pattern of God's being with his people that is most prominent, though, as it turns out, God chooses to show himself to be 'with us' in an escalated fashion through an actual virgin birth when Jesus takes on flesh and is born into the line of David.[18]

Characteristics of the Davidic ruler

While it seems unlikely that the child in Isaiah 7:14 should be identified as a Davidic ruler, the 'Immanuel' child points us to a prominent theme that grants perspective on the explicit promises concerning an ideal Davidic ruler. While the Davidic ruler is a lead human agent, his office is an outworking of what God is up to as he establishes and maintains his kingdom. While Judah's human rulers were failing to bring about justice (1:23), dying (6:1), wavering in faith (7:11–17) and being warned of exile (ch. 39), there is hope for a better ruler whom God is committed to raising up. There are four main passages in Isaiah that speak of a future Davidic ruler (9:6–7; 11:1–10; 16:5; cf. 32:1), and, instead of working through each passage, several key characteristics that are vital for understanding expectations pertaining to this lead agent will receive consideration.

The Davidic ruler is God's agent

Isaiah 9:1–7 and Isaiah 11 make it abundantly clear that the Davidic ruler is an extension of God's own plan and work.[19] In Isaiah 9:1–7 the centrality of God is evident in several ways.

First, throughout the passage, God is the primary actor.[20] In verse 1 it is God who will reverse Galilee's fortunes: he brought contempt to the area in the past, but will make it glorious in the future. In verses 3–4 the uses of the second person place a spotlight on God.

---

[18] It is debated how to understand the clause that the ESV translates as 'the virgin shall conceive' (7:14): (1) Many recognize that the term for 'conceive' in Hebrew is actually an attributive adjective (*hārâ*) meaning 'pregnant', which raises the possibility that the woman could already be pregnant (Gen. 16:11; Jer. 31:8). See Walton 1987: 290–291; Wegner 1992a: 130, n. 308; Wildberger 1991: 307–308. (2) While the Hebrew word *'almâ* can refer to a 'virgin', it seems to have the broader meaning of a girl who is mature enough to marry and have children. Even if the *'almâ* in 7:14 were a virgin at the time of Isaiah's message, her ensuing pregnancy would certainly have been understood as stemming from intercourse with a man. For an overview, see Wegner 1992a: 106–115; Wenham 1972.

[19] God's primacy is also apparent in 16:5 (divine passive, 'a throne will be established') and in 32:1.

[20] For similar reflections, see Goswell 2015: 102–106.

> *You* have multiplied the nation;
>> *you* have increased its joy;
> they rejoice before *you*
>> as with joy at the harvest . . .
> For the yoke of his burden,
>> and the staff for his shoulder,
>> the rod of his oppressor,
>> *you* have broken as on the day of Midian.

God is the reason behind the great increase in joy that the people are experiencing,[21] and the first among three reasons (9:4, 5, 6) for such joy is the recognition that God himself has delivered them from the oppressor (9:4). What is more, when verses 6–7 reflect upon the joy the Davidic ruler brings to the nation, the focus on God continues with the use of passive verbs:

> For to us a child is born,
>> to us a son is given . . .
>> (Isa. 9:6a)

This is a clear instance of the divine passive: God is the one who has given this child.[22] The final clause in verse 7 crystallizes this theocentric emphasis by stating, 'The zeal of the LORD of hosts will do this' (Isa. 9:7). God is the chief actor throughout 9:1–7, and he is the one who will provide the Davidic ruler.

Second, the primacy of God is apparent in 9:1–7 when we consider the names that the ruler will bear:

> Wonderful Counsellor, Mighty God,
>> Everlasting Father, Prince of Peace.
>> (Isa. 9:6b)

There are two ways of understanding these names. One position holds that these names describe the Davidic king. The interpretative crux for this position is the second name, 'Mighty God'. Since 'mighty God' refers to God in 10:21, interpreters like Oswalt and Motyer understand 'mighty God' as indicating that the Davidic ruler will

---

[21] Goswell (ibid. 103) highlights the hymnlike nature of this passage, which indicates that 'it is the deeds of YHWH that are celebrated'.
[22] Ibid. 105; Williamson 1998b: 33.

be divine.[23] Since this king is divine, the other titles make sense, for this divine-human king will naturally offer counsel far beyond human counsel, be everlasting in fatherly care and establish peace. There are a few challenges with this view, however. For one, it seems unlikely that Isaiah would conceptualize a Davidic ruler as being divine. While a king can be described as a 'son' of God (Ps. 2:7; 2 Sam. 7:14), the language of 'sonship' does not describe the ontological essence of the king as divine but rather the nature of God's relationship with that king. Perhaps, as Roberts argues, 'divine sonship' is metaphorical, even mythological, language that highlights how a human king could take up an office so dear to God and carry out God's plans in the world.[24] Another challenge with this position is that it seems to overlook how names often work, which leads to the second option for understanding these names.[25]

An increasingly favoured view is that these names primarily describe God rather than the human king. The foundation of this position is the recognition of how names work in Isaiah and elsewhere in the OT,[26] where names usually point to realities beyond the person bearing them. The names of Isaiah's children, Shear-Yashub ('a remnant shall return'; 7:3) and Maher-Shalal-Hash-Baz ('swift is the plunder; fast is the pillage'; 8:1), describe what Israel's experience would be, as do Hosea's

---

[23] Oswalt 1986: 245–247; Motyer 1993: 102–105. While Oswalt applies these titles directly to the nature of the king, Motyer suggests that the first two names relate to similarities with Immanuel and the second two refer to conditions stemming from the reign of this king. This division seems arbitrary, for there are elements in all of the titles that could entail conditions deriving from the reign (counsel could entail wisdom; might could entail victory; just as being a father entails fatherly care).

[24] Roberts 1997.

[25] Another objection against taking 'Mighty God' as describing the divinity of the king emerges in a study by Harris (1992: 188–204). In his examination of the application of 'God' to a human king in Ps. 45 he rightly observes that this is not an ontological description of the Davidic king as divine, but instead highlights the close relationship that God has with the Davidic king. The implication of this for Isa. 9:6 is that if 'Mighty God' describes the qualities of the Davidic king, then this title is not an ontological designation that the king is divine but instead a statement about the Davidic king's close relationship with God as God expresses his rule through the office of the Davidic king.

[26] Wegner 1992b; Goldingay 1999. Both Wegner and Goldingay divide these titles into two names. Wegner (1992b: 111) suggests 'wonderful planner [is] the mighty God; the Father of eternity [is] a prince of peace [or well-being]'. Goldingay (1999: 243) advocates for 'One who plans a wonder is the warrior God; the father forever is a commander who brings peace.' Both are influenced by Holladay (1978: 108–109), who advocates for three names, with the first and last describing the king and the middle being theophoric: 'Planner of Wonders; God the war hero (is) Father forever; prince of well-being'.

children – Lo-ammi ('not my people'; Hos. 1:9) and Lo-Ruhamah ('no compassion'; 1:6). Included among these are theophoric names that contain a divine name in them, usually 'el' or 'yah'. Eliezer (God of help), Elkhanah (God of grace), Hezekiah (YHWH is strong), Isaiah (YHWH saves), Immanuel (God with us) and Ishmael (God is hearing) are examples of names with a divine element in them. These names do not claim that the human bearing them is divine; instead, they express something about God. According to this view, the names in Isaiah 9:6 point to God, not the essence of the human ruler. During this era of radical reversal from gloom to joyful glory (9:1–2), from oppression to freedom (9:4) and from warfare to peace (9:5), it is fitting for the Davidic king who rules during this peaceful time to bear these names, for they point to the God who has brought about this glorious situation. Within the context of Isaiah the sight of an upright king ruling in Zion bears witness to God as the unsurpassable planner who has worked out his own plans wonderfully, while foiling the plans of the nations (cf. Isa. 8:10; 25:1; 29:14); as the mighty God who can save a remnant from the fiercest foe (10:21); as an everlasting father who has shown that his fatherly care and rule never cease (cf. 63:16; 64:7); as the 'prince (ruler) of peace' who brings about lasting peace unlike those rulers at the time of Isaiah (cf. 3:14; 31:9; 34:12).[27] The names of this Davidic ruler, then, point beyond the human office to King YHWH, who will wondrously save his people and establish a Davidic ruler in their midst. Mighty indeed is God!

Thus in 9:1–7 the prospect of a Davidic ruler's fulfilling his office is something only God himself can make happen, as is evident from God's serving as the chief actor in these verses. What is more, the very names that the Davidic ruler bears point beyond the human ruler to the divine king who, in his wisdom, might, fatherly care and governance, has put an end to war, brought joy to the nation and placed a Davidic ruler on the throne.[28] God, in his zeal, will bring this about. As Williamson puts it, 'The main focus of the passage, therefore, is on God's direct work on behalf of his people, and the provision of the royal figure is regarded as part of this. He serves as a sign of its gracious nature, as well as being, of course, a primary agent through whom God will work.'[29]

---

[27] Goldingay 1999: 241–243; Wegner 1992b: 112.

[28] Goswell (2015: 108) thinks the reference to David as a 'prince' (*sar*) in 9:6 instead of a 'king' is a choice to reserve the latter for God. This seems inconsistent with Goswell's (ibid. 107) view that these titles refer to God, not the human ruler.

[29] Williamson 1998b: 34.

Isaiah 11 also emphasizes God's involvement with an anticipated Davidic ruler. This is apparent in the imagery that opens this passage. While debate surrounds how best to understand the term often translated as 'stump',[30] the arboreal imagery unmistakeably points to a reality when all that exists is a small sign of potential, as only a root remains with a small shoot emerging from it. Just as God unexpectedly selected Jesse's youngest son, so Jesse's stump, which would be decimated through imperial threat, would again bear fruit. God will again raise up a ruler from the line of Jesse. Additionally, the role of God's Spirit in 11:2 indicates that the Davidic king is God's agent:

> And the Spirit of the LORD shall rest upon him,
>   the Spirit of wisdom and understanding,
>   the Spirit of counsel and might,
>   the Spirit of knowledge and the fear of the LORD.

The term 'Spirit' occurs four times in this verse. Just as God's Spirit is an indication of God's validation of King David's rule (1 Sam. 16:13–14), so God's Spirit will do the same with the future ruler from Jesse's line.[31] What is more, God's Spirit is an extension of God himself that empowers and equips his agents for his purposes, such as when God grants his Spirit to builders of the tabernacle (Exod. 28:3) or to the judges (Judg. 3:10; 6:34; 11:29; 13:25; 14:6, 19). In Isaiah 11 God's Spirit will endow the Davidic ruler with wisdom, which is vital for the task of ruling, as Solomon recognized, and is indicated by the final three uses of 'Spirit' being correlated with aspects of wisdom. Thus, as in Isaiah 9, in Isaiah 11 the Davidic ruler is God's agent. While one might be tempted to think of the Davidic ruler as an isolated central figure, the texts themselves demand that we place our hope not simply in a human king; rather, hope resides in God, the divine king, for if there ever would be a ruler from Jesse's line to reign amid the circumstances depicted in 9:1–7 and 11:1–10, then it would only be through the work of God and his empowering wisdom.

The Davidic ruler and a context of deliverance

Another prominent feature of the Davidic ruler is that he will rule in a context where deliverance from disaster has taken place. It is unclear, though, that the future Davidic ruler is a saviour and deliverer in

---

[30] See Wegner 1992a: 231–232.
[31] Marlow 2011: 225.

Isaiah. In Isaiah 9:1–7 God is the one who has saved his nation from their enemies:

> For the yoke of his burden,
>   and the staff for his shoulder,
>   the rod of his oppressor,
>   *you* have broken as on the day of Midian.
>   (Isa. 9:4)

Within the context of Isaiah 6 – 8 these oppressors are surely understood to be Assyria. The passage is clearly attributing the time when gloom turns into light and joy and when oppression ceases to YHWH's saving intervention. What is not clear in this passage, however, is whether YHWH has used the Davidic ruler as an agent to bring about God's salvation. The reason that this is ambiguous is because verses 6–7 are the last of three (9:4, 5, 6) explanatory verses (*kî*; 'because') given to clarify why joy has overtaken the nation (9:3). Does the final explanatory clause, where a Davidic ruler is given by God, illumine the previous explanations, conveying the idea that it is through the Davidic ruler that God broke the rod of the oppressor (9:4) and destroyed every garment of war (9:5)? Or is God's giving of a Davidic ruler one among three reasons given for the nation's joy? If the latter, the Davidic ruler is not understood as a saviour figure but instead is an agent for God in the aftermath of salvation.[32] What is certain in this passage is that God is receiving the glory for the nation's salvation (whether this was accomplished through a Davidic agent or not), and the description of the Davidic ruler emphasizes his role in the aftermath of salvation, as he promotes a peaceful kingdom.

In Isaiah 11 it is only in verse 4b where there is the faintest suggestion that the Davidic ruler may be a deliverer:

> and he shall strike the earth with the rod of his mouth,
>   and with the breath of his lips he shall kill the wicked.
>   (Isa. 11:4b)

While it is possible that Jesse's shoot will intervene against the wicked in a mighty act of judgment and deliverance, the parallel verses are concerned with the fair treatment of the powerless. Since the weapons in verse 4, 'rod of his mouth' and 'breath of his lips', are instruments

---

[32] See Goswell 2014: 96; 2015; Williamson 1998b: 33–34.

of speech, the focus here does not seem to be upon a mighty act of national deliverance, but rather upon how the upright decrees of this ruler will prevail against the wicked. As Smith puts it, 'The aim is not to present a negative view of uncontrolled slaughter of wicked people, but to emphasize that everything will be guided by principles of justice.'[33] Thus in 9:1–7 and 11:1–9 there is little evidence that the Davidic agent will act as a deliverer, for their focus is on the role of the ruler in the aftermath of salvation. The same holds true in 16:5 and 32:1, as we will see shortly.

The literary placement of 9:1–7 and 11:1–9 further emphasizes the Davidic ruler reigning in the aftermath of deliverance.[34] Isaiah 9:1–7 comes just after gloomy reflections upon life under judgment through Assyria (8:19–22). By placing a passage full of hope in God's deliverance (9:1–5), capped off with a vision of a Davidic ruler's reigning in peace (9:6–7), the hope is that an ideal ruler will emerge when judgment passes due to God's saving intervention. The placement of 11:1–9 after Isaiah 10 develops further the vision for a Davidic ruler's reigning in the wake of Assyria's demise. While mighty Assyria and its king will be cut down, just like an axe cutting the branches of a mighty tree (10:33–34), a humble shoot will sprout from a stump (11:1), presumably after Assyria falls.[35] Through arranging these texts in this way the vision of the Davidic ruler differs from the one we get in *The Return of the King*, where Strider's (Aragorn) kingship becomes evident when he leads his forces victoriously and bravely against Sauron. In the book of Isaiah it is God who is the saving warrior figure, as one sees, for example, in Isaiah 36 – 37 when God dramatically intervenes to save Jerusalem during the time of Hezekiah. While one cannot conclusively rule out the possibility that God will act through a Davidic ruler to deliver his people, when the book of Isaiah offers a vision of a Davidic ruler, its interest is in the reign of this agent in the aftermath of deliverance from Israel's foes. Hope resides in how the Davidic ruler will govern during the glorious era when deliverance has taken place.[36]

---

[33] G. V. Smith 2007: 273.

[34] Wegner (1992a: 305) believes that there is a fourfold pattern in the arrangement of the passages: (1) Assyria used to punish Israel, (2) a righteous remnant saved from Assyria, (3) God raises up a deliverer to bring Israel to victory over Assyria, and (4) the deliverer will establish a kingdom of peace and justice. It is unclear, however, how Wegner's second and third points work together, for if a remnant is already saved (by God) why is there a need for a Davidic king to deliver again?

[35] Beuken 2002; Wegner 1992a: 229–230; Williamson 1998b: 52.

[36] For a similar argument for Isa. 16:5, see Goswell 2014: 95–96.

The Davidic ruler will establish justice and righteousness
The chief task of the Davidic ruler in Isaiah is to be an agent of justice and righteousness. This feature appears in all four of the passages that speak explicitly of the Davidic agent. Isaiah 9:7[6] presents the Davidic agent's purpose:

> Of the increase of his government and of peace
>   there will be no end,
> on the throne of David and over his kingdom,
>   to establish it and to uphold it
> *with justice and with righteousness*
>   from this time forth and for evermore.
> The zeal of the LORD of hosts will do this.

It will be the Lord of hosts, the great king of the armies of heaven, whose zeal will bring about the Davidic ruler's perpetual reign, and of utmost importance is the recognition that this kingdom be anchored in justice and righteousness. Isaiah 11 shares this vision of a second David promoting justice and righteousness. God's Spirit will endow this ruler with wisdom so that the king will be able to bring about equity in the kingdom:

> And his delight shall be in the fear of the LORD.
> He shall not *judge* by what his eyes see,
>   or decide disputes by what his ears hear,
> but *with righteousness* he shall judge the poor,
>   and decide *with equity* for the meek of the earth;
> and he shall strike the earth with the rod of his mouth,
>   and with the breath of his lips he shall kill the wicked.
> *Righteousness* shall be the belt of his waist,
>   and faithfulness the belt of his loins.
>   (Isa. 11:3–5)

Since administering justice is a primary duty for a king, Isaiah 11 looks towards a time when even those with no economic, political or social capital will receive a fair hearing. In fact, just as clothing portrays God's nature and concerns in 59:17, so the garments in 11:5 metaphorically convey how this future ruler will exude righteousness. While the community was not 'seeing' or 'hearing' (6:10), this king will have a perception of a different order, not being influenced by any deception or temptations that would thwart justice.[37] Even the brief statements concerning the king in 16:5 and 32:1 share this emphasis:[38]

> then a throne will be established in steadfast love,
>   and on it will sit in faithfulness
>   in the tent of David
> one *who judges and seeks justice*
>   and is swift *to do righteousness*.
>
> (Isa. 16:5)

> Behold, a king will reign *in righteousness*,
>   and princes will rule *in justice*.
>
> (Isa. 32:1)

All four of these passages emphasize and clarify the Davidic ruler's role. '[T]his role is bound up as closely as it is possible to imagine with the maintenance of "justice" and "righteousness", terms which . . . stand as a sort of shorthand for the ordering of society as a whole in accordance with God's will.'[39]

The emphasis upon the Davidic ruler's role in establishing justice and righteousness is not surprising, for this is one of God's chief concerns. The book opens in Isaiah 1 with a summons for the audience to do justice and righteousness (1:16–17), a vision of God's transforming an unrighteous city of corrupt leaders into a city of righteousness (1:21–26), and the promise to redeem Zion in righteousness and justice (1:27). In Isaiah 5 God laments how his vineyard, Judah and Israel, has not produced the justice and righteousness he has hoped for (5:7). The powerful, as they amass houses and fields, are squeezing out poor inhabitants (5:8–9), are drunkards (5:11) and ignore God's works (5:12). Though injustice seems to be prevailing, an alternative destiny is stated in 5:15–16:

> Man is humbled, and each one is brought low,
>   and the eyes of the haughty are brought low.
> But the LORD of hosts is exalted in justice,
>   and the Holy God shows himself holy in righteousness.

---

[37] Wegner 1992a: 255; Williamson 1998b: 49.
[38] Goswell 2014: 97. See Williamson (1998b: 62–72), who argues that the statement in 32:1 is proverbial.
[39] Williamson 1998b: 70.

In language reminiscent of Isaiah 2 (vv. 9, 11–17) these verses assert that the tables will be turned, for there is no room for the pride of unjust humans when King YHWH assumes his rightful place of exaltation. Significantly, it is through justice and righteousness that YHWH will be exalted. Scholars are divided between whether the 'justice' and 'righteousness' in view in verse 16 belong to YHWH or to humanity. In other words, will God be exalted when he acts in righteous judgment towards the unjust, or will he be exalted when his people act in justice and righteousness? In support of the former position is the clear contrast with verse 15 between sinful humanity and God – God will be exalted in justice when he righteously levels proud, unjust humanity.[40] In support of the latter position is the fact that 'righteousness' and 'justice' in 5:7 clearly refer to human behaviour, so this may entail that the terms in 5:16 also refer to human action (cf. 1:17).[41] While I lean towards understanding 5:16 as referring to God's justice and righteousness (cf. 3:14), it may be unnecessary to limit the way through which God can express his justice and righteousness. God may choose to enact his justice and righteousness through his agents, thereby levelling the proud through them (cf. 11:4). As Moberly puts it, 'it is a basic prophetic axiom that YHWH acts in and through the actions of his servants . . . Thus YHWH's actions of justice and righteousness may be seen precisely in the actions of justice and righteousness performed by those accountable to him.'[42] God is committed to responding to injustice with his own justice and righteousness, and since the chief role of the Davidic ruler is to ensure justice and righteousness in 9:7 and 11:3–5, it is possible that we are to view him as an avenue through which God expresses his righteousness and justice amid his quest to set the world right. The important point here is that God cares about justice – his glory is tied to it – and this is evident in the mission of the ruler as God's agent.

God's plans to use human rule to establish justice and righteousness accord with the role David and his progeny undertook.[43] In 2 Samuel 8:15 we are told, 'So David reigned over all Israel; and David administered justice and equity to all his people' (2 Sam. 8:15, NRSV).

After David (cf. 2 Sam. 15:6), King Solomon is also extolled in the light of how God's wisdom enabled him to do 'justice' (1 Kgs 3:28). The Queen of Sheba praises God for providing a king like Solomon

[40] Williamson 2006: 375–376.
[41] Moberly 2001; Leclerc 2001: 61.
[42] Moberly 2001: 63.
[43] Schibler 1995: 97–98.

to Israel 'to do justice and righteousness' (1 Kgs 10:9, NASB). Even in a song of Israel, perhaps by Solomon, requests are made that God grant the king justice:[44]

> Give the king your justice, O God,
>   and your righteousness to the royal son!
> May he judge your people with righteousness,
>   and your poor with justice!
> Let the mountains bear prosperity for the people,
>   and the hills, in righteousness!
> May he defend the cause of the poor of the people,
>   give deliverance to the children of the needy,
>   and crush the oppressor!
>
>   (Ps. 72:1–4)

While Jerusalem's kings consistently abused their power and did not practise justice, Isaiah, along with Jeremiah (Jer. 23:5; 33:15), holds forth a vision of promise that is anchored deeply in Israel's history. During eras of injustice, the hope was that God would again use the office of David, as he had in the past, to bring a just and righteous order to God's society. The result of the just and righteous reign of the Davidic agent will be an era of great peace (9:7).

Summary and canonical reflections

The lead agent of King YHWH in Isaiah 1 – 39 is the Davidic ruler. How are we to understand this ruler? First, the Davidic ruler must be understood in the light of God's own kingdom activity, for it is God who provides and empowers the Davidic agent and creates the circumstances amid which he can rule. Second, the reign of the Davidic agent will operate amid an era of salvation, when oppression and judgment have passed. Third, the primary task of the Davidic ruler will be to establish God's justice and righteousness in the world through God's Spirit as an agent of God during the era of salvation.

Who is the referent of these hopes (9:1–7; 11:1–9; 16:5; 32:1)? A case can be made that most of these passages originally, before being placed in book form, could have been understood as referring to hopes associated with existing kings.[45] As anchored as Isaiah 1 – 12 is in the

---

[44] Williamson 1998b: 37–38.
[45] For a chart of views, see Laato 1988: 2. Heskett (2007: 58–60, 83–132) does not think that 7:14, 9:1–17 or 11:1–9 were originally messianic, though he thinks that they all take on a messianic flavour due to their placement in the book.

realities of the Assyrian era, it would be quite possible to understand 9:1–7 and 11:1–9 to refer to King Hezekiah, who ruled during a time when Sennacherib's armies were defeated, and later to King Josiah, who reigned during a time when Assyrian dominance was fading. What one finds, however, is that, even within the book of Isaiah, King Hezekiah fails and the dynasty of David is destined for exile (Isa. 39).[46] Though King Hezekiah does not fulfil these expectations, King Josiah emerges later as a strong candidate who pushed for reform, though he died unexpectedly, resulting in a chain of kings who failed in their task of promoting justice and righteousness (Jer. 22:11–17). With Isaiah's hope that a Davidic ruler would arise in the aftermath of Assyria's rule dissolving and with the prospect of the exile of the house of David to Babylon concluding Isaiah 1 – 39, there is a level of ambiguity concerning what we are to do with God's promises concerning a Davidic ruler. Some scholars claim that the absence of David in the second half of Isaiah in favour of an increasing focus on God as king indicates that the book of Isaiah gives up the hope for a Davidic king expressed in 1 – 39.[47] Others suggest that David does not disappear in the rest of the book, with the servant and messenger being the same messianic figure.[48] I will adopt a moderating position. As will become evident below, though David is not in focus in 40 – 66, this does not invalidate the hope for a Davidic king from 1 to 39.

While Hezekiah and Josiah did not fulfil the expectations of Isaiah's Davidic promises, the post-exilic era offered little hope either. Though Zerubbabel, a Davidic descendant, played an important role as governor, God's promises to David still awaited fulfilment (Hag. 2:20–23). It is Jesus Christ who offers an 'amen' to these promises from Isaiah, though in an unexpected fashion. The NT opens by stating that Jesus is the Christ, 'the son of David' (Matt. 1:1; cf. Luke 1:69; 2:4; 3:31), and is referred to as 'son of David' repeatedly (Matt. 9:27; 12:23; 15:22; 20:30, 31; 21:9, 15; Mark 10:47, 48; Luke 18:38, 39; Rom. 1:3). This connection between Jesus and David in the NT sits awkwardly, however, with the expectations of Isaiah. It was not during an era of salvation from political foes that Jesus came as a Davidic king, for Rome was still sovereign over Palestine before, during and after Jesus came. Jesus did not sit upon any throne in

---

[46] While scholars tend to emphasize the idealized portrayal of Hezekiah in Isaiah (Seitz 1991: 47–118), see Kennedy 2004 for a more scathing probe of Hezekiah's character.

[47] Berges 2014; Schmid 2005.

[48] Heskett 2007; Schultz 1995.

Jerusalem. This was probably the reason why he was mocked as 'king' throughout his trial, and even to his final breath on the cross (Matt. 27:29, 37, 42). He did not fit the mould of the expected Davidic ruler, as cross and crown were irreconcilable. Jesus did, however, earnestly embody the Davidic king's commitment to justice and righteousness, as he confronted systems of injustice, particularly religious ones (Matt. 23:23; Luke 11:42), and as he astounded people with his wisdom (Matt. 13:54; Mark 6:2; Luke 2:40, 52). He was the light to the desolate areas around Galilee (Matt. 4:15). Though his rule during his first coming did not manifest itself as one might expect, according to the book of Revelation, Jesus will rule as the heavenly Davidic king who has conquered and is able therefore to issue decrees (Rev. 3:7) and unleash God's justice in the world through the unfolding of the scroll (Rev. 5:5; 22:16; cf. Isa. 11:1). In fact, when Jesus comes again he will come as the rider who will issue righteous justice (Rev. 19:11) on behalf of his saints. As a result of his resurrection, he indeed reigns now upon the throne of David as the conquering king (Luke 1:32–33), and the realization of his mission for justice and righteousness will culminate when he comes again. Thus the hope for a Davidic ruler offers a canonical witness to Jesus' first and second coming as king, but his rule is realized in an unexpected fashion, which derives from the unexpected fusion in the NT between Isaiah's expectations regarding the Davidic ruler and the suffering servant.

The servant of the Lord in Isaiah 40 – 55

The transition to addressing an exilic context in Isaiah 40 – 55 naturally results in a different, though not entirely distinct, depiction of how God will use a lead agent to accomplish his kingdom plans. Instead of envisioning a centralized Davidic ruler who will establish justice and righteousness within Judah in the aftermath of Assyrian oppression (1 – 39), God's lead agent in Isaiah 40 – 55, the servant, takes on more of an international mission and undertakes the important task of reconciling Israel and the nations to God through suffering.[49] While the interpretation of the servant in Isaiah 40 – 55 is a much debated and vexing topic, I will set forth my understanding in as straightforward a manner as possible with trails in the footnotes leading to

---

[49] There is little space to examine the role that King Cyrus plays in God's plans of rebuilding Jerusalem, though one should observe that Cyrus is not God's servant but instead has a mission to God's servant (i.e. Israel) (45:4).

various debates for those interested.[50] I will argue that because Israel is unable to fulfil its task as God's servant to the nations (42:1–9) due to its own spiritual blindness (42:19), God will use an individual servant to achieve atonement for and effect spiritual change in Israel and all nations (49:1–13; 50:4–9; 52:13 – 53:12), with the result being a community of servants that is able to come to God's holy city and carry out Israel's mission.

Israel as God's (failing) servant in Isaiah 40 – 48

Isaiah 42:1–9 is the main passage in Isaiah 40 – 48 where God speaks of his plans to use a servant. While some scholars, especially more conservative ones, tend to claim that the servant in 42:1–9 is an individual Messiah,[51] the literary context points to the servant's being the nation of Israel, for nearly all of the other occurrences of the term 'servant' in 40 – 48, including those just prior to this in 41:8–9, apply to Israel as a nation.[52] Childs's observation here is important: 'For anyone who takes the . . . literary context seriously, there can be no avoiding the obvious implication that *in some way* Israel is the servant who is named.'[53] While it is not impossible that 42:1–9 could break the mould by speaking of an individual, the merits of the collective understanding of the servant in 42:1 as Israel commend themselves, not only due to this being the usual referent for the term in 40 – 48, but also in the light of how this passage fits into the drama of God's servant Israel failing in their task.

Isaiah 42:1–9 can be divided into two sections (1–4, 5–9), with the first being a description by YHWH of his servant's mission and the second being a direct statement from YHWH to his servant regarding this mission. While we will not work through every verse, the first verse warrants some initial reflection.

> Behold my servant, whom I uphold,
> my chosen, in whom my soul delights;

[50] For a survey of views prior to the modern period, see Laato 2012. For a survey of modern views, see North 1948; Rowley 1952: 1–32.

[51] Chisholm 2006: 393–401; Koole 1997: 208–239; Oswalt 1998: 108; G. V. Smith 2009: 161. Blenkinsopp interprets the servant as King Cyrus (2002: 210–211), though he acknowledges that it is equally plausible that the nation of Israel could be the figure.

[52] Isa. 41:8–9; 42:9[twice]; 43:10; 44:1–2, 21; 45:4; 48:20. See, however, 44:26, which probably refers to the prophet. Among many who identify the servant in 42:1–9 as Israel, see Laato 2012: 31–48; Lessing 2011: 131–132; Seitz 2004; Ward 1968; Wilcox and Paton-Williams 1988: 86; Williamson 1998b: 130–148.

[53] Childs 2001: 325, emphasis original. See also Goldingay and Payne 2006a: 212.

> I have put my Spirit upon him;
> he will bring forth justice to the nations.
>
> (Isa. 42:1)

The first line recalls 41:8–10, where God reassuringly calls Israel his 'servant' (*'ebed*) whom he has 'chosen' (*bḥr*) and 'upholds' (*tmk*).[54] By using similar terms the author indicates that we are dealing with another passage about God's servant, Israel, which further specifies Israel's mission. God's close association with the servant is evident through the use of first person pronouns ('I', 'my'), and the provision of God's Spirit highlights both God's favour towards the servant and God's empowerment for his task of bringing forth justice. The term 'justice' occurs three times in 42:1–4, so it is clear that God's chief purpose for Israel, his servant, is to carry forth justice.

A discerning reader should detect similarities between 42:1 and the task of the Davidic ruler as described in Isaiah 1 – 39. Like the Davidic ruler, the servant is an agent who receives God's 'Spirit' (42:1//11:2) and establishes 'justice' (42:1, 3, 4; 9:7[6]; 16:5; 32:1; cf. 11:4). Is the servant a (messianic) king in 42:1–9, as some claim?[55] While the focus on justice here certainly presents the servant 'to us in royal guise' to a limited extent,[56] several features point us away from understanding the servant in 42:1–9 as being identical to the royal figure from Isaiah 1 – 39.[57] (1) The immediate context surrounding Isaiah 42 repeatedly refers to the servant as the nation Israel.[58] (2) The *scope* of carrying out justice differs here, for it is 'the nations' (42:1) and 'the coastlands' (42:4) who are to be the prime recipients of God's 'justice' and 'instruction' through the servant.[59] (3) The overlap between the servant and the Davidic ruler with respect to justice and empowerment does not automatically lead to equating the two figures; instead, both

---

[54] Wilcox and Paton-Williams 1988: 86.

[55] Chisholm 2006: 393–401; Oswalt 1998: 108; G. V. Smith 2009: 161. Schultz (1995: 154–159) is more cautious, though he leans in the direction of understanding the servant, even in 42:3–4, as the same individual as the Davidic ruler from 1 to 39. For Schultz, a retrospective reading of Isa. 42 – 49 supports this understanding.

[56] Williamson 1998b: 132. He interprets the servant in 42:1–4 as Israel, albeit in 'royal guise' (135–144).

[57] It is of course possible that the servant in 42:1–9 is not the same individual as the Davidic agent of Isa. 1 – 39, while the servant in chapters 49, 50 and 53 could be the same as the Davidic agent. This will be assessed further below.

[58] Wilcox and Paton-Williams 1988: 87.

[59] Williamson 1998b: 137–140. The nations, however, are not completely out of view in 11:10. The movement of the nations there is centripetal (the nations coming to the king) while it is centrifugal with the servant (the servant going to the nations).

the servant and the Davidic ruler are empowered by God's Spirit and share in a common royal task of bringing forth justice because they are both agents of the same king. Is it possible for a judge and an ambassador to the United Nations to share in the common task of promoting justice, although their pursuits of justice manifest themselves differently based upon context and office? Just as a judge and ambassador need not be the same person, so the Davidic ruler and servant need not be identical just because they both share the common kingdom task of promoting justice. The Davidic ruler will establish justice primarily in a national sphere through regal power, but God's servant Israel will bring justice to the nations by announcing God's 'justice' (41:1, my tr.) and offering instruction in such a way that makes it clear that YHWH alone is the true God of all the earth (42:8).[60] Israel would carry out their task of bringing justice primarily as a messenger.[61] It is most likely, then, that though the servant in Isaiah 42:1 is not the same agent as the Davidic ruler from 1 – 39, they share a common 'royal' mission under King YHWH who, as his agents, will carry forth justice, albeit in unique ways in the light of their distinct contexts and roles.

The mission of 'justice' that Israel, God's servant, is to undertake manifests itself in a gentle manner. While one might expect God's justice for the nations to be full of wrathful destruction,[62] God's servant will have a gentle way of bringing about justice, as he will not carry on loudly in protest nor take advantage of power to crush bruised reeds or snuff out dim wicks (42:2–3). If one could imagine an exilic setting, the scene would be God's people, Israel, perhaps in the aftermath of the nations, experiencing judgment (i.e. bruised reeds), taking God's instruction and justice as a transforming light into a world of darkness. The political and spiritual component of this task becomes more explicit in the second half of this passage, particularly in 42:6b–7:

> I will give you as a covenant for the people,
> a light for the nations,
> to open the eyes that are blind,

---

[60] Goldingay and Payne (2006a: 212–223) translate *mišpāṭ* as 'decision', with the idea being that God's servant Israel will announce God's decision from the court scene in ch. 41.

[61] Note the parallel between servant and messenger in 42:19.

[62] There is some indication of wrathful destruction in 41:14–16, but Israel's role as servant will have a gentle side to it as well.

> to bring out the prisoners from the dungeon,
> from the prison those who sit in darkness.

As in verses 1 and 3, we again see that the purview of the servant's ministry is the nations. In fact, Israel themselves will be a covenant for the people, probably in the sense of establishing a relationship between God and the peoples,[63] functioning as a light for the nations. As a 'light', they will be in position to open the eyes of the blind, set prisoners free, particularly those sitting in darkness. While verse 7 could be understood literally, the language is probably figurative, with the confines of prison symbolizing the less than ideal life in exile and with 'blindness' indicating a spiritual darkness (29:18; 42:16, 18–19; 56:10). The servant will contribute to the reversal of these realities by bringing God's justice to the world and setting forth a new reality of covenant relationship between God and the nations; the servant, Israel, is to play a role in God's drama of reversing political oppression while summoning forth spiritual renewal.[64] With Abraham having been commissioned to be a blessing to all nations (Gen. 12:2–3) and with Israel serving as a signal to all nations of God's wisdom (Deut. 4:6), it is not a complete surprise that Israel is to be God's servant who brings God's justice and light to the entire world. Strategically positioned in exile, scattered among the nations, God's servant, Israel, is to carry forth God's mission of bringing justice and spiritual transformation throughout the world.

Isaiah 42:1–9 is not necessarily a description of who Israel in reality was, but, as Williamson puts it, this passage is 'an ideal held out before [Israel] as a vision and aspiration'.[65] It is an ideal in which Israel, who is or will be scattered throughout the world, receives a commission from God to be God's lead agent(s) in bringing justice and spiritual light to the entire world. There is a problem, however, that becomes explicit later in chapter 42. While God's servant is to open the eyes of the blind, the reality is that Israel is in no condition to fulfil this task:[66]

> Who is blind but my servant,
> or deaf as my messenger whom I send?

---

[63] In 42:5 the term 'people' (*'am*) clearly refers to humanity in general, which supports a similar interpretation in 42:6 (Koole 1997: 230–231).

[64] Ibid. 234–235; Goldingay and Payne 2006a: 229–230.

[65] Williamson 1998b: 142.

[66] Wilcox and Paton-Williams 1988: 88; Lessing 2011: 131–132.

> Who is blind as my dedicated one,
> or blind as the servant of the LORD?
> He sees many things, but does not observe them;
> his ears are open, but he does not hear.
> (Isa. 42:19–20)

Instead of being in a position to bring light to the nations, Israel finds itself in the very same circumstances. God's servant is blind just like the nations. In fact, though they should set free those in 'prison' (*byt kl'*; 42:7), they are in 'prison' (*byt kl'*; 42:22), as they remain unresponsive to God even after experiencing his judgment, presumably through exile (42:25). This poses a dilemma within the sweeping message of Isaiah 40 – 48. While God will use a foreign king, Cyrus, as his 'messiah' to rebuild Jerusalem (44:24 – 45:13) and to set God's servant Israel free from Babylon (48:20), there remains the dilemma of Israel's perpetual spiritual blindness and its inability to fulfil God's plans for them to open the eyes of a blind world. How will Israel become who they should be so that they can play their role in calling the nations to turn to God? How can a holy God welcome them home? The answer to this question comes through a shift in the servant motif in Isaiah 49 – 55. Thus in Isaiah 40 – 48 God's lead agent is the nation of Israel, his servant, who will ideally bring God's justice and instruction to all nations, though their spiritual blindness makes them incapable of fulfilling their task.

The suffering servant who restores Israel and the nations

With God's servant, the nation Israel, unable to fulfil its task, a new servant – the suffering servant – arises who will be God's lead agent in Isaiah 49 – 55, the second half of 40 – 55.[67] Three passages (49:1–13; 50:4–9; 52:13 – 53:12) deal with the servant's task, but instead of dealing with each passage in turn, I will reflect upon several significant features that are vital for understanding this servant.

The suffering servant is God's agent

Just as we saw with the Davidic ruler, the suffering servant and his mission must be understood in the light of what God is up to. The

---

[67] While the 'servant' in 42:1–9 is corporate Israel and in 49 – 55 is an individual, I understand them to be integrally related through sharing the same title ('servant'), and as the latter is an extension, development from the former. Hence they are treated categorically in this chapter as one lead agent, while acknowledging the need for nuance in this categorization.

agency of the servant depends completely upon the agency of God. In Isaiah 49:1–6, where the servant speaks of his identity and mission, God is the subject of most of the verbs:

> *The LORD* called me . . .
>   . . . *he* named my name.
> *He* made my mouth . . .
>   . . . *he* hid me;
> *he* made me . . .
>   . . . *he* hid me away.
> And *he* said to me, 'You are my servant,
>   Israel, in whom *I* will be glorified.' . . .
> And now *the LORD* says,
>   *he* who formed me from the womb to be his servant . . .
> *he* says . . .
> '*I* will make you as a light for the nations,
>   that my salvation may reach to the end of the earth.'

There is no doubt that the very existence, mission and identity of the servant in 49:1–6 rests upon the work and initiative of God himself. In fact, it will be through the servant's work that God gains glory for himself (49:3) and that God's salvation will reach the ends of the earth (49:6).[68] The servant also looks to God for vindication amid his wearying mission, for his 'right' and 'recompense' are with the Lord (49:4).

Isaiah 50:4–9 shares a similar God-centred outlook, though with different emphases. While the servant highlights his own obedience, it is the Sovereign Lord who makes this possible, for it is the Sovereign Lord who gives him a 'trained tongue' to speak words of comfort (50:4, my tr.) and wakens him and his ear for instruction (50:4–5). The Sovereign Lord helps him to not be humiliated (50:7, 9) and stands near to vindicate him (50:8). The servant's obedience depends wholly on the Lord, as does the servant's confidence that he will not be put to shame.

Isaiah 52:13 – 53:12 also places God at the forefront. At the beginning (52:13–15) and end (53:12) God is the speaker, referring to the servant as 'my servant' (52:13; 53:11) and declaring that his servant will be successful and receive vindication. Not only is God committed to the servant's exaltation, but several statements make it clear that the servant's suffering is all part of the divine plan:

---

[68] Gignilliat 2008: 133.

the LORD has laid on him
the iniquity of us all.
(Isa. 53:6b)

Yet it was the will of the LORD to crush him;
he has put him to grief . . .
(Isa. 53:10a)

The suffering of God's servant is wrapped up in God's own involvement in carrying out his plans. As Wilcox and Paton-Williams put it
succinctly, 'the servant's work is Yahweh's work'.[69]

In addition to these individual passages that testify that the servant
is God's agent, their literary context reinforces this point. Within
Isaiah 49 – 55 there is an alternation between 'servant songs' and
passages describing Zion's redemption. In the passages describing
Zion's redemption it often seems like God will act on his own to
accomplish his plans for Zion. There are indications, however, that
God will realize his promises, or at least some of them, through his
servant. Below are a few examples of this.

First, in Isaiah 51:4, which is part of an extended depiction of
Zion's restoration (51:1 – 52:12), God calls the nations to hear that
'I will set my justice for a light to the peoples [*lĕ'ôr 'ammîm*]'
(Isa. 51:4). Though Isaiah 51 does not specify how this will take place,
just prior to this, in 49:6, YHWH says of the servant, 'I will make you
as a light for the nations [*lĕ'ôr gôyîm*]' (Isa. 49:6). This association
may suggest that the suffering servant will be the means by which
God's light reaches the nations, though God's servant Israel previously
held this role (42:4, 6).

Second, God repeatedly promises that his 'salvation' (*yĕšû'â*;
51:6, 8; cf. 51:5) is coming, and, as we saw in chapter 2 above, the
culmination of God's salvation will be when his heralds announce
the 'saving' message to Zion that 'your God reigns' (52:7) as the
nations see 'the salvation of our God' (52:10). How will God's
salvation be accomplished? In Isaiah 49:6 YHWH says of his
servant:[70]

I will make you . . .
to be my *salvation* unto the end of the earth.

---

[69] Wilcox and Paton-Williams 1988: 95.
[70] For this translation, see Koole 1998: 1, 24; Goldingay and Payne 2006b: 166.

The literary context suggests that God may bring salvation for Zion through his servant.

Third, and perhaps most striking, there is hope in Isaiah 51 that the 'arm of the LORD' will awake and act, as it did in the exodus (51:5, 9). This hope culminates in the context of the announcement of good news that God reigns as king in Zion (52:7). During that time, one will say that

> The LORD has bared his holy arm
> before the eyes of all the nations . . .
> (52:10)

While the way in which God will lay bare his arm to redeem Zion is unclear initially, it is just after this in a servant passage that the 'arm of the LORD' surfaces in a question:

> Who has believed what he has heard from us?
> And to whom has the arm of the LORD been revealed?
> (Isa. 53:1)

This question assumes that the suffering servant is the means through which the arm of the Lord was revealed. As Goldingay and Payne state, 'Given where the revelation came (in this humiliated servant), it is not surprising that the people failed to see it.'[71] Significantly for our purposes, since the revelation of God's arm correlates in some fashion with the establishment of God's rule as king in Zion (52:7, 10), the suffering servant seems to be an agent whom God the king uses to establish his reign in Zion before the purview of all nations. Thus by considering how statements about God's plans to redeem Zion coordinate with the servant motif, the arrangement of Isaiah 49 – 55 seems to suggest that the suffering servant will be a significant agent through whom God acts to bring salvation to Zion and reveal his arm amid the establishment of God's kingship.

At this point we may ask whether the servant in Isaiah 49 – 55 is divine. Some point to the application of the clause '[he will be] high and lifted up' (*yārûm wĕnissā'*) to the suffering servant in 52:13, which correlates with the same pair of verbs that describe YHWH in 6:1 ('high and lifted up'; *rām wĕnissā'*) and 57:15 ('high and lifted

---

[71] Goldingay and Payne 2006b: 298.

up'; *rām wĕnissā'*), as evidence for the servant's divinity.[72] This observation, along with the way in which God's actions manifest themselves through the servant (see above), leads Gignilliat to infer that 'the narrative identity of the servant and of Yahweh act in a perichoretic relationship', which leads to his strong claim that the narrative flow invites us to see the servant as having 'a divine identity that at a minimum hints at later trinitarian formulations'.[73] While I empathize with Gignilliat's concern to allow the literary context to inform the way we comprehend the servant's identity, it seems more natural to understand the statements about the servant in a straightforward fashion – as an agent through whom God acts.[74] Instead of being a designation of divinity, the expression 'he shall be high and lifted up' (52:13) indicates a reversal in status that is befitting for God's servant. This verb pair ('to be high' and 'to be lifted up') not only describes deity in Isaiah but also refers to proud humanity (2:12), the cedars of Lebanon (2:13), and mountains and hills (2:14) that will be brought low before the Lord. While God alone will be exalted over the wannabes in the last day, Isaiah 52:13 tells us that God will transform the suffering servant's lowly status to such an extent that he will be deserving of honour usually fit only for Yahweh; this will not be due to a shared ontological identity, but instead will be due to the servant's having faithfully carried out his role in God's kingdom plans.[75]

In summary, there is little doubt that the suffering servant is God's agent in Isaiah 49 – 55. While it may be inaccurate to claim that God's servant is the only means through which God will act in Isaiah 40 – 55,[76] it is certainly true that God's servant will be a significant agent through whom God's kingdom purposes will be realized. As Schultz puts it, 'the Servant . . . is merely Yahweh's agent whose role is subordinate to the divine purposes for Israel and the nations . . . The sending of the [servant] is first and foremost a demonstration of God's sovereignty.'[77] The servant songs themselves testify to the servant as God's agent, and their placement next to passages that depict God's restoration of Zion leaves the impression that God's

---

[72] See also 33:10.
[73] Gignilliat 2008: 132, 136. See also Bauckham 1998: 50–51.
[74] Wilcox and Paton-Williams 1988: 95.
[75] G. V. Smith 2009: 436.
[76] The term 'justice' does not appear as a feature of the servant's mission in Isa. 49 – 55, but instead is taken up by God (51:4) and later by God's servants (56:1; 58:2).
[77] Schultz 1995: 164.

plans of salvation will unfold through his mission with the servant. Indeed, God's work through his suffering servant will play a vital part in the realization of the gospel of God's reign on Zion (52:7, 10; 53:1).

The servant is not Israel
While in Isaiah 40 – 48 the servant is Israel, the relationship between the servant and Israel transitions in Isaiah 49 – 55. In several respects, particularly in 49:1–7, God's servant is closely associated with the nation Israel.[78] The servant has the same name of 'Israel' (49:3; cf. 41:8–9; 44:1–2, 21), a similar purpose of bringing glory to God (49:3; cf. 44:23) and light to the nations (49:6; cf. 42:6), and the same origin (44:2, 24; 49:2, 5) as the servant Israel does in Isaiah 40 – 48. Despite these similarities, it is a mistake to equate God's servant in 49 – 55 with the Israel of 40 – 48 who were blind and unable to fulfil their task. A chief reason for this is 49:5, where an aspect of the servant's mission is to 'bring Jacob back to [God] and gather Israel to [God]' (cf. 49:6). How can the servant be Israel and also have a mission to themselves?[79] A distinction between the servant and Israel is also apparent in Isaiah 52:13 – 53:12. There the speaker uses the first person plural ('us' and 'we'), which suggests that the speaker, in solidarity with others in Israel, is reflecting upon the servant.[80] A distinction is also apparent when one observes that the servant is an innocent one who suffers for Israel, the rebellious one.[81] Thus the servant in Isaiah 49 – 55 closely resembles Israel, so much so that he bears the name Israel and takes up parts of its mission,[82] but the servant is not Israel, for he has a mission to reach Israel.

---

[78] On the interpretation of this figure as a corporate referent, see Berges 2012; Hägglund 2008: 22–32; Laato 2012: 9–48; Ward 1968. Laato and Ward speak of a faithful remnant, and Berges and Hägglund (only for Isa. 53) identify the servant as those who returned from exile. While I prefer an interpretation of the servant as an individual for 49 – 55, it is possible that the servant might have been understood originally to be a faithful remnant who had a mission to reach the rest of Jacob. Williamson (1998b: 150) is open to the servant in 49:1–6 being the prophet along with his supporters.

[79] Wilcox and Paton-Williams 1988: 89.

[80] Since 'we' and 'us' always refer to Israel within the OT, it is likely that Israel is speaking (Heskett 2007: 176–177).

[81] Zion's 'rebellion' (*pešaʿ*) leads to exile (50:1), while the suffering servant is an intermediary for the 'rebellion' (*pešaʿ*) of many (53:12).

[82] Williamson 1998b: 148–152.

The servant suffers as part of his prophetic and priestly task
While the servant Israel had the primary task of bringing justice to the nations in Isaiah 40 – 48, albeit with some prophetic dimensions to it, the suffering servant's mission in Isaiah 49 – 55 is far more prophetic and priestly.[83] We will begin by considering his role as a prophet.[84] In Isaiah 49:1–6 the first description of the servant's mission relates to speaking – God has made the servant's mouth like a sharp sword (49:2).[85] The same is true in Isaiah 50:4–9, where the servant's opening line is

> The Lord God has given me
> the tongue of those who are taught,
> that I may know how to sustain with a word
> him who is weary . . .
>
> (Isa. 50:4)

It seems, in fact, as one reads on, that the servant's obedient, unrelenting commitment to conveying what God is teaching him (50:5) is what leads to all of the humiliation and suffering that he is experiencing. If this is the case, the servant's lament that 'I have laboured in vain' in 49:4, which is reminiscent of prophetic failure such as that experienced by Jeremiah,[86] is due to resistance to his word. The mission

---

[83] Some believe that the suffering servant is the Davidic king. Treat (2014: 70–71) offers six reasons for this: (1) the title 'servant' applies to kings (Isa. 37:35), (2) common anointing for justice, (3) botanical imagery (11:10; 53:2), (4) mention of David in 55:3, (5) royal characteristics of victory (52:12–13) and burial with the rich (53:9), (6) the Targum adds 'messiah' after 'my servant' in 52:13. While there is some merit to Treat's list, the evidence is not so clear: (1) The title 'servant' can also apply to figures other than a king in the OT, such as Abraham (Ps. 105:42), Moses (Exod. 14:31; Num. 12:7–8), Joshua (Josh. 24:29; Judg. 2:8); (2) justice need not be limited to the duties of a king (see the earlier discussion of Israel as servant in Isa. 42); (3) botanical imagery can also refer to the community (6:13; 37:31; 61:3b); (4) on 55:3, it is unclear if this verse is promising a Davidic king (see below under the heading 'Summary and canonical reflections'); (5) being exalted is not evidence of royal victory, and a burial with the rich is more likely negative in 53:8, not a sign of royal status; (6) the Targum of Isa. 53 was written after Christ, and though the servant is called 'Messiah' the Targum inserts other lines to offer a militaristic component to the Messiah that overshadows the vicarious suffering (see Laato 2012: 129–163).

[84] Many hold that this servant is a prophetic individual, with some suggesting that this stems from the experience of Deutero-Isaiah (see also 48:16b). Cf. Childs 2001: 385; Hermisson 2004; Heskett 2007: 147; Janowski 2004; Seitz 2004; Wilcox and Paton-Williams 1988; Williamson 1998b: 151–154.

[85] Proclamation is apparent in 49:9a. Though Koole (1998: 10) believes the servant's speech involves royal decrees of justice, 'justice' is not in the foreground in 49:1–6 as it was in 42:1–4.

[86] Williamson 1998b: 154; Jer. 15:15–18; 17:14–17; 20:7–18.

of the servant is 'to bring Jacob back to [God]; / and that Israel might be gathered to him' (49:5), but the servant's audience is resisting God's words that are spilling forth from his prophetic tongue. The servant is taking up the office of Moses and the prophets,[87] but, just as the prophetic word had been resisted throughout Israel's history, the servant will suffer a great deal in his prophetic ministry.

While it might at first seem that the servant's ministry should be fulfilled through the spoken and prophetic word, there is a gradual clarification throughout these passages that it will be through suffering that the servant's mission is accomplished. This is not entirely unexpected because prophets throughout Israel's history suffer and serve as intercessors with God for his rebellious people.[88] In 49:1–6 there are glorious promises from God swirling about, such as God's statement that 'in [you] I will be glorified' (3b) or God's lofty purpose for appointing the servant to be God's salvation that brings Jacob and all nations to God (49:6). Despite these affirming words, the servant's experience does not seem to align with these expectations:

> But I said, 'I have laboured in vain;
> I have spent my strength for nothing and vanity;
> yet surely my right is with the LORD,
> and my recompense with my God.'
>
> (Isa. 49:4)

As noted above, the servant's labour in speaking the prophetic word, as sharp as his tongue is, has seemed futile. In the light of this futility the servant looks to God alone to set the record straight; if the servant's mission is to be accomplished, the servant knows that it will only be through God's upholding his end of the mission. God responds by assuring his suffering servant that there will be a time of vindication when his mission will be accomplished:

> Thus says the LORD,
> the Redeemer of Israel and his Holy One,
> to one deeply despised, abhorred by the nation,
> the servant of rulers:

---

[87] For an extended defence of Moses as the backdrop, see Hugenberger 1995.

[88] For comparisons between the suffering servant and Moses' suffering and intercession, see Hugenberger 1995: 135–136.

149

> 'Kings shall see and arise;
>> princes, and they shall prostrate themselves;
> because of the LORD
>> . . . who has chosen you.'
> Thus says the LORD:
> 'In a time of favour I have answered you;
>> in a day of salvation I have helped you;
> I will keep you and give you
>> as a covenant to the people,
> to establish the land,
>> to apportion the desolate heritages,
> saying to the prisoners, "Come out",
>> to those who are in darkness, "Appear."'
>> (Isa. 49:7–9a)

Although the servant is despised and abhorred, the eye of faith recognizes that this is not the end of the story. There will be a time when even kings and princes will see what God does through his servant, and they will fall before God in submission. The mission of the servant will continue with his playing a key role as a covenant to the people and as a means of setting people free from prison and establishing the land.

In Isaiah 50:4–9 the servant also describes the suffering and rejection he has experienced:

> I gave my back to those who strike,
>> and my cheeks to those who pull out the beard;
> I hid not my face
>> from disgrace and spitting.
> But the Lord GOD helps me;
>> therefore I have not been disgraced . . .
> He who vindicates me is near.
>> (Isa. 50:6–8a)

As noted above, the context for this suffering is the servant's obediently learning from God and conveying God's word to the weary. Amid this, the servant is being abused, and, in fact, he is bravely facing this opposition because he is confident that God will intervene. What will God's intervention look like? How will God's mission for his prophetic servant be accomplished amid such suffering and opposition?

150

Isaiah 52:13 – 53:12 gives a definitive and clarifying answer to how the servant's suffering fits into God's mission. While the prophetic servant spoke in the first person in 49:1–6 and 50:4–9, there is a shift in speakers in 52:13 – 53:12, with God and the community speaking. This gives the impression that the speaker in 49:1–6 and 50:4–9 has met his fate of death, and now, in the aftermath, the purpose of the suffering of the prophetic servant is becoming clear. The prophetic task seems to have brought about this suffering, but this was all part of God's plan for God's servant to fulfil a priestly atoning purpose.

Some doubt that the servant's suffering is vicarious in the sense of its being a substitutionary sacrifice of atonement. The strongest resister is Whybray.[89] Linguistically, he shows that the evidence to support vicarious suffering in Isaiah 53 is weak. The combination of the verb 'to bear' (*śbl*) and the noun 'iniquity' (*'āwôn*) in 53:11, 'he shall bear their iniquities', occurs elsewhere only in Lamentations 5:7, where an exilic community speaks of bearing the iniquity of their sinful fathers as they experience harsh treatment in the wake of exile.[90] Additionally, the combination of 'to bear' (*ns'*) and 'sin' (*ḥṭ'*) found in 53:12, 'he bore the sin of many', almost always refers to a retribution principle that the person who sins will 'bear' their own sin (Lev. 20:20; 22:9; 24:15; Num. 9:13; 18:22; Ezek. 23:49), not the sin of someone else (Ezek. 18:20; cf. Lev. 19:17).[91] What is more, combinations that one might expect to occur in contexts of sacrifice, such as 'wounded' (*ḥll*) with 'transgression' (*peša'*), 'crushed' (*dk'*) with 'iniquity' (*'āwôn*), 'chastisement' (*mûsār*) with 'peace' (*šālôm*), and 'lay' (*pg'*) with 'iniquity' (*'āwôn*) in 53:5–6, appear only in this passage.[92] These linguistic observations, according to Whybray, point to an understanding whereby the servant does not suffer *in the place* of the others, but instead he suffers *as a result* of the sins of others. What is this 'servant song' conveying, then, if it is not a vision of vicarious suffering? According to Whybray, this is a corporate 'hymn of thanksgiving' written in the aftermath of the prophet, Deutero-Isaiah, being released from prison, where the community confesses that they indeed are sinners for having rejected the prophet and now they can see God's

[89] Whybray 1978.
[90] Ibid. 29–30.
[91] Ibid. 30–31. See Hägglund (2008: 82–94) on *nś' 'wn* (to bear iniquity), a slightly different formulation from what we find here. He argues that the combination usually does not convey the sense of 'atonement', although he does believe Ezek. 4:4–8 demonstrates vicarious suffering by a prophet that could have evoked a change of heart from the audience.
[92] Whybray 1978: 60–63.

vindication of his servant in the prophet's deliverance.[93] The servant, then, has not suffered vicariously in the place of exiles, but instead he suffered because of the sins of the exiles – primarily their sinful disposition towards him as a prophet – and this awakens repentance in them. He did not suffer in their place, but due to their sinful treatment of him.

While Whybray helpfully identifies some linguistic ambiguities in the debate, there are good reasons for maintaining that the servant's suffering is vicarious and has an atoning effect. For one, there are several terms that clearly point to some sort of atoning function. In 52:15 we read, 'so shall he sprinkle [nzh] many nations' (Isa. 52:15). The verb 'to sprinkle' (nzh) occurs twenty-four times in the OT and nearly always relates to priestly activity.[94] Priests would sprinkle water to cleanse Levites amid ordination (Num. 8:7) or to cleanse unclean people and objects (Num. 19:18–19, 21). When oil was sprinkled, blood would be part of the ritual too, as the two were used to cleanse lepers (Lev. 14:7, 16, 27) or to consecrate priests and their garments for service (Exod. 29:21; Lev. 8:30). Blood was the most common item that was sprinkled. It was sprinkled to atone for the impurity of the community that impinges upon the holy space, in front of the tent of meeting (Num. 19:4), beside the altar (Lev. 5:9), upon the altar (8:11; 16:19), in front of the veil (Lev. 4:6, 17) and, on the Day of Atonement, in front of and upon the mercy seat (16:14–15). Whether it is to enable a leper (Lev. 14) and others who are unclean (Num. 19:18–19, 21) to be part of the holy community and have access to the sanctuary, or to enable priests (Exod. 29:21; Lev. 8:11, 30) and Levites (Num. 8:7) to fulfil sacred tasks safely, or to atone for the sin of the priests and the community (Lev. 16), there is a common objective in the priestly act of sprinkling: to enact purification in order to enable people who might otherwise be excluded to relate to a holy God in his holy community and holy place.

What does the use of 'sprinkle' (nzh) convey in Isaiah 52:15? When one looks just prior to this passage, God's 'holy' arm has been revealed as YHWH takes up residence as king in Zion (52:7–10), which leads to an exhortation for the audience to leave Babylon and not to touch

---

[93] Ibid. 134–135.

[94] Two exceptions are when the verb refers to the splattering of blood (2 Kgs 9:33; Isa. 63:3; cf. Lev. 6:27). The oddity of 'sprinkling' through human suffering leads some to offer alternative interpretations, such as nzh (to leap) from Arabic (Koole 1998: 272–273) or yzh (to startle) from a different root (Hägglund 2008: 38). For the traditional understanding of this term, see Heskett 2007: 186–187.

anything unclean (52:11–12). Presumably, the sense is that a grand return to Zion, the city of the holy king, requires that anyone returning be pure. Isaiah 52:15, then, is probably conveying the tremendous news that the suffering servant's 'sprinkling' will effect a purification that will enable not only exiled Jews but also 'many nations' to approach the holy king and be part of the holy community.

Another term, 'guilt offering' (*'āšām*), found in 53:10 conveys a similar priestly idea:[95]

> Yet it was the will of the LORD to crush him;
> he has put him to grief;
> when his soul makes an offering for guilt [*'āšām*],
> he shall see his offspring . . .

A 'guilt offering' (*'āšām*) did not always have to be an animal sacrifice. When the Philistines incurred guilt for capturing the ark, they followed priestly instruction by sending five golden tumours and five golden mice back with the ark as a 'guilt offering' (1 Sam. 6:3, 4, 8, 17).[96] When someone wrongs another, the offender is to send the victim an *'āšām* with 20% interest to make restitution (Num. 5:7–8). In the majority of the occurrences of 'guilt offering' (*'āšām*), however, the offering is a sacrificial animal.[97] Whether a person sins against God's holy things (Lev. 5:15–16), breaks a holy commandment (5:18–19), wrongs a neighbour (6:6[5:25]), is leprous (14:12–14, 17, 21, 24–25, 28), sexually mistreats a slave pledged to another man (19:21–22), touches a dead corpse as a Nazirite (Num. 6:12), or becomes guilty in any way (Lev. 5:6, 7), the guilt incurred requires that reparation be made in the form of an animal sacrifice, a 'guilt offering' (*'āšām*; 7:1, 2, 5, 7, 37; Num. 18:19; Ezek. 40:39; 42:13; 44:29; 46:20).[98] At the core of the *'āšām* was the idea that guilt had been incurred, so reparations needed to be made either towards the injured party or, most often,

---

[95] On *'āšām*, see Averbeck 1997.

[96] Janowski (2004: 69) suggests that the use of *'āšām* to refer to an animal sacrifice occurs later than its use in Isa. 53:10, so he prefers to interpret 53:10 in the light of 1 Sam. 8 and Gen. 26:10, where *'āšām* is not a sacrificial animal. This simply means that the servant 'tak[es] over the consequences of others' actions'. Averbeck (2012: 46–47), however, is correct that making a sharp distinction between the animal sacrifice and other means of reparation is unnecessary, for both deal with 'guilt-incurring encroachments' and even a sacrificial understanding of the servant is a figurative statement.

[97] Blenkinsopp (2002: 351) links *'āšām* in 53:10 with the idea of sacrifice.

[98] A monetary equivalent was acceptable at some points in history (Lev. 5:15; 2 Kgs 12:17).

towards God. Removing guilt through blood would bring about forgiveness (Lev. 19:22) and atonement (Lev. 5:6, 16–17; 7:7; 14:21; 19:22), resulting in a restored standing with God amid the holy community. As we consider Isaiah 53:10, the surprising twist is that it is not a sacrificial ram that is presented as a guilt offering. Instead, '"[the servant's] soul" becomes the very offering itself'.[99] By offering his life the servant's suffering wipes out the guilt of the many, so that they (his offspring) can be restored to God. Averbeck captures well how this fits into the setting of Isaiah 40 – 55:

> the suffering of the Isaiah 53 Servant was as essential to the restoration of the exiled people back to their Promised Land as the guilt offering was for the restoration of the skin-diseased person to the community. Reparation for the violation of sancta needed to be made so that they could be restored.[100]

The suffering of the servant, then, takes away the guilt of the 'many' exiles (53:11, 12) and 'many nations' (52:15) so that there can be 'peace' (53:5) between them and God.[101]

With the atoning purpose of the servant's suffering clearly in view from 52:15 and 53:10, the vicarious suffering in this passage can be more readily recognized and understood. The dynamic between the 'we–us' and 'he–him' in verses 4–6 expresses the vicarious way the servant suffered for others:[102]

> Surely he has borne *our* griefs
>   and carried *our* sorrows . . .
> But he was pierced for *our* transgressions;
>   he was crushed for *our* iniquities;
> upon him was the chastisement that brought *us* peace,
>   and with his wounds *we* are healed.
> All *we* like sheep have gone astray . . .
>   and the LORD has laid on him
>   the iniquity of *us* all.
>
> (Isa. 53:4–6)

---

[99] Heskett 2007: 202.

[100] Averbeck 2012: 59.

[101] Laato (2012: 3) observes that 'peace' in 53:5 is the outcome of the servant's sufferings, a result of atonement.

[102] On the interplay between the 'I–my', 'we–us', 'he–him' and 'they–them–their', see Clines (1976: 37–40), who highlights how all voices revolve around the servant ('he–him').

Even when YHWH returns as speaker, he understands the suffering of the servant in the same way as the 'we' group:

> <u>he</u> was cut off out of the land of the living,
>> stricken for the transgression of *my* people? . . .
> . . . the righteous one, my servant,
>> [will] make many to be accounted righteous,
>> and <u>he</u> shall bear *their* iniquities. . . .
> . . . <u>he</u> bore the sin of many,
>> and makes intercession for the transgressors.
>>> (Isa. 53:8, 11, 12)

While the traditional logic in Israel was that sinners deserve their own punishment, this servant passage declares that 'for some mysterious reason Yahweh has diverted the ills that should have fallen on the community onto this [suffering servant]'.[103] While strange, this is not out of touch with priestly activity, where sacrifice could achieve expiation for the people.[104]

Since God's servant Israel could not fulfil their mission, it is an individual servant whom God establishes to reconcile Israel and the nations to God. Though the servant is a prophetic figure, the rejection and suffering he experiences is God's surprising means of achieving restoration for Israel and the nations; through suffering the prophet takes on a priestly role of sprinkling many nations and is even like a sacrificial animal, serving as the guilt offering that enables Israel and the nations to return from exile to a holy God, back to the holy place as part of the holy community.[105]

Summary and canonical reflections

In Isaiah 40 – 55 the servant is a lead agent in God's kingdom plans. Within chapters 40–48 Israel is God's servant, whose task is to bring God's justice and instruction to the entire world. The problem is that God's servant is blind (42:19), so even though Cyrus will rebuild Jerusalem (44:24 – 45:10), Israel will be unable to fulfil their part of God's mission. This leads to chapters 49–55, where an individual servant takes on aspects of Israel's mission, though the servant's primary task will be to reconcile Israel and the nations to God. While

---

[103] Blenkinsopp 2002: 351.
[104] Heskett 2007: 214.
[105] Dumbrell 1985: 126.

it seems that it will be through his prophetic role that the servant will accomplish this mission, it turns out that the servant's vicarious suffering amid his prophetic mission will fulfil a priestly and sacrificial function that will enable the exiles and all nations to be with God in his kingdom. As a result of the servant's mission, a community of 'servants' (54:17; 56:6; 63:17; 65:8, 9, 13, 14, 15; 66:14) will arise to take up Israel's mission of bringing God's justice to the world (56:1; 58). Throughout these chapters it is apparent that the servant can be understood only as an agent in the outworking of God's activity and God's plan. Surprisingly, however, though one might expect the laying bare of God's holy arm as he establishes his reign as king to be an expression of raw power and force (52:7–10), we find that a significant element in the establishment of God's reign will be the use of a suffering servant to enable the undeserving to have a place in God's holy kingdom.

We can now ask the vexed question concerning 'who' the suffering servant is in Isaiah. Is the servant identical to the hoped-for Davidic ruler from Isaiah 1 – 39? Part of the answer depends on how one interprets Isaiah 55:3b:

> and I will make an everlasting covenant with you [all],
> even the sure mercies of David.
>
> (JPS)

The challenge in interpreting this verse revolves around the relationship between the everlasting covenant and the sure mercies of David.[106] Is God promising to make a new covenant through a Davidic ruler?[107] Or is God promising an everlasting covenant that is analogous to the way he previously showed steadfast love to David?[108] The latter interpretation seems most likely in the light of verses 4–5, where God recounts how he previously made David an international attraction (v. 4) and then uses this as an analogy for how God's community will attract many nations when God beautifies his people (v. 5).[109] The

---

[106] There is debate concerning whether the 'sure mercies of David' is a subjective (Beuken 1974; Caquot 1965) or objective (Williamson 1978) genitive. Williamson convincingly demonstrates how the context establishes it as an objective genitive.

[107] Koole 1998: 414–415; Oswalt 1998: 438–439; G. V. Smith 2009: 500–502.

[108] Blenkinsopp 2002: 370; R. J. Clifford 1983: 32.

[109] Admittedly, there is a level of ambiguity in v. 5 concerning whom 'you' (masculine singular) refers to. While this could be referring to a future Davidic ruler, connections between v. 5 and Isa. 60 make it likely that Zion, or at least the community being addressed in 55:1–3, is in view. The verb in 'for he has glorified [$p'r$, piel] you' (55:5)

reference to David in verse 3, then, is not offering a promise concerning a future Davidic king, but instead is envisioning how the future glory of God's people under an everlasting covenant will be akin to David's earlier international renown. Though some explain this as a democratization of earlier promises to David that rules out earlier promises concerning David in the book,[110] an analogy drawn between David's previous experience of blessing and Israel's future blessing does not automatically cancel the hopes of a Davidic ruler from earlier in the book; it merely shows that the primary interest in Isaiah 55 is upon the restoration of God's people, with the Holy One in their midst (55:5).[111]

If it is correct that there is no explicit promise concerning David in 55:3, the question still remains whether David is simply 'implied' when passages speak of the servant.[112] Rowley captures the relationship between the Davidic ruler and the servant well:

> Both the Davidic Messiah and the Servant were conceived of as agents in the establishment of the divine rule in all the earth, but they were different conceptions of the means whereby this should be accomplished.[113]

Rowley goes on to state that the common bond between these distinct agents is a shared root in royal court ritual.[114] I believe, however, a better answer is already emerging in Rowley's statement quoted above. Commonality between the Davidic ruler and the servant is found in their both being agents, albeit differing ones, in the expression of God's 'divine rule'. With a focus on life in the land after foreign

---

occurs elsewhere in the piel only in Isa. 60:7, 9, 13, which speak of God's glorifying Zion. What is more, Isa. 60 shares with 55:5 a vision of nations coming to Zion. In this understanding a shift from the plural in v. 3 ('with you all', my tr.) to the singular in v. 5 retains the same audience. On the ability to retain the same referent amid a shift from plural to singular, see Goldingay and Payne 2006b: 374.

[110] E.g. Baltzer and Machinist 2001: 470–471; Childs 2001: 435–436; Goldingay and Payne 2006b: 372–373; Sweeney 1997; Westermann 1969: 283–284; Williamson 1998b: 116–130. Most draw upon Eissfeldt's essay (1962b) on the reuse of Ps. 89 in Isa. 55 as evidence for a democratization of the Davidic promises, but Eissfeldt (1962b: 203) is unsure whether or not Isa. 40 – 55 renounces the Davidic kingdom.

[111] Laato (1992: 244–245) argues that the democratization of Davidic language to the people 'did not exclude messianism'; instead, it encourages the remnant to envision how God's royal rule will be manifest through his people as they await the fulfilment of Davidic messianic hopes from earlier in Isaiah.

[112] Chisholm 2006: 396–397.

[113] Rowley 1952: 54.

[114] Ibid. 86.

imperial domination, Isaiah 1 – 39 announces that God, the king, will use a Davidic ruler to establish justice and righteousness within society. With an emphasis upon how sinful exiles and all nations can partake in Zion's restoration when God returns as king, Isaiah 40 – 55 anticipates that God will use a suffering servant to remove guilt so that a new community of servants may fit within God's holy kingdom. A differentiation between the Davidic ruler and God's servant does not mean that the exilic period led the book of Isaiah to give up on earlier hopes for a Davidic ruler, as some scholars infer;[115] instead, both agents are compatible, with the servant enabling a people to return to God's land guilt free and bringing justice to the nations and with a Davidic ruler maintaining justice once the nation is re-established.

If the servant is not a coming Davidic ruler, is the servant an eschatological figure at all? For the most part,[116] scholars recognize the future oriented force of the 'servant' feature within the final form of the text, even if they assert that the sufferings of a historical figure may reside in the backdrop.[117] In fact, the ambiguity of this passage seems to be a feature in the text that points us to an open future. Caird captures the openness of the servant passages well when he describes them as

a Situation Vacant advertisement: it describes in some detail a person whose identity is not yet known to the writer. . . . It is as though he had published an advertisement, 'Wanted, a servant of the Lord', accompanied by a job description. He was undoubtedly aware that many famous men, such as Moses and Jeremiah, had sat for the composite portrait he was drawing. What he could not know was that in the end there would be only one applicant for the post.[118]

Whether or not one agrees with Caird's assumption that the writer knew of Jeremiah's suffering, Caird captures the ambiguity inherent in this passage. The book of Isaiah does not resolve who exactly would fulfil the role of God's suffering servant.

[115] Berges 2014; Schmid 2005; Williamson 1998b: 113–129.

[116] Laato (2012: 46–47) argues that the suffering servant (an exilic remnant) did not accomplish its mission, for there is still need for another agent in 61:1–3 and the community remains divided in Isa. 56 – 66.

[117] E.g. Hermisson (2004: 46–47) identifies the suffering of Deutero-Isaiah as the background, but argues that the breadth of the prophetic office looks to the future for further fulfilment.

[118] Caird 1980: 57–58.

An unexpected merger happens in the coming of Christ.[119] It turns out that Jesus, fully divine and fully Davidic, takes on the mission of the servant. As Jesus healed many in his earthly ministry, Matthew conceptualizes this in the light of Jesus as God's suffering servant who takes our infirmities upon himself (Matt. 8:17; Isa. 53:4) and as God's servant Israel who brings gentle justice (Matt. 12:18–21; Isa. 42:1–4).[120] Additionally, with Jesus comprehending that his mission was to suffer, to lay down his life for his flock and to give his life as a ransom for many (Mark 10:45; Isa. 53:10), as he journeyed silently (Mark 14:61) to the cross, the gospel writers used allusions and echoes to frame Jesus' death in the light of the suffering servant's vicarious suffering to reconcile the world to God.[121] It is for this reason that Philip could begin with Isaiah 53:7–8 to explain the gospel of Jesus when answering the Ethiopian's question concerning whom the passage was speaking about (Acts 8:32–33). It is Jesus who has sprinkled many nations with his blood and has given his life as a guilt offering so that we can be reconciled to the holy God.

What is more, Jesus' own sufferings as a suffering servant aim to create a community of servants. As Clines aptly states:

> the figure of the servant presented by the poem has the potency to reach out from the confines of a historical past and from the poem itself and to 'seize' the reader and bend him to a new understanding of himself and of the direction of his life. The reader can, in the presence of this, the central *persona* of the poem, cease to be the active subject interrogating the text, and become the one who is questioned and changed by the text.[122]

As Christian communities read Isaiah 52:13 – 53:12 in the light of its witness to Christ, the suffering servant's death does more than achieve atonement for sin. It creates a community of servants who are willing to suffer and serve like their master (1 Peter 2:20–25). What is more, Paul understood from Isaiah 49:6 his own mission in the light of God's

---

[119] Pre-Christian interpreters did not merge the Davidic king and the suffering servant; see Rowley 1952: 61–88. On the earliest interpretations of the suffering servant, see Hengel with Bailey 2004; Laato 2012: 49–128. Hengel is more favourable towards seeing messianic (though perhaps not Davidic) associations being made with the suffering servant in early interpretations. Laato and Hengel recognize the importance of Zech. 9 – 14 in this regard.

[120] Williamson 1998b: 142–144; E. R. Hayes 2012.

[121] France 1968.

[122] Clines 1976: 63–64.

servant being a light and salvation to the Gentiles; if this was Jesus' mission, Paul shares in it too as his servant (Acts 13:47). Thus, though the book of Isaiah does not present the Davidic ruler and the servant as identical figures, we find an unexpected and glorious merging of two unique offices and purposes in one person, Jesus Christ.

God's messenger in Isaiah 56 – 66

The final lead agent in the book of Isaiah appears in Isaiah 61:1–3. It will be helpful at this point to recall the chiastic arrangement of Isaiah 56 – 66 set forth in chapter 3 above:

A. Faithful outsiders to be in God's service upon salvation (56:1–8)
    B. Confronting the faithless insiders with judgment and assuring the faithful with salvation (56:9 – 59:8)
        C. Prayer for forgiveness and restoration (59:9–15a)
            D. The warrior king judges the wicked and redeems the repentant (59:15b–21)
                E. Zion's international renown amid King YHWH's glory and his messenger (60 – 62)
            D'. The warrior king judges and saves the nations (63:1–6)
        C'. Prayer for forgiveness and restoration (63:7 – 64:12[11])
    B'. Confronting the faithless insiders with judgment and assuring the faithful with salvation (65:1 – 66:17)
A'. Faithful outsiders to be in God's service upon salvation and judgment (66:18–24)

Isaiah 56 – 66 centres on Zion's transformation as the international capital city of the king (60 – 62), level E of the chiasm, in the aftermath of God's coming as the warrior king to save and judge (59:15b–20; 63:1–6), level D. This eschatological vision of God as king who will transform Zion through salvation and judgment seeks to motivate a community of divided loyalties to turn in repentance to God that they may share in Zion's glories, levels A–C of the chiasm. Amid Zion's eschatological transformation, a lead agent emerges in Isaiah 61:1–3 who will declare the good news that God's rule is breaking in. Two questions pertaining to the identity and the purpose of this lead agent will guide our reflections on this passage.

Who is the figure in Isaiah 61:1–3?

There is debate concerning the identity of the agent in Isaiah 61:1–3. For some interpreters, especially if they equate the Davidic king with the servant, the figure in 61:1–3 is the Davidic king/servant. Since the Davidic king (11:2), the servant (42:1; 48:16) and the agent in 61:1–3 have the 'Spirit of the Lord', the claim is that this is the same individual.[123] The problem with this view is that connections with the Davidic ruler are forced, for a common empowerment by God's Spirit is not sufficient evidence to draw a conclusion that they share the same identity.[124] Could these not be three distinct individuals who have a common source of empowerment? The tasks of this figure are more like those of a herald for God, than of a kingly figure. For these and other reasons, I remain unconvinced that the figure in 61:1–3 is a royal figure akin to the Davidic ruler from 1 to 39.

The connections between the servant and Isaiah 61:1–3 are far stronger. Like servant Israel (42:1) and the suffering servant (48:16), the Spirit of God (42:1; 48:16) resides upon the agent of Isaiah 61:1–3, who also has a task of dealing with the 'dim' (*khh*; 42:3–4; 61:3) and reaching 'prisoners' (49:9; 61:1) as he operates during the era of God's 'favour' (*rāṣôn*; 49:8; 61:2). Additionally, just as the servant had a prophetic role as God's spokesperson, so does the agent in 61:1–3. What is more, the use of the first person in 61:1–3 resembles the same style as the 'servant songs' in 49:1–6 and 50:4–9. There are several differences, however, between the agent in 61:1–3 and the servant that incline me not to equate the two figures. For one, there is no indication that the agent in 61:1–3 is suffering or will suffer to fulfil God's purposes (49:1–13; 50:4–9; 52:13 – 53:12).[125] Additionally, the ministry of God's servant has more of a universal, international focus, while the agent in 61:1–3 operates in more of a specific locale, with a particular ministry to those mourning for Zion.[126] Finally, the figure in 61:1–3 takes on features of figures other than the servant, such as the heralds of good news from 40:9 and 52:7, the prophet Isaiah who is 'sent' (6:8), the anonymous voices who are calling out in 40:1–5 and, perhaps, Cyrus who is also anointed (45:1). So, though this figure may

---

[123] Oswalt 1998: 563; Koole 2001: 268–270; G. V. Smith 2009: 631.
[124] There are other lines of evidence used to identify this figure as a 'king' that will be critiqued below.
[125] Beuken 1989b: 439; Whybray 1975: 240.
[126] Whybray 1975: 240; Williamson 1998b: 187.

relate in some fashion to the servant, it seems unlikely that the figure in 61:1–3 is identical to the servant.

Another view stems from the final point raised above, that Isaiah 61:1–3 offers a composite portrait of a future figure. As Williamson puts it, these verses present 'a character who somehow gathers to himself every available role in Deutero-Isaiah related to the work of announcing and inaugurating God's salvation'.[127] With the endowment of the Spirit, he takes up the task of the servant (42:1) and even the Davidic king (11:1). As the 'anointed', he takes up the aim of Cyrus, YHWH's anointed (45:1). As one who is sent, he is like the prophet whom YHWH sends (6:8). As one called to 'comfort', 'proclaim' and 'herald glad tidings', he is like those commissioned in 40:1–11, 41:27 and 52:7 with proclaiming God's salvation. These, and a few other associations, lead Williamson and Stromberg to see the agent in 61:1–3 as 'a composite character who single-handedly takes up God's plan where a host of earlier figures had left it off'.[128] While I agree that Isaiah 61:1–3 draws to mind a wide range of earlier figures and features in the book's message, we can say more than that this is a 'composite figure'. The task of this agent is quite specialized around the mission of proclamation. It seems fitting to understand this figure primarily as a prophetic messenger. This agent is not a 'do it all' sort of figure, as he does little that Cyrus was tasked with, does not suffer vicariously like the suffering servant, and does not instantiate justice from a throne like a Davidic ruler. For this reason I agree with Beuken and Childs that the agent in 61:1–3 is a prophet who takes on the task of preaching the good news, just like the prophet Isaiah, the heralds and the servant were to do.[129]

What is the purpose of this messenger?

I have already been advocating for understanding the figure in 61:1–3 as God's messenger, but it is now time to justify this and flesh this passage out.

---

[127] Williamson 1998b: 184.

[128] Stromberg 2009: 269. For Williamson and Stromberg, the composite nature of this figure stems from these verses being written by a post-exilic literary prophet who is drawing upon earlier Isaianic traditions.

[129] Childs 2001: 503; Beuken 1989b: 415–424. They claim that this spokesperson is one of the offspring of the suffering servant. For others who view this agent as a prophet, see Blenkinsopp 2003: 221; Gregory 2007: 480–481; Westermann 1969: 365–367. The Targum added 'the prophet said' before this passage.

The spirit of the Lord GOD is upon me,
> because the LORD has anointed me;
> he has sent me to bring good news to the oppressed,
>> to bind up the broken-hearted,
>> to proclaim liberty to the captives,
>>> and release to the prisoners;
>>> ²to proclaim the year of the LORD's favour,
>>>> and the day of vengeance of our God;
>>> to comfort all who mourn;
>>> ³to provide for those who mourn in Zion –
>>> to give them a garland instead of ashes,
>>>> the oil of gladness instead of mourning,
>>>> the mantle of praise instead of a faint spirit.

(NRSV)

As we will see, this messenger's role is inextricably tied to the rule of God as king.

The arrangement of 61:1–3 above aims to highlight the discourse logic of these verses. The statement that 'the Spirit of the Lord is upon me' serves as the foundation of this unit. While kings such as Saul (1 Sam. 10:10; 16:14) and David (1 Sam. 16:13) were said to have God's Spirit, as does the future Davidic ruler in Isaiah 11:2, prophets also had the Spirit of God upon them (Num. 11:29; 1 Sam. 10:10; 19:20; Mic. 3:8; Zech. 7:12).[130] Context must determine what task or office the Spirit is empowering an individual for. The reason for the endowment of God's Spirit is because God has anointed this figure for a particular task. Again human recipients of an 'anointing' could fulfil a range of offices, such as priests (Exod. 28:41; 30:30; 40:13, 15), kings (Judg. 9:8, 1 Sam. 9:16; 10:1; 15:1, 17; 16:12–13; 1 Kgs 1:39), and even prophets (1 Kgs 19:16; Ps. 105:15). The seven infinitives that follow make it clear that this anointing is for the role of a prophet. What is important to observe at this point is that it is the empowerment of God's Spirit that provides the basis for the work of this messenger. The messenger will be a vehicle through whom God works by his Spirit; the messenger is an agent of God.

The seven infinitives – aligned vertically in the text above – display the purpose (61:1–2) and results (61:3) of the messenger's mission: '1 to bring good news . . . to bind up . . . to proclaim . . . 2 to proclaim . . . to comfort . . . 3 to provide . . . to give'. In the first five the

---

[130] Westermann 1969: 365.

emphasis upon proclamation is unmistakeable. The verbs 'to bring good news' (*bsr*) and 'to proclaim' (*qr'*) most likely inform how the prophet will 'bind up' and 'comfort' in his mission; binding the broken-hearted and comforting those who mourn will take place through heralding the good news. Verse 3 transitions to highlight the results that stem from the prophet's ministry. If we allow verses 1–2 to inform our reading of verse 3, the prophet's mission of proclamation will bring about a reversal from ashes, mourning and faintness to glory, gladness and praise. Westermann expresses this relationship between purpose in verses 1–2 and results in verse 3 when he states, 'All that he has to do is speak. Nevertheless, in and through this proclaiming he is to effect a change on those to whom he is sent.'[131] While some will want to claim far more for this figure, such as that he is some sort of conquering, saviour figure,[132] the role of this agent is to be a messenger. This prophetic figure will draw attention to what God, the king, is doing, not necessarily to what the prophet is doing.

As one considers the task of proclamation and the content of the message here within the context of Isaiah, it is striking how closely these concepts relate to God's reign as king. Three observations will establish this.

First, we are not told explicitly what the 'good news' is that the prophet will proclaim in 61:1. He has been anointed to bring good news, but what is it? When the verb 'to bring good news' (*bśr*) occurs in Isaiah, the 'gospel' message is that God is coming as king. In 40:9 Zion is to take on the role as the one proclaiming the good news to the cities of Judah that God is coming as a mighty and tender king. In 52:7 the herald whose feet scurry across the mountains to bring good news declares the message that 'your God reigns'. Indeed, 41:27 anticipates a time when God will give to Zion a 'herald of good news'.[133] Within those same contexts in chapters 40 and 52 the concept of comfort also emerges (40:1; 52:9), as it does in 61:2. The good news – the comforting news – that the agent in 61:1–3 will bring is that ' "God reigns" and his eschatological kingdom is about to begin'.[134] This of course fits well within the context of Isaiah 59:15 – 63:6, for

---

131 Ibid. 366.
132 E.g. Oswalt (1998: 564) claims that the servant/messiah 'is not only the preacher of the good news – he *is* the good news, able to give (v. 3) what he announces' (emphasis original). While some claim that 61:10 portrays the messenger as a military figure (59:17–18), vv. 10–11 indicate that the messenger will be a recipient of salvation and will live righteously, just like the rest of the community (Beuken 1989b: 432–438).
133 Childs 2001: 505; Williamson 1998b: 180–182.
134 G. V. Smith 2009: 634; cf. Blenkinsopp 2003: 223.

the pulse of this section is all about how God will come as the saving warrior king to take up his reign in Zion that will result in Zion's glory. Since this message is for the 'oppressed' and for 'all who mourn', particularly for Zion, the prophetic figure will serve as a herald of good news, whom the Spirit will empower to utter a message that will bring life to the despairing hearts of the faithful. The news is that the coming of the king is at hand.

Second, the concept of 'proclaiming liberty to the captives' points us to the king who makes such freedom possible. The word translated as 'liberty' is *dĕrôr*, which can be traced back to the Jubilee in Leviticus 25:10 when Israelite slaves were to be set free during every fiftieth year.[135] Since the land was God's holy land and the people in it were his, the law in Leviticus 25 expresses God's desire for Israelite slaves to return to their land and their families. The outworking of this law in Israel's history was sketchy and inexact, as one finds Jeremiah confronting King Zedekiah for not following through on enforcing his previous proclamation of *dĕrôr* that slaves should be set free (Jer. 34:8, 15). There it is the king who issues the 'order' (*qr'*) for *dĕrôr*, which is parallel to what one finds in Mesopotamia where kings would decree the release of slaves.[136] Since a king was responsible for the land and its people, it is fitting for a king to be the one who would be responsible for issuing a judicial decree for the release of slaves in the *dĕrôr*. Does this suggest that the figure in 61:1–3 is a king instead of a prophet, as some claim?[137] Not necessarily. The proclamation of *dĕrôr* in 61:1 is not a precise judicial decree; instead, this is a poetic expression by the prophet that functions figuratively, conveying far more than the manumission of slaves.[138] Through a parallel with 'release to prisoners' the focus here is clearly upon the reversal of oppression, which is certainly a major challenge facing the community in the light of chapters 58–59. The prophet's declaration of *dĕrôr* draws upon an ancient tradition as a metaphor for announcing the arrival of an entirely new socio-economic order when

---

[135] On the background to *dĕrôr* and its manifestations throughout the OT and intertestamental times, see Bergsma 2007.

[136] Ibid. 20–26.

[137] Ibid. 200; Chisholm 2006: 401–402.

[138] There is a range of metaphorical interpretations: release from exile (Bergsma 2007: 202–203) or from 'extended exile' that reached through the post-exilic period (Gregory 2007: 483–488); '"liberation" of the community from its frustrations' (Whybray 1975: 241); a reversal of socio-economic exploitation of all kinds (Beuken 1989b: 419–420; cf. Williamson 1998b: 185); 'a metaphorical release from any past social or spiritual enslavement' (G. V. Smith 2009: 635).

oppression will cease.[139] While these words are not necessarily those of a king issuing a precise legal decree, the only reason that the prophet can envisage and announce such liberty is because God, the warrior king, will soon defeat the foes of injustice (59:15–20) and reign as king in Zion. While the anointed prophet is the one declaring freedom from oppression, this proclamation points ultimately to the king who will bring about a new era where there is freedom in all realms of life.

Third, God's kingship comes to mind in 61:2, when the messenger declares

> the year of the LORD's favour,
>   and the day of vengeance of our God.

These phrases coordinate most closely with 34:8 and 63:4, though also with 35:4 and 59:17. The correspondence between 34:8, 61:2 and 63:4 is unmistakeable:

> For the LORD has a day of vengeance,
>   a year of recompense for the cause of Zion.
>   (Isa. 34:8, NASB)

> to proclaim the year of the LORD's favour,
>   and the day of vengeance of our God . . .
>   (Isa. 61:2)

> For the day of vengeance was in my heart,
>   and my year of redemption had come.
>   (Isa. 63:4)

These passages use the day–year formula, with all of them speaking of a 'day of vengeance' but with variation concerning the modifier for the 'year' formula: year of recompense, favour and redemption. By choosing 'favour' in 61:2 there is an explicit link back to 60:7 and 10, where sacrifice will again be viewed favourably (60:7) and where God schematizes Zion's experience around when God struck Zion in his anger and the new era of 'favour' when God will have mercy on Zion (60:10).[140] The era of favour according to chapter 60 will be a

---

[139] Beuken (1989b: 419) clarifies that instead of being judicial, this is 'a prophetic program, the ideal perception of a new socio-economic order'.

[140] Though some emphasize how 'favour' relates to the servant in 49:8 (Beuken 1989b: 424), the nearer context in 60:7, 10 is a stronger connection.

time when God's presence as the glorious king will be so great that all nations will come to Zion with gifts and tribute to build up Zion. The 'day of vengeance' in 61:2 corresponds with 34:8 and 63:4 (cf. 35:4; 59:17).[141] In these contexts YHWH is coming as a warrior king in both judgment and salvation. What is important to note here is how the expressions in 61:2 are forging connections within the literary context of 59:15 – 63:6. By coordinating with the 'day of vengeance' in 63:4 (cf. 59:17) and the concept of 'favour' in 60:7 and 10 we are able to fill in the gaps regarding what the 'year of the LORD's favour' and 'the day of vengeance' refers to in 61:2. The anointed messenger is declaring that YHWH is coming as a warrior king in saving judgment (63:1–6; cf. 59:15–20), and this will usher in a new era of favour in which Zion becomes glorious because the glory of King YHWH will dwell there (ch. 60).

In summary, the agent in 61:1–3 is a prophetic figure, for all of his actions entail proclamation. This prophetic figure shares in the tasks of earlier figures of the book of Isaiah, particularly with the herald of good news (40:9; 41:27; 52:7) and the servant. As one looks at the task and message of this herald, it becomes clear that one can only understand this figure in the light of the coming of God as king. As a herald of good news, this agent, along with the heralds from 40:9 and 52:7, is declaring that God is coming as the saving king. As one proclaiming 'liberty', this prophet is announcing the reversal of all systems of oppression because the divine king will be on the throne and will defeat the forces of injustice (59:15–20). As one declaring the 'year of the LORD's favour' and the 'day of vengeance', this agent's message sits squarely within the vision of Isaiah 59:15 – 63:6, in which the warrior king will come in vengeance to set things right by judging all that is evil (59:15–20; 63:1–6) and will usher in a time of favour for Zion as he resides there as the king of glory. The chief purpose, then, of the figure in 61:1–3 is to be a Spirit-anointed messenger who brings life to the faithful – those who are mourning for Zion's desolation – by declaring the good news that God is coming as king and will transform all that is evil.

Canonical reflections

The office of the prophet has a prominent place in the outworking of God's plans throughout redemptive history, as the legacies of Moses and the Former and Latter Prophets bear witness. Indeed, the prophet

---

[141] The only occurrence of this phrase outside Isaiah is in Prov. 6:34.

Malachi also anticipates that some sort of messenger figure will play an important role in God's eschatological plans (Mal. 3:1; 4:5–6), though the tasks of Malachi's messenger revolve around calling for repentance while the figure in Isaiah 61:1–3 primarily offers words of comfort. With Isaiah 61:1–3 being set within an eschatological context in Isaiah 56 – 66, readers would look to an open future for a prophet, not necessarily because the prophet is the answer, but because the prophet will be a signal that points to the in-breaking of God's kingdom, when all oppression will be overturned.

When Jesus unrolled the scroll of Isaiah in the synagogue in Nazareth in Luke's Gospel, he read words from Isaiah 61:1–2 in Luke 4:16–21, with phrases from 58:6 and perhaps 42:7 intermingled by Luke. By reading these words and declaring their fulfilment Jesus presents himself as the fulfilment of the expectation of a Spirit-anointed messenger who is declaring the in-breaking of the reign of God in his preaching ministry throughout Galilee (4:14–15). Luke offers a further interpretation of Jesus' action by adding a few phrases from elsewhere in Isaiah to the scriptural quotation. By adopting a reading of the LXX in 61:1b, which adds 'recovery of sight to the blind' to establish further correlation with the role of the servant in 42:7, Jesus' role as messenger blends with that of Isaiah's servant (cf. Luke 2:30–32). Additionally, Jesus' reception of the Holy Spirit in his baptism, where he is declared to be God's 'Son' (cf. Ps. 2:7), presents Jesus as the hoped-for Davidic king. In this way, Luke coordinates the distinct roles of Isaiah's various agents and brings them together in the person of Jesus. Jesus, the one anointed by the Spirit as Davidic king (3:22) and the one who takes up the mission of the servant (4:18; cf. 2:30–32), is also the one who is fulfilling the expectations of the prophet from Isaiah 61. What is more, in Luke 3:4–6 Jesus' ministry is also portrayed as the coming of God himself that was anticipated in Isaiah 40:3–5. This means that Jesus is not only the messenger but is also the message; Jesus is the in-breaking of the very reign of God that will fulfil Isaiah's expectations of oppression being over-turned.[142] This becomes apparent later in Luke 4 when he overcomes oppressive spirits and heals many. Thus, as God sovereignly unfolds his plans, Isaiah 61:1–3 bears witness to Jesus as both the expected

---

[142] Luke adds Isa. 58:6 ('to set the oppressed free', NIV) to the quotation in Luke 4:18 to emphasize how Jesus embodies Isaiah's entire vision of transformation that reaches into all realms of oppression.

messenger and the embodiment of the message concerning God's rule in this world.

Conclusion

A subtext within this chapter has been a concern to offer middle ground between alternative interpretations. Among some conservative evangelicals the tendency is to treat all three figures in Isaiah as the same Davidic 'Messiah'. On the other hand, the majority of scholars, including some evangelicals, tend to see these figures as distinct, and, furthermore, to claim that hopes for a Davidic king expressed in 1 – 39 are replaced in 40 – 66 by a democratization of God's earlier promises to David and an exclusive focus on God as king.

The case made above is that the Davidic ruler, the servant, and the anointed messenger are distinct figures in the outlook of the book of Isaiah, for they have fairly distinct purposes and operate in differing contexts. The Davidic ruler will be God's agent in maintaining justice within Israel in the aftermath of deliverance from their oppressors. The servant will be God's instrument among the nations in reconciling Israel and the nations to God through his suffering so that they may dwell with God, the holy king, in his holy city. The anointed messenger will emerge on the brink of the eschatological in-breaking of God's coming as the warrior king who will reign in Zion to declare the gospel to the disheartened faithful. It is not unexpected for Isaiah to envision multiple lead agents in the light of other prophetic literature. As Boda argues, Haggai, Zechariah and Malachi envision royal, prophetic and priestly figures who will all play an important role in the establishment of God's kingdom.[143] The claim here also does not undermine the New Testament's application of all three of Isaiah's figures to Jesus; instead, it displays the grandeur of Jesus and the surprise of recognizing how one person, Jesus Christ, can take on the role of all three figures, while also being the very God of these agent figures.

While a Davidic figure is virtually absent from the final half of the book,[144] his absence does not warrant the claim that the hopes for a Davidic king earlier in the book are defunct. It is indeed true that David's task of ensuring justice is shared by God's servant Israel. This

[143] Boda 2007.
[144] On Isa. 55:3, see above. There could be a veiled allusion in 65:25 to a Davidic ruler in the new creation, as it quotes from parts of 11:6–9. If there is, the focus still remains on God, for specifying how a Davidic ruler will fit into these future plans is not of ultimate importance in the book.

does not mean, however, that the servant's commission is a replacement of earlier hopes for a Davidic ruler. The shift to God's servant as an agent of justice occurs because these chapters are addressing an exilic context, when there was no Davidic king and when they were among the nations. As lead agents of the same king, the Davidic ruler would bring justice to a settled homeland and the servant (Israel) would bring God's justice throughout the entire world in the wake of exile. The servant Israel is not usurping the role of the Davidic king, but shares in the kingdom task of being God's agent of justice in a new context. As for the absence of David in 40 – 66, this merely indicates that the Davidic ruler is not a point of emphasis in the final part of the book, not that we are to dismiss such hopes from earlier in the book.[145] The book of Isaiah's chief aim is to grant a vision of God, the king, coming to establish his universal kingdom through judgment and salvation, so it is in keeping with the aims of the entire book for the book to end on this note. It is not unreasonable to infer, however, that, in the post-exilic era and beyond, a Davidic ruler could still fit into the outworking of the plans of God, the king, but this remains secondary within the ultimate vision of Isaiah. For whether it is the Davidic ruler in the homeland, the servant suffering as a prophet in the wake of exilic realities, or the anointed messenger on the cusp of the eschaton, these figures are merely agents of God that point to the work of God, the king, who will reign in glory in the aftermath of an astonishing work of salvation and judgment. So, while a tendency in the church may be to give one-sided attention to messianic figures in the OT and the debate concerning which passages qualify as 'messianic' predictions of Jesus, the book of Isaiah reminds us that such figures must always be understood in the light of the broader purposes, reign and person of God the king.

---

[145] See Schultz 1995.

Chapter Five

The realm and the people of God's kingdom

If God is the king of the kingdom and if he will use lead agents to prepare for and maintain it, two questions naturally arise. *Where* is God's kingdom? And, *who* are the people of God's kingdom? These questions in many respects are inseparable, as we will see below. God's kingdom, according to Isaiah, is not an immaterial, spiritual reality of displaced selves in a displaced context. God's kingdom is 'placed', if you will, with people in the midst of it. Though the topics of place and people in Isaiah certainly warrant book-length treatments, the aim here is to offer an orientation to how place and people interrelate amid a common connection under God's kingship in Isaiah. The first half of this chapter will present a bifocal view on 'place' by balancing the universal scope of God's reign with a particularized expression of it in Zion. This will lead to some reflections on the nature of the community that will inhabit the realms of God's kingdom as his people.

A bifocal view of the realm of God's kingdom

Place is inescapable, for to be human is to be so in a place. Whether we sleep, wake, eat, fast, work, play, worship, vacation, stay-cation, cry, rejoice, suffer or heal, all of these experiences occur in places we inhabit. For this reason a defining feature of place is the recognition that it is 'a quintessentially *human* concept in that it is part of our creatureliness'.[1] There is a solid theological rationale for this in the early chapters of Genesis. In Genesis 1 the creation of humanity occurs only after God makes the 'earth' into an inhabitable world, when the uninhabitable earth from Genesis 1:2 finds the waters receding, light shining upon it, vegetation springing from it and animals filling it as creation progresses. Humans are then created to image God as vicegerents upon it. In Genesis 2 a more particularized

---

[1] Bartholomew 2011: 2, emphasis original.

sense of place develops, where God creates a garden within which he sets first Adam and later Eve (2:15). To be human according to Genesis 1 – 2 is to exist in a place in relationship with God and that place. While the expulsion of Adam and Eve from Eden frustrated the notion of God's people being in a particular place,[2] the rest of the storyline of Scripture revolves around promises concerning a land, preparations for dwelling in it, inhabiting it, losing it through exile, and anticipations of a dramatic recovery of 'place' with God inhabiting a New Jerusalem and the new heavens and new earth.[3] The message of God's kingdom in Isaiah fits directly into this drama of recovering 'place'.

Genesis 1 and 2 establish a schema concerning place – the universal (the world) and the particular (Eden).[4] This schema can be useful for conceptualizing the realm of God's kingdom in Isaiah. Just as bifocal glasses enable one to see both near and far, so the 'realm' of God's kingdom can be seen from universal and particular perspectives. On the one hand, God's kingdom is universal – all of heaven and earth is the realm of God's kingdom. On the other hand, there is a particularized view of God's kingdom – Zion is its centre point.

The cosmos as the universal realm of God's kingdom

The recognition that YHWH is creator of heaven and earth provides a basis for grasping that the realm of God's kingdom is everywhere. Isaiah's prayer in chapter 37 captures the essence of this: 'O LORD of hosts, God of Israel, enthroned above the cherubim, you are the God, you alone, of all the kingdoms of the earth; you have made heaven and earth' (Isa. 37:16). What is the evidence that Israel's king, YHWH, is indeed the supreme God over all the kingdoms of the earth? Since he is the maker of heaven and earth, God's royal reach even encompasses the Assyrian Empire. As a result, Isaiah, Hezekiah and God's people can trust in God in the face of Assyria's threat.

Isaiah 40 – 55 also affirms that God is the creator of heaven and earth, which reiterates God's sovereign kingship, as we saw in chapter 2 above. The rhetorical importance of God's status as creator becomes evident in several questions in Isaiah 40:

---

[2] Ibid. 9–31.

[3] On land in the OT, see Brueggemann 1977.

[4] This schema emerges from reflection on the categories of general presence and special presence from Strange (2004) and parallels between Zion and Eden identified by Levenson (1985: 127–137).

> Lift up your eyes on high and see:
>> who created these?
> He who brings out their host by number,
>> calling them all by name,
> By the greatness of his might,
>> and because he is strong in power
>> not one is missing.
>
> (Isa. 40:26)

> Have you not known? Have you not heard?
> The LORD is the everlasting God,
>> the Creator of the ends of the earth.
> He does not faint or grow weary;
>> his understanding is unsearchable.
>
> (Isa. 40:28)

Why is it so important for Israel to know that God is mindful of all the stars that he created? Why must they know that the creator does not grow weary and has unfathomable wisdom? In between verses 26 and 28 there is a glimpse of what the audience is struggling with:

> Why do you say, O Jacob,
>> and speak, O Israel,
> 'My way is hidden from the LORD,
>> and my right is disregarded by my God'?
>
> (Isa. 40:27)

Addressing the context of exile, God's people wonder if he has the power to help and if he even cares. As the creator, God's jurisdiction reaches outside Judah; it reaches to the furthest corners of the universe. Surely, he is mindful of their situation and has the power to bring about his purposes. Similar claims that God is the creator of heaven and earth are scattered throughout Isaiah 40 – 55 (44:24; 42:5; 45:12, 18; 51:12, 13; 54:5), and in nearly every case these claims aim to encourage the exiles, for if God's power extends beyond Israel and Judah, they have no need to fear because the powerful creator is their maker and redeemer.[5]

---

[5] On the debate concerning the relationship between salvation and creation in Isa. 40 – 55, see R. J. Clifford 1993: 5–8. Lee's (1995) placement of salvation and creation under YHWH's sovereignty proves helpful.

Since God created heaven and earth, there is a basis for hope that he will create again. Isaiah 65:17a states:

> For behold, I create new heavens
> and a new earth . . .

While Isaiah 40 – 55 used the verb 'create' (*br'*) to appeal to God's previous acts of creation, Isaiah 65:17a uses *br'* to declare that God will create again. Yes, 'God created the heavens and the earth' in the beginning (Gen. 1:1), but he will also create a new heaven and new earth in the future. The second half of the verse casts light on what this declaration may mean for the audience:

> the former things shall not be remembered,
> or come into mind.
>
> (Isa. 65:17b)

What former things is Isaiah referring to? Just prior to this verse, in verse 16, God is speaking about the 'former troubles', where the same Hebrew word for 'former' occurs in verse 17.[6] When one looks at 65:18–25, the reversal of the former things entails the 'restoration of Jerusalem and its people, extremely long life, ownership and use of the land, productive labour, success in birth, attentiveness from the Lord, and safety from threatening animals'.[7] The focus is more upon 'social and political transformation' than upon material changes to creation,[8] though the two are not mutually exclusive. God will be creating a reality where all is as it should be; distress and turmoil will be no more.

Before dwelling further on the meaning of God's promise to create a new heaven and new earth in 65:17, Isaiah 66:1 deserves our attention. This is the clearest statement in Isaiah that God is king of heaven and earth:

> Thus says the LORD:
> 'Heaven is my throne,
> and the earth is my footstool.'
>
> (Isa. 66:1)

---

[6] Blenkinsopp 2003: 286–287.
[7] Stromberg 2011b: 91–95, esp. 94.
[8] Blenkinsopp 2003: 286.

The 'throne' symbolizes royal power. In fact, this reminds us of Isaiah 6 where Isaiah saw the 'Lord' sitting upon the throne. As for 'footstool', this term usually refers to Zion as the place from where God exercises his rule (1 Chr. 28:2; Pss 99:5; 132:7; Lam. 2:1).[9] In Isaiah 66:1 God's footstool is the entire earth. *Where* is the realm of God's kingdom? How far does God's jurisdiction reach? Since heaven is God's throne and the earth is his footstool, it is clear that God's reign fills heaven and earth. There is a tension, however, in this profession that God's dominion extends over heaven and earth right now and for all times: How can he be king of heaven and earth when all things are not in submission to him? It is at this point that the first three chapters of this book are so important. God is indeed the king of all the kingdoms of the earth for all times, but as we have seen, Isaiah is looking for a time when God will come in his divine glory, when faith shall become sight, when what Isaiah professes about God's universal kingship will be realized (24:23; 59:15b – 63:6; 66:18–24). Perhaps it is this kind of tension that led Jesus to pray to the Father in heaven that his already existing kingdom would come. As we will see in the next section, the chief way of comprehending what the universal realm of God's kingdom will be like is by taking a closer look at the particularized realm of God's reign in Zion.

Zion as the particularized realm of God's kingdom

As the king over heaven and earth (66:1) and as the creator, there is a strong basis for the declaration that God will create a new heaven and new earth (65:17). What does this look like? The verses surrounding 65:17 tell us that the answer is found through considering what Jerusalem will be like in that era. In verse 18 we read:

> But be glad and rejoice for ever
> in that which I create;
> for behold, I create Jerusalem to be a joy,
> and her people to be a gladness.

While in verse 17 God says he will 'create' (*br'*) a new heaven and a new earth, in verse 18 God states that he will 'create' (*br'*) Jerusalem to be a delight. This creates a parallel between God's creation of the universe and God's creation of a particular place, Jerusalem. Some of the features in this New Jerusalem will be

---

[9] Beuken 1989a: 54–56.

> no more shall be heard in [Jerusalem] the sound of weeping
> and the cry of distress. . . .
> They shall build houses and inhabit them;
> they shall plant vineyards and eat their fruit.
> They shall not build and another inhabit;
> they shall not plant and another eat . . .
> . . . They shall not hurt or destroy in all my holy mountain . . .
>
> (Isa. 65:19, 21–22, 25)

In the New Jerusalem there will be joy instead of crying (65:19), no untimely death (65:20), no systems of oppression that confiscate homes and food (65:21–22), and there will be no more conflict (65:25). Curses, particularly those from Sinai, will be erased. Life will be as it should be. The setting for this ideal life is 'in [Jerusalem]' (65:19) and 'in all my holy mountain' (65:25). Why does God focus on Jerusalem's future in a context where he is announcing that he will create a new heaven and a new earth? The reason for this is because what God does for Jerusalem is a sample of what he will do throughout the entire heaven and the earth. Jerusalem is a microcosm of the universal realm of God's kingdom.[10]

An illustration may clarify the point being made here. What if God said this? 'I'm going to make a new world. In Chicago there will no longer be a children's hospital, for there will be no more sick children. Everyone will be able to find fulfilling employment and enjoy the fruits of their labours, for those on the south side will have the same opportunities as those in the western suburbs. Fourth of July gatherings at Grant Park will no longer be a time of fear, for rivalries and violence will be no more.' In this hypothetical scenario God describes new life in Chicago as a sample of what life will be like throughout the entire world. In a similar way, by describing what life will be like in God's particular realm, Zion, one can conceptualize what new creation might entail for the entire world.

---

[10] Levenson 1984; Berges 1998: 506; 2002: 14–15. The claim that Jerusalem is a microcosm often stems from symbols of creation in the temple (1 Kgs 7:23–26) and parallels between creation and temple construction (Levenson 1985: 142–145). For Levenson (1985: 138), the tension between God's omnipresence and particular presence in the temple leads him to state, 'the Temple is the epitome of the world, a concentrated form of its essence, a miniature of the cosmos'. Blenkinsopp (2003: 286) speaks of the cosmic vision as a 'panorama'. For alternative understandings, see Westermann (1969: 408–409), who thinks 'heaven' and 'earth' are just metaphors for Jerusalem, and Koole (2001: 449–451), who thinks 'earth' refers to Canaan and 'heaven' to an ability to relate to God.

The illustration above, however, has its limits. The choice of Jerusalem is strategic. Could Samaria, Jericho, Bethlehem, Cairo, Damascus or Babylon have served this purpose of envisaging the new creation? No. Ever since David chose Jerusalem to be his capital and God inhabited the temple in Zion, Yahweh's presence as king has been inextricably tied to Zion. Yes, Zion is a symbol, even of the entire cosmos, but Zion is also an actual place in the 'theo-topological' outlook of Israel. It is a geographical reference point that is to orient the entire world around God's kingship. Or, as Levenson puts it in his discussion of Zion, 'geography is simply a visible form of theology'.[11] In Isaiah the realm of God's kingdom is universal, but the universal, cosmic scope of God's kingdom has a centre point in Zion. Zion, then, is not just an illustration of God's plans for the rest of the world, but it is also a hub around which the rest of God's kingdom finds its orbit.

There are numerous passages that explicitly envisage Zion as the capital city of God's international kingdom.[12] The book's first passage that speaks of 'the latter days', Isaiah 2:2–4, envisions a scene where Zion has risen to prominence worldwide. Since God dwells there as the wise king, all nations stream there to receive God's instruction. It can be inferred from this passage that 'Yahweh's sovereignty as king extends not simply over Judah, of course, but over all nations; when the nations come streaming to His throne in Jerusalem they are acknowledging Him as their rightful sovereign.'[13]

Another passage that demonstrates how Zion will be the capital city of God's kingdom appears in 24:23 in coordination with 25:6–8. As an explanation for why God can enact worldwide judgment, it is because

> the LORD of hosts reigns
> on Mount Zion and in Jerusalem . . .
> (Isa. 24:23b)

Not only does YHWH's reign on Zion provide a basis for how far God's judgment can reach, but it also provides the basis for all nations streaming to Zion to partake in a feast hosted by the king (25:6). Again Zion is the focal point for God's rule, which entails that the

---

[11] Levenson 1985: 116.
[12] On the Zion tradition in Isaiah, see Dekker 2007: 282–337.
[13] Jensen 1973: 90.

rest of the universal kingdom will come to Zion for a feast to align with YHWH.

The second half of the book shares the same outlook. In Isaiah 40 – 55 the grand expectation that God will come as king from Isaiah 40:1–11 culminates in 52:7–12. All nations will see it when YHWH returns to Zion amid the heralds announcing the good news that 'Your God reigns' (52:7). This leads to a call for people to depart from wherever they are to come to the house of the Lord (52:11–12). In Isaiah 56 – 66 its central section envisions nations from across the world streaming to Zion with tribute for their king (60:5–14). A similar scene concludes the book where all nations will come to God's holy mountain to worship before the Lord (66:19–24). Zion is clearly the hub of an international kingdom.

Whether it is Isaiah 2:2–4, 24:23, 25:6–8, 33:20–22, 40:9–11, 52:7–10, ch. 60 or 66:18–21, Zion is the city of YHWH, the king. This corresponds with Ollenburger's conclusion to his study on Zion that 'the central theological notion evoked by the symbol of Zion is the kingship of Yahweh'.[14] What is more, Zion is the capital of a kingdom that stretches far beyond Judah, which is evident by the many passages that depict other nations coming to Zion. Thus, though the realm of God's kingdom is the entire cosmos, the centre point of this is Zion, which in some respects is a microcosm of God's intention for the entire world.

In the light of these reflections it is no surprise that Zion's destiny is central to the overall narrative of the book of Isaiah.[15] In Isaiah 7 Aram and Israel come against Jerusalem and its king, Ahaz. In Isaiah 36 – 37 King Sennacherib of Assyria comes against Jerusalem and its king, Hezekiah. On both occasions, Assyria wrought havoc upon Judah, but God preserves the city of Zion. God's ability to deliver Zion from Assyria provides an important basis for the hope that God will do it again in the future. It is in the aftermath of this threat that the book of Isaiah opens, where Zion is described like a 'booth in a vineyard' (1:8), tottering on its last leg. Though God had preserved Zion, the dreadful news is announced that another wave of judgment will come through a future empire (1:5, 20, 24–25), Babylon, with the result being exile and devastation for Jerusalem (ch. 39).[16] There are hopes, though, that God will use a Persian king, Cyrus (44:26–28), to

---

[14] Ollenburger 1987b: 146.
[15] Webb 1990: 68–72; Dumbrell 1985.
[16] On Isa. 36 – 39, see Seitz 1991.

rebuild the city of Jerusalem when the exiles return. The book of Isaiah looks forward to a far greater, eschatological restoration of Zion (2:2–4; 25 – 26; 60:13–14; 65:18; 66:18–21).[17] Thus there is a movement in the book of Isaiah from Zion's being under threat and delivered during the Assyrian era, to Zion's fall to Babylon, to hope for restoration through Cyrus, and ultimately to Zion's greater restoration when God returns. As Sweeney puts it when he tries to capture the overall eschatology of Isaiah:

> the book of Isaiah is fundamentally concerned with Zion or the city of Jerusalem, insofar as Jerusalem is the site of YHWH's holy Temple, which in turn symbolizes YHWH's role as the sovereign creator of the entire universe, including Israel, Judah, and the nations at large.[18]

God's mission is for his kingdom, and this entails his plans to reveal his sovereign rule before all nations at Zion.

So, in summary, *where* is God's kingdom? A bifocal outlook is required. On the one hand, God's kingdom stretches throughout the entire universe. While this is true right now, as his throne is in heaven and his footstool upon the earth, the book of Isaiah envisages a day when the realm of God's kingdom will be fully realized, with every inch of creation living in joyful submission to God. On the other hand, the realm of God's kingdom can be most fully seen by looking at what will transpire on Zion, God's holy mountain. As the capital city of God's kingdom, Zion is to be the centre point around which the rest of the kingdom finds its orientation. Zion's significance as a place, as the hub of the kingdom, however, derives entirely from the king who resides there.

Canonical reflections

This is not the place to enter into debate regarding whether and how physical Jerusalem fits into God's plans on this side of the cross. The original readers of Isaiah, though, would certainly have retained a material, physical understanding of Isaiah's promises concerning Zion, though this would not diminish their sensitivity to the symbolic associations attached to Zion. As one looks to the NT, Jerusalem in

---

[17] On the movement concerning YHWH's kingship in Zion from Isa. 24 – 27 to 52 to 66, see Beuken 2009.
[18] Sweeney 2014: 180.

many respects was an initial 'hub' for apostolic ministry. This is not, however, because Jerusalem had an exclusive claim on God's reigning there as king. The church was the temple of the Holy Spirit, and, since the church was growing worldwide, the realm of God's kingdom is more universal in focus in the NT. His reign encompasses the entire world and can most readily be seen amid those people who submit to him. Nevertheless, the NT retains the OT's geographical outlook as it looks to the future, to a time when all will recognize God as king. The story of the Bible concludes by intertwining the particular with the universal. Revelation 21 says, 'Then I saw a new heaven and a new earth . . . And I saw the holy city, new Jerusalem, coming down out of heaven from God . . . And I heard a loud voice from the throne saying, "Behold, the dwelling place of God is with man. . . ."' (Rev. 21:1–3).

Adopting the same bifocal vision from Isaiah, Revelation 21 conceptualizes the realm of God's kingdom from a universal and particular vantage point. God reigns over the entire cosmos now (Revelation 4 – 5), though this will be fully realized in the new heaven and new earth (21:1). The New Jerusalem will be the centre point of the new creation, with the nations coming from across the world to bring glory to this city, where the Lord and the Lamb dwell (Rev. 21:22–26; cf. Isa. 60:3, 10–11). This, of course, corresponds with how the Bible begins and how Isaiah envisions the realm of God's kingdom. God reigns over the entire universe, though his reign can also be seen in a particular place like Jerusalem, which is the centre of his kingdom.

The people of God's kingdom

When one speaks of the realm of God's kingdom, it is impossible for the people within God's kingdom to be far from view. This is apparent time after time when Zion clearly refers to the people who are associated with the city. For example, when God states in Isaiah 1:21 that his 'faithful city' has become a 'whore', the city is not literally a whore. The 'city' is a figure of speech for the people who inhabit Zion, and perhaps even Israel and Judah as a whole.[19] Examples like this can be multiplied throughout the book. So, when we ask, 'What do kingdom people look like in Isaiah?', we are also asking, 'What should those who inhabit the realm of God's kingdom be like?' A simple answer to these questions is that they will reflect the nature of their

[19] On Zion as a reference for all of Israel, see Levenson 1985: 136–137.

king. I will highlight several emphases within Isaiah regarding the nature of God's kingdom people.

A purified and redeemed community

The book of Isaiah opens by confronting an audience that is not embodying what God's people should be like. As a result, they are referred to as rebellious children (1:2), stupider than donkeys (1:3), a 'sinful nation', 'a people laden with iniquity', 'offspring of evildoers', 'children who deal corruptly' (1:4), sick and wounded while seeking no remedy (1:5–6), like Sodom and Gomorrah (1:10), unjust (1:15–17, 23), whorish (1:21) and even God's enemy (1:24). While our initial inclination might be to focus upon what God's people should be *doing* instead, such as trusting God or practising justice, the foundation of Isaiah rests upon *what God will do* to create the kingdom community that he is after. As Jenner puts it, 'the key to the restoration of faded glory [in Zion] is in the hands of YHWH'.[20] There are two different, though not unrelated, paths in the unfolding of God's mission to create a kingdom people.

Purifying a kingdom people

The first path is God's plans to create a *holy people*, often through purifying judgment.[21] In Isaiah 1 God announces that

> I will turn my hand against you [Zion]
> and will smelt away your dross as with lye
> and remove all your alloy.
>
> (Isa. 1:25)

Presumably, this is referring to how God uses Assyria (10:5–6) and later Babylon (ch. 39) to bring judgment against Israel and Judah. In the aftermath of this judgment Zion will go from being a faithless whore (1:21) to being a faithful, righteous city (1:26). This same movement unfolds in chapters 2–4, where depictions of God's plans to judge his sinful city through a siege by a foreign power (3:1 – 4:1) precede a glimpse of what will remain in the aftermath of this judgment (4:2–6):

> And he who is left in Zion and remains in Jerusalem will be called holy, everyone who has been recorded for life in Jerusalem, when

[20] Jenner 2011: 171.
[21] Webb 1990: 72.

the Lord shall have washed away the filth of the daughters of Zion and cleansed the bloodstains of Jerusalem from its midst by a spirit of judgment and by a spirit of burning. (Isa. 4:3–4)

It is significant to note that the remnant after judgment will be called 'holy'.[22] This also corresponds to God's answer to Isaiah's question concerning how long the prophet would speak to a hardened people. It would last until judgment and exile (6:11–12) had come, but the result of this judgment would be a 'holy seed' (6:13), a remnant who would become God's holy people. Why is there such an interest in the early part of the book on God's creating a holy people? The answer comes in Isaiah 6. The king whom Isaiah sees sitting upon the throne is 'holy, holy, holy' (6:3), so it is fitting that the holy king will set out to create a people who are fit to be in a holy kingdom.

As the story of God's creation of a holy people progresses, one expects that God's use of Assyria and later Babylon will produce a 'holy' people. The second half of Isaiah, however, reframes God's mission. A significant portion of Israel and Judah remain recalcitrant, blind even after God's judgment. This is clearly stated in Isaiah 42, where we read about how God's blind servant Israel responded to his sending foreign nations to punish them:

> So [God] poured on [Israel] the heat of his anger
>   and the might of battle;
> it set him on fire all round, but he did not understand;
>   it burned him up, but he did not take it to heart.
>   (Isa. 42:25)

Instead of creating a holy people, God's judgment through Babylon does not impact Israel as one might expect.[23] As a result, there is a reframing of how God will create a holy people in the light of the suffering servant and God's coming in eschatological judgment. Through the priestly suffering of God's servant many nations will be 'sprinkle[d]' (52:15) and his life will serve as an 'offering for guilt' (53:10). The result of this will be 'offspring' (53:10) of the servant, as is indicated with the term 'servant' occurring only in the plural after

---

[22] On Zion's transformation through purging and repentance, both of which are brought about by YHWH, see Jenner 2011: 170–171.

[23] Webb (1990: 77) thinks that Babylonian exile achieves its purpose of purification (48:10). Isa. 40 – 48, however, paints a bleak picture of Israel's spiritual condition.

chapter 53 (54:17; 56:6; 65:9, 13–15; 66:4).[24] It is God's 'servants' who will inherit God's 'holy mountain' (56:6–7).

What is more, there is an even greater judgment looming in Isaiah 56 – 66. When God comes in judgment in the future, it will not be to purify the wicked to make them righteous; instead, when God comes as the warrior king in 59:15b–20 and 63:1–6, his judgment will sweep away the wicked who remain, while saving the repentant (59:20).[25] The result will be that all of the 'impurities' in Zion will be swept away, and as Isaiah 60 – 62 envisages Zion's glory in the aftermath of God's judgment, 'they shall be called The Holy People ' (Isa. 62:12). This title is fitting, for earlier in chapter 60 God's people will be called

> the City of the LORD,
> the Zion of the Holy One of Israel.
> (60:14)

As the city of the Holy One – the king whom Isaiah saw on his throne earlier in chapter 6 – the king's people will be like him: 'The Holy People'. One path in the story of God's people in Isaiah, then, is about a holy king creating a holy people through judgment; they will be washed by the blood of the servant and inhabit Zion as 'The Holy People' in the eschatological era in the aftermath of his judgment of the wicked and the salvation of the repentant.

Redeeming a kingdom people

A second path in God's mission to create a people is intertwined with the first. As he creates a holy people, these people are also recipients of his *salvation and redemption*. In the opening chapter of Isaiah the rhetorical climax declares that 'Zion shall be *redeemed* by justice' (Isa. 1:27). With Zion's redemption in view from the start of the book, this sets the stage for what is to come. In chapter 12, which closes the opening section of the book and prepares for Isaiah 35 and 40,[26] there is a vision of a time when a song will be sung:

> I will give thanks to you, O LORD,
> for though you were angry with me,

---

[24] On the significance of YHWH's 'servants' in 54 – 66, see Beuken 1990.

[25] Gregory (2007: 494–495) also observes the development in Isaiah from anticipations of purifying the wicked to expectations that the wicked will be eradicated.

[26] On the strategic role of chs. 12 and 35 in relationship to 40 – 66, see Rendtorff 1993a: 146–169.

> your anger turned away,
>> that you might comfort me.
> Behold, God is my salvation;
>> I will trust, and will not be afraid;
> for the LORD GOD is my strength and my song,
>> and he has become my salvation.
>> > (Isa. 12:1–2)

When this song is set in its context in 1 – 12, it appears just after the hope that God will vanquish Assyria (ch. 10) and restore Judah and Israel to the land under a Davidic king (ch. 11). By praising God as their 'salvation' the book opens by emphasizing that the holy king who will bring judgment against his people will save his people from their oppressors too. In fact, a major reason for delight is that the Holy One of Israel will be great in their midst as their saviour (12:6).

Amid the universalizing tendencies in Isaiah 13 – 27, we again see praise for God as a saviour. Upon God's establishing his rule on Zion (24:21–23), nations will stream to Zion for a feast hosted by the king (25:6–8). At that time they will exclaim:

> Behold, this is our God; we have waited for him,
>> that he might save us.
> This is the LORD; we have waited for him;
>> let us be glad and rejoice in his salvation.
>> > (Isa. 25:9)

Similarly, part of a song sung in Judah will be:

> We have a strong city;
> he sets up salvation
> as walls and bulwarks.
>> (Isa. 26:1)

An important aspect of God's salvation within Isaiah 25 – 26, and also the entire book (cf. 41:17; 49:13; 51:21; 54:11), is that God's salvation is on behalf of the 'poor'. Who are the poor and afflicted? On the one hand, they are those who previously experienced God's judgment in exile; the great hope is that a new era of salvation will come for them (41:17; 49:13; 51:21; 54:11). This dynamic is captured in the depictions of Mother Zion who has been depleted but now finds her city full of children and being renewed (49:14–26; 52:1–6;

54; 66:7–14). On the other hand, there are those who are 'afflicted' because they are victims of oppressive forces. It is the latter who seem to be in view in chapters 25–26. While some may emphasize how God graciously saves sinners, which is certainly true in Isaiah, it is also the case that God saves the powerless who are abused by earthly powers. Often they are oppressed because they are aligning themselves with God instead of the ways of the world (cf. 66:5). This is why God's people will sing:

> You have been a stronghold to the poor,
> a stronghold to the needy in his distress . . .
> (Isa. 25:4a)

Amid this song, there will be a dramatic reversal of the lofty, arrogant powers that have oppressed the lowly. Guess who will get to join in God's saving judgment against the 'arrogant city'?

> The foot tramples it,
> the feet of the poor,
> the steps of the needy.
> (Isa. 26:6)

These people will experience and even participate in their own reversal of fortune,[27] and praise God for saving them from the evil powers of arrogant oppression when he establishes his reign on Zion.

In Isaiah 28 – 33 hopes for salvation again cap off a section of the book. A prayer opens chapter 33:

> O LORD, be gracious to us; we wait for you.
> Be our arm every morning,
> our salvation in the time of trouble.
> (Isa. 33:2)

A statement of confidence near the end of this chapter brings it to a close:

> The LORD is our king; he will save us.
> (Isa. 33:22)

---

[27] Berges 1999: 165.

It is this confidence that God will save his people as their king that orients a reader to look with the eye of faith to a time beyond the judgment coming through Babylon.

This motif develops in Isaiah 35 and throughout 40 – 55. While judgment for Zion still awaits, Isaiah 35 offers a vision of an era of radical transformation. As God's people look towards that time, they are to say to one another:

> Be strong; fear not!
> Behold, your God
>   will come with vengeance,
> with the recompense of God.
> He will come and save you.
>   (Isa. 35:4)

Amid their journey on the holy highway back to Zion, we are told that

> the redeemed shall walk there.
> And the ransomed of the LORD shall return
>   and come to Zion with singing.
>   (Isa. 35:9b–10a)

These hopes of redemption for the exiles and confidence that God will come to save his people are prominent in Isaiah 40 – 55. This is apparent in the close parallels between 35:4 and 40:9–10 and between 35:10a in 51:11.[28] The grand hope for exiles is that when God comes as king to redeem his people, they will return to Zion with great joy – they will be with their king. This hope of salvation culminates in 52:7–10, when the one 'who publishes salvation' declares that 'your [Zion's] God reigns'. It is at this time that the waste places of Jerusalem break forth with joy because God has redeemed his people (52:9).

Isaiah 56 – 66, especially at its centre, also emphasizes the salvation of God's servants. Isaiah 59:15–20 and 63:1–6 frame chapters 60–62 with visions of the warrior king coming to 'save' his people. God puts on the 'helmet of salvation' (59:17) to save (59:16) his repentant people (59:20), not necessarily from their own personal sin, but from the rampant injustice around them (59:15–16). In 63:1–6 the warrior covered in blood identifies himself as 'mighty to save' (63:1) and

---

[28] Rendtorff 1993a: 157; Webb 1990: 76.

explains that the bloodbath he created was actually due to his own arm working 'salvation' (63:5). Because God came as a warrior king 'to save' his repentant people, Zion's walls would come to be called 'salvation' (60:18) and those inhabiting Zion would not only be called 'The Holy People' but also 'The Redeemed of the LORD' (62:12; cf. 59:20).

In summary, when speaking of God's people in Isaiah, we have to start with what God will be doing to create a kingdom people. There are two major paths in God's endeavour. One path relates to God's purifying a people that they may be holy. While it initially seems that this will take place through judgment from foreign empires, it will be through God's suffering servant that God's people become holy and through God's eschatological judgment of the wicked that Zion can be called 'The Holy People'. The second path relates to God's redeeming his people when he comes as king, not only from their own sin, but also from oppressive powers that afflict his people. Praise often appears in conjunction with the idea that God will save his people (cf. 12:2–3; 25:1–5, 9; 26:1–6; 35:10; 51:11); redemption leads to praise. Since God is a holy king (ch. 6) and a saving king (25:9; 33:22; 40:9–11; 52:7; 59:17; 63:1, 5), it is only appropriate that God's kingdom people, the people of Zion, be called 'The Holy People, / The Redeemed of the LORD' (62:12).

An obedient and just community

While the foundation of who God's people are rests upon what God has done to create them, it is evident throughout Isaiah that God's people should reflect their king. In fact, there is a tension between God's sovereign action and human responsibility, for it will be those 'who turn from transgression' who experience God's salvation (59:20), and the call to do 'justice' and 'righteousness' is motivated by God's coming salvation (56:1). So, there is a tension between God's resolve to purify and save and the need for God's people to obey him.[29]

The ultimate litmus test – in terms of behaviour – for belonging to God's community is whether or not one responds obediently to God's word. This is apparent when one considers how the book opens and closes.[30] While Jeremiah and Ezekiel open with stories about the 'call' of the prophet, Isaiah opens with a challenging confrontation. Two

---

[29] See Houston 1993 for an insightful study on the tension between divine sovereignty and human involvement, and the already but not yet in Isaiah's kingdom message.

[30] On responding to God's word in Isa. 1 and 65–66, see Liebreich 1956: 277; Conrad 1991: 83–102; Jang 2012.

rhetorical climaxes in Isaiah 1 force readers to make a choice as they start the book:

> If you are willing and obedient,
>   you shall eat the good of the land;
> but if you refuse and rebel,
>   you shall be eaten by the sword . . .
>   (Isa. 1:19–20)

> Zion shall be redeemed by justice,
>   and those in her who repent, by righteousness.
> But rebels and sinners shall be broken together,
>   and those who forsake the LORD shall be consumed.
>   (Isa. 1:27–28)

God is committed to restoring Zion (1:26), so the question for readers or hearers from the start of the book is whether they will be among the 'obedient' (1:19) and those who 'repent' (1:27; cf. 59:20) who will experience the time of restoration. The conclusion of the book in Isaiah 65 – 66 conveys a similar message, though it has a different tone. Instead of a lawsuit-like call to repentance from Isaiah 1, Isaiah 65 – 66 depicts the contrasting eschatological destinies that await God's servants and the apostates. The dividing line between these two groups is abundantly clear. God's sword and fire (65:12; 66:16; cf. 1:20) await those who have not listened to his words (65:1, 12; 66:4). Those who tremble at God's word (66:2, 5), however, will inherit YHWH's holy mountain. God's servants approach God's word as God's word, recognizing the dangers of ignoring it and the delights of embracing it. By opening and closing the book with an emphasis upon responding obediently to God's word, a major purpose of the book is clear: kingdom people should obey the voice of their king as they await his coming judgment and salvation.

A prominent expression of obedience in Isaiah involves upholding righteousness and justice.[31] During the time of Isaiah, injustice was running rampant. Leaders were making laws that put the poor at a disadvantage (10:1–2). Bribery was influencing Judah's judges (1:23). The goods of the poor were stolen by the rich (3:14), and the powerful would dispossess the poor in a quest for more and more

---

[31] On the hendiadys of *mišpāṭ* and *ṣedāqâ*, see Weinfeld 1992.

real estate (5:8). It was no wonder that God lamented over his beloved vineyard (5:7). Instead of bearing lush grapes, Israel and Judah's fruit was putrid, bearing 'bloodshed' (*miśpāḥ*) instead of 'justice' (*miśpāṭ*) and an 'outcry' (*ṣĕʿāqâ*) instead of 'righteousness' (*ṣĕdāqâ*). Since God is exalted by justice and righteousness (5:16), the behaviour of the people was certainly not reflective of or pleasing to the king.

Amid such rampant injustice, the book of Isaiah calls forth a people who will embody God's desires for justice and righteousness. While the future Davidic ruler will take a lead in this matter (9:7; 11:3–5; 16:5),[32] other leaders and the community as a whole were to share in the quest for social justice, even before and prior to the establishment of a Davidic king. Since Isaiah 1 and 58 are the chapters that most fully highlight what it could look like to practise justice (cf. 56:1), I will draw upon these two chapters to suggest three ways that they envisage justice being carried out.

First, justice looks like advocating for the vulnerable, for those who can easily be overlooked within society.[33] As Weinfeld puts it, 'doing [justice/righteousness] is . . . bound up with actions on behalf of the poor and the oppressed'.[34] The book of Isaiah opens on this note:

> cease to do evil,
>   learn to do good;
> seek justice,
>   correct oppression;
> bring justice to the fatherless,
>   plead the widow's cause.
>   (Isa. 1:16b–17)

Justice is very active here. The people are to 'learn', 'seek', 'correct', 'bring justice' and 'plead'. One cannot get away with saying, 'I am not oppressing anyone directly.' Kingdom people must get involved when they see injustice; they are to be advocates for the poor.

Second, justice looks like setting captives free, as we see in Isaiah 58. Instead of fasting for their own self-interest (58:3), they need to seek the sort of fast God desires:

---

[32] Weinfeld (ibid. 237–241) emphasizes the importance of the king in establishing and enforcing laws of justice in society.

[33] On Isa. 1:16–17 as a call for 'advocacy', see M. Gray 2006: 88.

[34] Weinfeld 1992: 235–236.

Is not this the kind of fasting I have chosen:
to loose the chains of injustice
   and untie the cords of the yoke,
to set the oppressed free
   and break every yoke?

               (Isa. 58:6, NIV)

Understanding the context of these verses is important. More than likely, the oppressed referred to here have sold themselves into slavery due to debt or bankruptcy.[35] Perhaps they had some difficult harvests, and then they had to borrow money they could not repay, which ultimately led to their enslavement to pay off their debt. God calls for wealthy landowners to have a vision for setting these slaves free. Surely they might legally have a right to demand the services of the slave indefinitely, but they should be willing to give up what might rightfully be owed to them for the sake of the freedom of another. This is true fasting, and by setting captives free, they 'keep alive the redeeming activity of God toward his people' when he redeemed them out of slavery from Egypt.[36]

Third, it is not enough just to set people free to fend for themselves, as if they will have the resources available to survive on their own.[37] Justice is sharing with those in need, feeding the hungry, housing the homeless and clothing the naked:

Is it not to share your food with the hungry
   and to provide the poor wanderer with shelter –
when you see the naked, to clothe them,
   and not to turn away from your own flesh and blood?

               (Isa. 58:7, NIV)

Justice involves not turning away from a fellow human being when they are in need. A true fast is when one is willing to give of one's own possessions for the sake of another.

These three insights into what justice looks like in practice are by no means exhaustive. They are illustrative, however, of what God's kingdom community should be like. Since God 'love[s] justice' (61:8) and even enters the fray because he is so appalled by the injustice in

---

[35] Blenkinsopp (2003: 179) notes how 'to set free' relates to slaves in Exod. 21:26–27; Deut. 15:12–13, 18; Jer. 34:8–16.

[36] Polan 1986: 208.

[37] M. Gray 2006: 78–81, esp. 79.

this world (59:15), it is fitting for his servants to advocate for the vulnerable, set captives free and provide for those in need. The people should be like their king, for they are beneficiaries of God's own justice and righteousness.

A community that trusts God

Another characteristic of God's kingdom people that we will briefly consider is trust. The notion of trust is illustrated in the contrasting stories of two kings. In Isaiah 7 King Ahaz of Judah faces a major threat, as King Rezin of Aram and King Pekah of Israel come to mount a joint attack against Jerusalem and Ahaz. In the second verse in the narrative the narrator reveals the internal response of Ahaz and Jerusalem: 'the heart of Ahaz and the heart of his people shook as the trees of the forest shake before the wind' (Isa. 7:2). God's message through Isaiah to King Ahaz addresses this: 'Be careful, be quiet, do not fear, and do not let your heart be faint' (Isa. 7:4).

God then offers Ahaz evidence – a sign (7:11) – to prove that God can be trusted. King Ahaz, however, declines God's offer (7:12), and thereby shows a lack of trust in God.

In Isaiah 36 – 37 King Hezekiah is faced with a similar threat as Assyria surrounds Jerusalem. The spokesperson for Sennacherib, king of Assyria, begins his verbal assault by challenging Hezekiah concerning whether Hezekiah has misplaced his trust by turning to YHWH (36:4–9).[38] Instead of shaking like a tree, King Hezekiah turns to Isaiah to intercede. Isaiah returns with this message: 'Do not be afraid because of the words that you have heard' (Isa. 37:6). Hezekiah displays his trust in God, as he turns directly to God when Sennacherib again threatens Jerusalem and its king (37:14) and trusts in him as the 'God . . . of all the kingdoms of the earth' (37:16). When we compare these stories, the difference is obvious. Though both kings are under threat in Jerusalem and are told to not be afraid, King Hezekiah demonstrates what trust looks like as he turns to YHWH for intervention.

In addition to these narratives the expression 'do not fear' occurs ten times in Isaiah,[39] especially in the second half of the book. For example, God assures his servant Israel saying:

> fear not, for I am with you;
> be not dismayed, for I am your God;

[38] On the theme of trust here, see Smelik 1986: 78.
[39] Isa. 10:24; 35:4; 40:9; 41:10, 13, 14; 43:1; 44:2; 51:7; 54:4.

> I will strengthen you, I will help you,
> I will uphold you with my righteous right hand.
>> (Isa. 41:10; cf. 41:13–14)

Though God's people experience his judgment through exile, he is assuring them that he will be with them. They do not need to fear, for God himself will help them and take hold of their right hand (41:13), as he upholds them with his right hand (41:10).

Along with the exhortations 'Do not fear', the concept of trust is a regular topic in the book.[40] In a warning against foreign alliances[41] Isaiah laments:

> Woe to those who go down to Egypt for help
>> and rely on horses,
> who trust in chariots because they are many
>> and in horsemen because they are very strong,
> but do not look to the Holy One of Israel,
>> or consult the LORD!
>>> (Isa. 31:1)

Later in the book, there is a call for trust when there seems to be no light:

> Who among you fears the LORD
>> and obeys the voice of his servant?
> Let him who walks in darkness
>> and has no light
> trust in the name of the LORD
>> and rely on his God.
>>> (Isa. 50:10)

When all else seems bleak, God's kingdom community trusts in their God, their king. This is why they can sing:

> Behold, God is my salvation;
>> I will trust, and will not be afraid;
> for the LORD GOD is my strength and my song,
>> and he has become my salvation.
>>> (Isa. 12:2)

---

[40] Olley 1999: 66–69.

[41] On whether or not Hezekiah entered into a foreign alliance with Egypt, see Seitz 1991: 75–81.

Thus if the Holy One of Israel is the God of all the kingdoms of the earth (37:16), as Hezekiah professes in his prayer of faith, his kingdom people should trust in him.

A national and international community

The nations are constantly in view throughout Isaiah. This has led one scholar to state that it is Isaiah instead of Jeremiah who most deserves the title 'a prophet to the nations' (Jer. 1:5).[42] While I resonate with that point, it is important to observe how the superscriptions at the start of Isaiah (1:1; 2:1) offer a better frame of reference, for they specify that Isaiah's vision is 'concerning Judah and Jerusalem'. The motif of the nations can be understood only in the light of Jerusalem and the one who resides there as its king, for the nations find their place in God's kingdom in connection to Zion.[43] Why else would a scene of nations streaming to King YHWH in Zion (2:2–4) follow the superscription in 2:1? My point in this section is that God's purposes for his particular people in Zion, Israel, intertwine with his mission to incorporate all nations into his kingdom.[44]

The beginning (2:2–4) and end of Isaiah (66:18–24) envision how the nations will be part of God's kingdom.[45] In Isaiah 2:2–4 there is a vision of the 'latter times' where all nations will stream to Zion to receive instruction from YHWH. This vision is ironic in the light of its placement next to Isaiah 1, where those Israelites who should be God's people are actually disobeying God. When chapter 1 is read with 2:2–4, Israel is called to imitate what the nations will be doing in the future – obeying God's instruction (2:5; cf. 1:10, 19). This strategic juxtaposition establishes a trajectory for the rest of the book. God's mission is not simply to create Israel into an obedient, faithful city (1:26); his plans involve obedient nations becoming a part of his kingdom too (2:2–4). This, in fact, is how the book of Isaiah ends in 66:18–24. In a recapitulation and development of the vision of Zion's international renown from chapter 60, Isaiah 66:18–24 depicts a scene where nations receive word of YHWH's glory in Zion and come to pay homage to him. YHWH will even take some from the nations to serve

---

[42] Davies 1989: 105.
[43] Davies (ibid. 119–120) agrees that Jerusalem ideology undergirds the motif of the nations.
[44] For helpful overviews of the 'nations' throughout Isaiah, see Davies 1989; Oswalt 2006; Schultz 2009. On Isa. 40 – 55 in particular, see van Winkle 1985.
[45] Davies 1989: 94–95; Oswalt 2006: 42–43; Schultz 2009: 129–131.

as his priests, and they will join in the Sabbath and New Moon festivals that God rejected in the opening chapter of the book (1:13; 66:23). In both 2:2–4 and 66:18–24 God's prominence in Zion serves as a reference point for why the nations would come there. By closing the book of Isaiah on this note it is unmistakeable that a major feature of the book's message is that God's kingdom community will consist of many nations, though these passages aim to evoke jealousy and repentance within Israel simultaneously.

While it is easy for Gentile readers to resonate with mentions of the 'nations' in the passages above, both texts assume that Zion's restoration intertwines with the inclusion of the nations. YHWH's commitment to Israel and Zion is the means through which YHWH's universal interests will unfold. This will be evident by revisiting some of the passages I have covered earlier in this book. In Isaiah 6 the holy king will judge his nation to such an extent that all that remains in the land is a small remnant, a holy seed (6:13). There is hope, however, in chapter 11 that, after Israel's oppressors fall, Israel and Judah will be restored and many nations will then flock to the banner of David (11:10). In the oracles against the nations (13 – 23) YHWH will also judge many nations, which to some extent is part of YHWH's gracious act in restoring Israel (14:1–3). What is more, God's judgment of these nations will result in African nations streaming to Zion with gifts (18:7), so it seems that Zion's restoration goes hand in hand with international judgment and invites a response by the nations to profess allegiance to YHWH. With Zion in Judah as a centre point of blessing, even Egypt and Assyria will travel on a highway that passes through Judah, experiencing the blessing that comes through Judah. They even take on the status of being God's people and the work of his hands (19:24–25). From an eschatological vantage point, the feast hosted by YHWH in 25:6–8 will include 'all the peoples' (*kol-hā'ammîm*); they will be attendees (25:6) and the beneficiaries of God's abolishing death (25:7). While verses 6–7 highlight the destiny of 'all the peoples' (*kol-hā'ammîm*), a shift to the singular occurs when God specifies that it is the 'reproach of his people [*'ammô*] he will take away from all the earth' (25:8b).[46] This shift from plural to singular displays how God's particular commitment to Israel endures, even as God establishes his rule over all nations. God's work of salvation will remove the disgrace associated with his people Israel and be a means through which the nations can join in the feast.

---

[46] Blenkinsopp 2000: 358; Kaiser 1974: 200; Polaski 2001: 192.

In Isaiah 40 – 55 the tension between the desolation of Zion and exile draws attention regularly both to God's commitment to restore Zion and how the nations fit into his plans. On the one hand, a chief concern of Isaiah 40 – 55 is to announce that Zion's demise is not the end of the story. Though Mother Zion feels abandoned (49:14), God is promising that her children will soon be coming home, even with kings and queens serving as their nurses and chauffeurs (49:17, 20–23). Though Zion drank the cup of wrath before, their oppressors will soon drink the cup of wrath as Zion is restored to prominence (51:17–23). Indeed, YHWH will call Zion back like a deserted wife (54:5–6); his anger struck Zion in judgment in the past, but the city will shine beautifully in the future (54:7–15). These hopes concerning Zion's restoration centre upon God's return to Zion to reign as king (40:9–11; 52:7–10). God, then, is clearly committed to Israel, to the restoration of Zion. On the other hand, the nations are regularly in view amid God's plans to restore Zion. Though God's servant Israel (corporate) should serve as God's means of being light and serving as a covenant with the nations (42:6),[47] the suffering servant takes up the task of restoring both Israel and the nations to God (49:5–6), which the nations witness (49:7; 52:15) and find themselves sprinkled by his blood (52:15). What is more, all flesh will see God's glory when he takes up residence as king in Zion (40:5; 52:7–10). In fact, as Israel experiences blessings that are analogous to David's, all nations will come running to Israel because of the beauty that the Holy One of Israel has given to Zion (55:5). Thus throughout Isaiah 40 – 55 God's mission to restore desolate Zion and Israel will coincide with and even be the means through which all nations find blessing under the rule of YHWH in glorious Zion.

In Isaiah 56 – 66 the nations are in view both at the edges and the centre of its chiastic structure. At its edges there are unexpected portrayals of faithful foreigners having a place of service in YHWH's house on his holy mountain (56:1–8; 66:18–24). At the centre the glory of God the king will shine so brightly that all nations will stream there with gifts of tribute. While the nationalistic focus of Isaiah 60 is explicit, as the rebuilding of Zion is paramount, it is less clear how the nations fit into this vision. Strawn contends that there is no war scene in Isaiah 60, so the gifts from the nations are not instances

---

[47] '[C]ovenant for the people' in 42:6 likely refers to how Israel is to enable the nations to experience God's salvation (van Winkle 1985: 454–456).

of demanded tribute, but are rather instances of gift giving amid pilgrimage.[48] Stansell, however, argues that this is a scene of conquered peoples being forced to fuel YHWH's building projects, as is evident in the emphasis upon a reversal of power with enemies (60:14), kings being held as prisoners (60:11) and the role of foreigners as the manual labourers (60:10, 12).[49] In my opinion the text invites us to a balance between these poles. With Stansell I agree that there is an emphasis upon how Israel's oppressors will find a reversal of status in the future when Zion is restored. Verse 6, however, depicts the nations streaming to Zion with praise on their lips,[50] so there is also a sense of pilgrimage here. Importantly, as Maier observes, these nations 'have to accept a serving role' as they join in YHWH's kingdom as he restores Zion.[51] Thus the place of the nations amid Zion's restoration in Isaiah 60 is multi-perspectival: pilgrims coming to worship (60:6), former oppressors finding the tables turned (60:14), labourers who build Zion's walls (60:10), those in danger of perishing if they do not submit (60:12). In Isaiah 56 – 66, then, there is a clarification that all of the faithful will inherit Zion (59:20), regardless of ethnicity (56:1–8; 66:18–24), though being a part of the kingdom community will come through benefiting from Zion's restoration as the capital of the entire world, with the holy king in its midst. The nations, however, will take on a serving role, though with very high standing, even serving as priests.

In summary, I assume that most who will read this book are Gentiles, so our tendency is to get excited about the many references to the nations being part of God's kingdom community in Isaiah. We need to be careful, however, not to overlook how it is that the nations come to become participants in God's kingdom. It is upon witnessing a spectacular display of God's saving and holy kingship when he judges all that is evil and saves and restores Israel and Zion (40:5; 52:10; 60:1; 66:18) that the nations then come to align themselves with the king in Zion as members of his kingdom community (2:2–4; 25:6–9; 60).[52] God's kingdom people will consist of the faithful from Israel and all nations.

---

[48] Strawn 2007: 107–108. His point is weakened when one observes that divine warrior texts (59:15–20; 63:1–6) frame Isa. 60 – 62.

[49] Stansell 2009: 238–239.

[50] Schultz (2009: 141) thinks that the rest of ch. 60 reveals that the praise in v. 6 is 'coerced'.

[51] Maier 2008: 194.

[52] Schultz (2009: 127) has a similar thesis.

Summary and canonical reflections

Reflection on God's kingdom people in Isaiah must begin with the acknowledgment that it is God who is creating his people. From the opening chapter of Isaiah, God's people are a faithless and sinful lot, yet he will purify a people for himself and save them (1:21–28). His people are also afflicted by various sorts of oppression and injustice (25:3; 57:15; 59:15–16; 66:5), yet he will intervene to set things right (26:6; 59:15–20; 66:5). God's people are fundamentally recipients of his purifying and saving action. This corresponds with God's work in Christ, who came not for the righteous but the unrighteous (Luke 5:32; Rom. 5:6–8) and also came to help the poor in spirit know that the kingdom of heaven is theirs (Matt. 5:3). It is chiefly through Christ's work on the cross and his resurrection that God by his Spirit creates a 'holy nation' (1 Peter 2:9) who are recipients of a great salvation (Heb. 2:3).

A distinguishing feature of God's people is that they will obey the voice of their king, as is highlighted in the calls to obey in Isaiah 1 and at the end of the book in the depiction of two eschatological destinies that hinge upon whether one trembles at God's word (66:2, 5). This accords with the people of God in Christ, for kingdom people are the good soil that holds to God's word (Luke 8:15) and those who build their house on Jesus' words (Matt. 7:24–27). Paul labours to bring about the *obedience* that stems from faith (Rom. 1:5) among the nations. It is through promoting justice that obedience is often on display in Isaiah, for becoming an advocate, setting captives free and sharing one's goods with those in need can be costly. Jesus (Matt. 23:23), James (Jas 1:27) and Paul (Gal. 2:10) share this same outlook, for promoting justice for the vulnerable is a mark of the church's religious identity. Along with being a people who pursue justice, God's kingdom people should also trust in God. As an analogy, just as Judah and Israel were to trust in God instead of foreign powers and to look to him as they wait for the restoration of Zion after exile, so Christians are to trust that they are and will be saved from the day of wrath (Rom. 5:9) and trust that God is the sovereign king who will overthrow all that is evil.

God's kingdom people will be from all nations in Isaiah, though the nations will become part of God's kingdom in the wake of his salvation and restoration of Zion. Since Jesus was the Jewish Messiah, God's remarkable, saving intervention shines as a spotlight both in and upon Israel. With John the Baptist baptizing Jews in the Jordan, a reconstitution of Israel was taking place (Luke 3:1–20) around the repentant. What is more, Jesus' choice of twelve disciples clearly parallels the twelve tribes of Israel, a start of a 'new Israel'. The apostles, who were all Jewish, pick up on this, and they therefore replaced Judas to bring the number back to twelve after Jesus' ascension (Acts 1:12–26). God was intervening in Jesus in a spectacular fashion to create a new believing community within Israel, and it is through the life, death and resurrection of the Jewish Jesus that the nations stand in awe as they see both Israel's salvation and their own in the Christ (Rom. 9 – 11; Eph. 2:11–22).

Conclusion

We began this chapter by asking two questions that we can now answer. Where is the realm of God's kingdom in Isaiah? For all times, God's dominion is over the entire cosmos, for his throne is in heaven and his footstool on earth (66:1), though Isaiah anticipates a new heaven and a new earth when all realms will be in harmony with the king (65:17). In the outworking of God's plan Zion will be the central hub of God's kingdom (2:2; 24:23; 40:9–11; 52:7; 60; 66:18–24), through which the entire world will align with the king. Thus bifocal vision is necessary when considering the realm of God's kingdom. From a big picture vantage point, the entire cosmos is the realm of God's kingdom. From a narrower vantage point, Zion is the microcosm and capital of God's kingdom, for it is the place where God will dwell as king.

Who are the people of God's kingdom in Isaiah? Since God is a holy king and a saving king, his people are those whom God makes holy through purifying judgment (1:24–26; 4:2–6) and the blood of the servant (52:13 – 53:12) and are those who are or will be saved by their king (12:1–2; 25:9; 33:20; 52:7; 59:15–20). Since God is a king who is to be revered and is committed to justice (5:16), God's kingdom people should obey his word and be his agents in promoting justice (1:17; 56:1; 58). Since God is the God of all the kingdoms of this earth, his people are to trust him, even amid foreign threat. Since God will save Zion dramatically, this will result in many nations becoming part of his kingdom alongside Israel. Kingdom people, then, will reflect their king, who is holy, who saves, who demands justice, who is worthy of obedience and trust, and who maintains his covenant love for Israel as a means of saving the nations.

Conclusion

> If one were asked what the book of Isaiah 'is about', this
> would be the answer: the kingship of God now visible to the
> eye of faith and to be made visible to all in the new world
> that is about to dawn.
>
> (Houston 1993: 34)

As we bring this study on kingdom in Isaiah to a close, it is unnecessary to recap all of our findings, for each chapter has multiple
summaries within it. Instead, I would like to conclude with a brief
reflection upon how this project fits into the quest to 'imagine' the
kingdom. Within theology imagination is not simply the ability to
dream up the impossible or the unreal. 'The theo-dramatic imagination that fuels Christian play is altogether different: it is the ability
to form mental images of what is *really* present – the kingdom of God
– even though it cannot be perceived empirically with the senses.'[1] A
theo-dramatic imagination stems from the powerful ability of the
imagination to create a 'synoptic vision' from Scripture;[2] through
this lens we can see how the kingdom of God is the reality within
which we live, move and have our being. As one inhabits the world
of Scripture, the imagination kicks into gear, creating networks of
coherence concerning the whole of Scripture, resulting in a synthetic
sense of God's purposes in the world and how humanity fits into this
drama.[3] As one enters the world of the text, the Spirit works through
the text to shape its readers into kingdom people and a unified vision
of God's ways with his world and his people emerge. In many respects,
this book is my attempt to express the networks of coherence that
have been forming as I have been inhabiting the world of Isaiah in
ecclesial, classroom, devotional and academic contexts. It seems that
the book of Isaiah is inviting us to imagine the kingdom of God.

The book of Isaiah's vision of the kingdom centres in upon its king.
A holy king reigns in the present (Isa. 6), which meant that judgment
against the wicked, especially among God's people, was immanent

---

[1] Vanhoozer 2005b: 416, emphasis original.
[2] Ibid. 281.
[3] Ibid. 377. On the creation of networks of coherence in the reading process, see
Iser 1980: esp. 119–125.

during the pre-exilic era. This same king, however, would also save his people – as he did earlier from Sennacherib (36 – 37) – out of exile and establish his reign on Zion (40:1–11; 52:7–10). These anticipations of judgment and salvation that are initially set within the pre-exilic and exilic eras fuse with and culminate in the anticipation of an eschatological era when God will come climactically as a warrior king (59:15–20; 63:1–6; 66:16–18) and then reign victoriously as the saviour king over his international kingdom (25:6–9; 33:22; 60; 66:18–24).

In the establishment and maintenance of God's kingdom several lead agents emerge. A Davidic ruler will promote justice and righteousness within society after God establishes his kingdom (9:1–7; 11:1–5; 16:5). A servant, through suffering, will enable Israel, God's blind and sinful servant, and even many nations to be purified that they might enter the holy city as part of God's kingdom (49:1–6; 52:13 – 53:12). There will also be an anointed messenger who declares to Zion that they are on the very cusp of God's coming to establish his kingdom; freedom is near (61:1–3)!

Where will this kingdom be? God's kingdom will stretch over the entire universe, as he creates a new heaven and a new earth. At the same time God's kingdom will find particular expression in Zion, the capital of his international kingdom. The inhabitants of God's kingdom will consist of those who have experienced the purification and salvation of the king. They will be those who trust and obey the king and join him in promoting justice. They will be a people from Israel and all nations. The book of Isaiah invites its readers to live in the light of this vision of God's kingdom.

As we look further down the line of canonical witness, Isaiah's kingdom vision bears witness to the remarkable news that God, the king, has come in Jesus. Yet, surprisingly he comes in the form of a man and takes on the roles of all three of God's lead agents. What is more, there is a reconfiguration of the realm of God's kingdom, since it is the church that is the temple of the king, although there continues to be the expectation that God's kingdom will be fully realized in the new heaven and new earth, with the New Jerusalem at its centre. God's kingdom people are his church from among all nations, recipients of salvation and purification, who obey their Lord and are his ambassadors of justice in the world.

As this book comes to a close, I am under no illusion that I have written the final or exhaustive word on the subject. It is ultimately Scripture – not secondary discourse, such as this book – that should have the ultimate say in how one envisions the message of Isaiah amid life in the world as we know it. This book will have accomplished its goals if its readers are eager to traverse the terrain of Isaiah, and, as they do, find that being alert to the kingdom motif enables them to navigate better and appreciate the jagged, yet breathtaking, message of the book of Isaiah.

Appendix:
Teaching series outline

Upon reading *The Book of Isaiah and God's Kingdom* some may be inspired to preach a series on Isaiah or teach an adult-education class on Isaiah. While each teacher and pastor will certainly need to wrestle with how best to organize a series on Isaiah, my hope is that the templates below will be helpful food for thought.

Option I: Textual–thematic series in Isaiah

It may not be feasible or wise for you and your church to preach a chapter-by-chapter series through the book of Isaiah. You may choose instead to preach from 'representative' thematic texts from Isaiah to help your congregation encounter God's message through the book of Isaiah.

Theme 1: God, the king of Zion and the world

Sermon 1: The holy king (Isa. 6)
Sermon 2: The saving king (Isa. 52:1–9; cf. ch. 35 and 40:1–11;
        Rom. 10:14–17; Matt. 3:1–4; 4:12–17)
Sermon 3: Revering the international king who stoops
        (Isa. 60; 66:1–2; 57:14–21)

Theme 2: The lead agents of the king

Sermon 1: The tale of two Davidic kings (Isa. 7; 36 – 37)
Sermon 2: The Davidic king as God's agent of justice (9:1–7
        or 11:1–9; cf. 16:5; 32:1–8)
Sermon 3: A suffering servant (52:13 – 53:12)
Sermon 4: God's anointed messenger (61:1–3)

Theme 3: The community of the king

Sermon 1: A community of justice (Isa. 1; cf. chs. 5, 56, 58)
Sermon 2: A community of trust and joy (Isa. 12; cf. 30:15; 32:17)
Sermon 3: An international community (Isa. 56:1–8; Mark 11:17;
        cf. Isa. 2:2–4; 25:6–8; 42:1–6; 66:18–24)

Theme 4: The domain of the king

Sermon 1: A particular domain: Zion, city of the king
(Isa. 60 – 62)
Sermon 2: A cosmic domain: new heaven and new earth
(Isa. 65:17 – 66:24)

Option II: Sequential–expository series in Isaiah

In the light of *The Book of Isaiah and God's Kingdom* another possibility for a series could be to work sequentially through each subsection of the book. While some could preach through every chapter, the outline below presents a template for working sequentially through the subsections of Isaiah by focusing on structurally significant or representative passages. While not every chapter is covered, the congregation would obtain a significant grasp of the flow and arrangement of the book. The outline amounts to approximately half a year of sermons, which divides into five different sessions.

Part I: The holy king must judge, but hope remains (Isa. 1 – 12)

Isaiah 1 – 5: Introduction to Isaiah's message of judgment
and hope
Sermon 1: Repent! Judgment is coming on the unjust
(Isa. 1; cf. 2:6–22; 3:1 – 4:1; ch. 5)
Sermon 2: Hope for Zion: obedience and cleansing
(Isa. 2:2–5; 4:2–6)

Isaiah 6: A vision of the holy king: perspective on the nature
of Isaiah's message
Sermon 3: The holy king who must judge but will forgive
(Isa. 6)

Isaiah 7 – 12: Judgment with a foolish king and hope for a just king
Sermon 4: Faith or frenzy: Ahaz and God's response of
judgment with a glimmer of hope (Isa. 7; cf. ch. 8;
9:8 – ch. 10)
Sermon 5: Hope for a faithful king (9:1–7; chs. 11–12)

Part II: YHWH's sovereignty in judgment and salvation of the world (Isa. 13 – 27)

Isaiah 13 – 23: Oracles about and against the nations
    Sermon 1: The crumbling of the proud and powerful
        (Isa. 13:1 – 14:23)
    Sermon 2: Worship among the nations after judgment
        (Isa. 19)

Isaiah 24 – 27: A cosmic vision of judgment and salvation
    Sermon 3: Be terrified sinners: the king will curse the world
        for sin (24:1–23)
    Sermon 4: Celebrate faithful: the king will save his people
        (chs. 25–26)

Part III: Back to reality – judgment, trust and signs of hope (Isa. 28 – 39)

Isaiah 28 – 33: Woes against mistrust and hope for a king
    Sermon 1: Misplaced trust (30:1–17; cf. 31:1–5)
    Sermon 2: A righteous king, a righteous city
        (ch. 32; cf. ch. 33)

Isaiah 34 – 35: Cosmic judgment or renewal
    Sermon 3: What is your destiny? (Isa. 34 – 35)

Isaiah 36 – 39: Historical bridge – God can save, but Zion's exile
        awaits
    Sermon 4: God can save Zion through a faithful king!
        (Isa. 36 – 37)
    Sermon 5: Zion's redemption is not complete – exile awaits
        (Isa. 39)

Part IV: After judgment – comfort while waiting for the king to return (Isa. 40 – 55)

Isaiah 40 – 48: Waiting confidently when God seems absent
    Sermon 1: Wait confidently – God will come as a tender king
        (Isa. 40:1–31)
    Sermon 2: Wait confidently – idols do not compare with the
        Lord (Isa. 44:9–20)

Isaiah 49 – 55: God the king, the servant and Zion's comfort
    Sermon 4: God the king will come to save (52:7–12)
    Sermon 5: The suffering servant accomplishes atonement
        (52:13 – 53:12)
    Sermon 6: Accepting the invitation to experience the
        restoration (Isa. 55)

Part V: Responding to the final judgment and salvation (Isa. 56 – 66)

    Sermon 1: In or out of the kingdom community? Obedience,
        ethnicity and religiosity (56:1–8; ch. 58)
    Sermon 2: A warrior king who is coming to save and judge
        (59:15–21; 63:1–6)
    Sermon 3: The king's glory shines amid the darkness (60:1–22)
    Sermon 4: The anointed messenger of the king (61:1–3)
    Sermon 5: The king is making all things new – don't miss out
        (65:17–25)

Bibliography

Abernethy, A. T. (2014a), *Eating in Isaiah: Approaching Food and Drink in Isaiah's Structure and Message*, BIS 131, Leiden: Brill.

––––––– (2014b), 'Theological Patterning in Jeremiah: A Vital Word Through an Ancient Book', *BBR* 24: 149–161.

Ackroyd, P. R. (1987), 'Isaiah 36–39: Structure and Function', in *Studies in the Religious Tradition of the Old Testament*, London: SCM Press, 105–120.

Altmann, P. (2011), *Festive Meals in Ancient Israel: Deuteronomy's Identity Politics in Their Ancient Near Eastern Context*, BZAW 424, Berlin: de Gruyter.

Ames, F. R. (2014), 'The Red Stained Warrior in Ancient Israel', in B. E. Kelle, F. R. Ames and J. L. Wright (eds.), *Warfare, Ritual, and Symbol in Biblical and Modern Contexts*, Ancient Israel and Its Literature 18, Atlanta: Society of Biblical Literature, 83–109.

Aune, D. E. (1998), *Revelation 17–22*, WBC 52C, Nashville: Thomas Nelson.

Averbeck, R. A. (1997), '*'āšām*', in *NIDOTTE* 1: 553–566.

––––––– (2012), 'Christian Interpretations of Isaiah 53', in D. L. Bock and M. Glaser (eds.), *The Gospel According to Isaiah 53: Encountering the Suffering Servant in Jewish and Christian Theology*, Grand Rapids: Kregel, 33–60.

Balogh, C. (2008), '"He Filled Zion with Justice and Righteousness": The Composition of Isaiah 33', *Bib* 89: 477–504.

Baltzer, K., and P. Machinist (2001), *Deutero-Isaiah: A Commentary on Isaiah 40–55*, Hermeneia, tr. M. Kohl, Minneapolis: Fortress.

Barr, J. (1999), *The Concept of Biblical Theology: An Old Testament Perspective*, London: SCM Press.

Barstad, H. M. (1989), *A Way in the Wilderness: The 'Second Exodus' in the Message of Second Isaiah*, JSSM 12, Manchester: University of Manchester Press.

Bartelt, A. H. (2004), 'The Centrality of Isaiah 6–8) Within Isaiah 2–12', *Concordia Journal* 30: 316–335.

Bartholomew, C. G. (2004), 'Biblical Theology and Biblical Interpretation: Introduction', in C. G. Bartholomew, M. Healy, K. Möller and R. Parry (eds.), *Out of Egypt: Biblical Theology and Biblical Interpretation*, Scripture and Hermeneutics Series 5, Grand Rapids: Zondervan, 1–17.

———— (2011), *Where Mortals Dwell: A Christian View of Place for Today*, Grand Rapids: Baker.

Bartholomew, C. G., and M. W. Goheen (2004), *The Drama of Scripture: Finding Our Place in the Biblical Story*, Grand Rapids: Baker Academic.

Bauckham, R. (1998), *God Crucified: Monotheism and Christology in the New Testament*, Carlisle: Paternoster.

Beale, G. K. (1991), 'Isaiah VI 9–13: A Retributive Taunt Against Idolatry', *VT* 41: 257–278.

———— (1999), *The Book of Revelation*, NIGTC, Grand Rapids: Eerdmans.

Berges, U. (1998), *Das Buch Jesaja: Komposition und Endgestalt*, Freiburg: Herder.

———— (1999), 'Die Armen im Buch Jesaja: Ein Beitrag zur Literaturgeschichte des AT', *Bib* 80: 153–177.

———— (2002), 'Der neue Himmel und die neue Erde im Jesajabuch: Eine Auslegung zu Jesaja 65:17 und 66:22', in F. Postma (ed.), *The New Things: Eschatology in Old Testament Prophecy. Fss. for Henk Leene*, Maastricht: Uitgeverij Shaker, 9–15.

———— (2011), 'Zion and the Kingship of Yhwh in Isaiah 40–55', in A. L. H. M. van Wieringen and A. van der Woude (eds.), *'Enlarge the Site of Your Tent': The City as Unifying Theme in Isaiah. The Isaiah Workshop – De Jesaja Werkplaats*, OtSt 58, Leiden: Brill, 95–119.

———— (2012), *The Book of Isaiah: Its Composition and Final Form*, tr. M. C. Lind, Sheffield: Sheffield Phoenix.

———— (2014), 'Kingship and Servanthood in the Book of Isaiah', in R. J. Bautch and J. T. Hibbard (eds.), *The Book of Isaiah: Enduring Questions Answered Anew. Essays Honoring Joseph Blenkinsopp and His Contribution to the Study of Isaiah*, Grand Rapids: Eerdmans, 159–178.

Bergsma, J. S. (2007), *The Jubilee from Leviticus to Qumran: A History of Interpretation*, VTSup 115, Leiden: Brill.

Beuken, W. A. M. (1974), 'Isa. 55, 3–5: The Reinterpretation of David', *Bijdragen* 35: 49–64.

———— (1989a), 'Does Trito-Isaiah Reject the Temple? An Intertextual Inquiry into Isa. 66. 1–6', in S. Draisma (ed.), *Intertextuality in*

Biblical Writings: Essays in Honour of Bas van Iersel, Kampen: J. H. Kok, 53–66.

———— (1989b), 'Servant and Herald of Good Tidings: Isaiah 61 as an Interpretation of Isaiah 40–55', in J. Vermeylen (ed.), *The Book of Isaiah. Le livre d'Isaïe: Les oracles et leurs relectures. Unité et complexité de l'ouvrage*, Leuven: Peeters, 411–440.

———— (1990), 'The Main Theme of Trito-Isaiah: "the Servants of YHWH"', *JSOT* 47: 67–87.

———— (1991), 'Jesaja 33 als Spiegeltext im Jesajabuch', *ETL* 67: 5–35.

———— (2000), *Isaiah II: Isaiah 28–39*, vol. 2, HCOT, Leuven: Peeters.

———— (2002), '"Lebanon with Its Majesty Shall Fall. A Shoot Shall Come Forth from the Stump of Jesse" (Isa 10:34–11:1): Interfacing the Story of Assyria and the Image of Israel's Future in Isaiah 10–11', in F. Postma (ed.), *The New Things: Eschatology in Old Testament Prophecy. Fss. for Henk Leene*, Maastricht: Uitgeverij Shaker, 17–33.

———— (2003), *Jesaja 1–12*, tr. Ulrich Berges, HTKAT, Freiburg: Herder.

———— (2004), 'The Manifestation of Yahweh and the Commission of Isaiah: Isaiah 6 Read Against the Background of Isaiah 1', *CTJ* 39: 72–87.

———— (2009), 'YHWH's Sovereign Rule and His Adoration on Mount Zion: A Comparison of Poetic Visions in Isaiah 24–27, 52, and 66', in A. J. Everson and H. C. P. Kim (eds.), *The Desert Will Bloom: Poetic Visions in Isaiah*, Ancient Israel and Its Literature 4, Atlanta: Society of Biblical Literature, 91–107.

———— (2010), 'Woe to the Powers in Israel that Vie to Replace YHWH's Rule on Mount Zion! Isaiah Chapters 28–31 from the Perspective of Isaiah Chapters 24–27', in M. N. van der Meer, P. van Keulen, W. van Peursen and B. Romeny (eds.), *Isaiah in Context: Studies in Honour of Arie van der Kooij on the Occasion of His Sixty-Fifth Birthday*, VTSup 138, Leiden: Brill, 25–43.

Blenkinsopp, J. (2000), *Isaiah 1–39: A New Translation with Commentary*, AB 19, New York: Doubleday.

———— (2002), *Isaiah 40–55: A New Translation with Introduction and Commentary*, AB 19A, New York: Doubleday.

———— (2003), *Isaiah 56–66: A New Translation with Introduction and Commentary*, AB 19B, New York: Doubleday.

Blomberg, C. (2002), 'Interpreting Old Testament Prophetic Literature in Matthew: Double Fulfillment', *TrinJ* 23: 17–33.

Boda, M. J. (2007), 'Figuring the Future: The Prophets and Messiah', in S. E. Porter (ed.), *The Messiah in the Old and New Testaments*, Grand Rapids: Eerdmans, 35–74.

———— (2012), 'Biblical Theology and Old Testament Interpretation', in C. G. Bartholomew and D. J. H. Beldman (eds.), *Hearing the Old Testament: Listening for God's Address*, Grand Rapids: Eerdmans, 122–153.

Brendsel, D. J. (2014), *'Isaiah Saw His Glory': The Use of Isaiah 52–53 in John 12*, BZNW 208, Berlin: de Gruyter.

Brettler, M. Z. (1989), *God Is King: Understanding an Israelite Metaphor*, JSOTSup 76, Sheffield: Sheffield Academic Press.

———— (1993), 'Images of YHWH the Warrior in Psalms', *Semeia* 61: 135–165.

Briant, P. (1995), 'Social and Legal Institutions in Achaemenid Iran', in J. M. Sasson (ed.), *CANE* 1, Peabody: Hendrickson, 517–528.

———— (2002), *From Cyrus to Alexander: A History of the Persian Empire*, tr. P. T. Daniels, Winona Lake: Eisenbrauns.

Brownlee, W. H. (1964), *The Meaning of the Qumrân Scrolls for the Bible: With Special Attention to the Book of Isaiah*, New York: Oxford University Press.

Brueggemann, W. (1977), *The Land: Place as Gift, Promise, and Challenge in Biblical Faith*, Philadelphia: Fortress.

———— (2008), 'Faith in the Empire', in R. A. Horsley (ed.), *In the Shadow of Empire: Reclaiming the Bible as a History of Faithful Resistance*, Louisville: Westminster John Knox, 25–40.

Brunner, H. (1987), 'Die Gerechtigkeit Gottes', *ZRG* 39: 210–225.

Bürki, M. (2013), 'City of Pride, City of Glory: The Opposition of Two Cities in Isaiah 24–27', in J. T. Hibbard and H. C. P. Kim (eds.), *Formation and Intertextuality in Isaiah 24–27*, Ancient Israel and Its Literature 17, Atlanta: Society of Biblical Literature, 49–60.

Caird, G. B. (1980), *The Language and Imagery of the Bible*, Philadelphia: Westminster.

Calvin, J. (1979a), *Calvin's Commentaries*, vol. 7, tr. W. Pringle, Grand Rapids: Baker.

———— (1979b), *Calvin's Commentaries*, vol. 8, tr. W. Pringle, Grand Rapids: Baker.

Caquot, A. (1965), 'Les "grâces de David". A propos d'Isaïe 55/3b', *Semitica* 15: 45–59.

Carr, D. M. (1995), 'Isaiah 40:1–11 in the Context of the Macro-structure of Second Isaiah', in W. R. Bodine (ed.), *Discourse Analysis of Biblical Literature: What It Is and What It Offers*, Semeia, Atlanta: Scholars Press, 51–74.

Carson, D. A. (1991), *The Gospel According to John*, PNTC, Grand Rapids: Eerdmans.

Carvalho, C. L. (2010), 'The Beauty of the Bloody God: The Divine Warrior in Prophetic Literature', in J. M. O'Brien and C. Franke (eds.), *The Aesthetics of Violence in the Prophets*, New York: T. & T. Clark, 131–152.

Childs, B. S. (2001), *Isaiah*, OTL, Louisville: Westminster John Knox.

Chisholm Jr, R. B. (2006), 'The Christological Fulfillment of Isaiah's Servant Songs', *BSac* 163: 387–404.

Cho, P. K. K., and J. Fu (2013), 'Death and Feasting in the Isaiah Apocalypse (Isaiah 25:6–8)', in J. T. Hibbard and H. C. P. Kim (eds.), *Formation and Intertextuality in Isaiah 24–27*, Ancient Israel and Its Literature 17, Atlanta: Society of Biblical Literature, 117–142.

Clements, R. E. (1980), *Isaiah and the Deliverance of Jerusalem: A Study of the Interpretation of Prophecy in the Old Testament*, JSOTSup 13, Sheffield: University of Sheffield.

——— (1990), 'The Immanuel Prophecy of Isa. 7:10–17 and Its Messianic Interpretation', in E. Blum, C. Macholz and E. Stegemann (eds.), *Die Hebräische Bibel und ihre zweifache Nachgeschichte: Festschrift für Rolf Rendtorff zum 65. Geburtstag*, Neukirchen-Vluyn: Neukirchener Verlag, 225–240.

——— (1994), 'The Politics of Blasphemy: Zion's God and the Threat of Imperialism', in I. Kottsieper, J. van Oorschot, D. Römheld and H. M. Wahl (eds.), *Wer ist wie du, Herr, unter den Göttern? Studien zur Theologie und Religionsgeschichte Israels. Festschrift für O. Kaiser*, Göttingen: Vandenhoeck & Ruprecht, 231–246.

——— (1997), '"Arise, Shine; For Your Light Has Come": A Basic Theme of the Isaianic Tradition', in C. C. Broyles and C. A. Evans (eds.), *Writing and Reading the Scroll of Isaiah: Studies of an Interpretive Tradition*, VTSup 70.1, Leiden: Brill, 441–454.

Clifford, H. (2010), 'Deutero-Isaiah and Monotheism', in J. Day (ed.), *Prophecy and Prophets in Ancient Israel: Proceedings of the Oxford Old Testament Seminar*, London: T. & T. Clark, 267–289.

Clifford, R. J. (1983), 'Isaiah 55: Invitation to a Feast', in C. L. Meyers and M. O'Connor (eds.), *The Word of the Lord Shall Go Forth: Essays in Honor of David Noel Freedman in Celebration of His Sixtieth Birthday*, Winona Lake: Eisenbrauns, 27–35.

—————— (1984), *Fair Spoken and Persuading: In Interpretation of Second Isaiah*, New York: Paulist Press.

—————— (1993), 'The Unity of the Book of Isaiah and Its Cosmogonic Language', *CBQ* 55: 1–17.

Clines, D. J. A. (1976), *I, He, We, and They: A Literary Approach to Isaiah 53*, JSOTSup 1, Sheffield: JSOT Press.

Cole, R. L. (2011), 'Isaiah 6 in Its Context', *STR* 2: 161–180.

Conrad, E. W. (1991), *Reading Isaiah*, Minneapolis: Fortress.

Cross Jr, F. M. (1953), 'The Council of Yahweh in Second Isaiah', *JNES* 12: 274–277.

Cunha, W. de A. (2013), '"Kingship" and "Kingdom": A Discussion of Isaiah 24:21–23; 27:12–13', in J. T. Hibbard and H. C. P. Kim (eds.), *Formation and Intertextuality in Isaiah 24–27*, Ancient Israel and Its Literature 17, Atlanta: Society of Biblical Literature, 61–75.

Darr, K. P. (1994), *Isaiah's Vision and the Family of God*, Louisville: Westminster John Knox.

Davies, G. I. (1989), 'The Destiny of the Nations in the Book of Isaiah', in J. Vermeylen (ed.), *The Book of Isaiah. Le livre d'Isaïe: Les oracles et leurs relectures. Unité et complexité de l'ouvrage*, Leuven: Peeters, 93–120.

De Jong, M. J. (2011), 'A Note on the Meaning of Besedeq in Isaiah 42,6 and 45,13', *ZAW* 123: 259–262.

Dekker, J. (2007), *Zion's Rock-Solid Foundations: An Exegetical Study of the Zion Text in Isaiah 28:16*, Leiden: Brill.

Dumbrell, W. J. (1985), 'The Purpose of the Book of Isaiah', *TynBul* 36: 111–128.

Ehring, C. (2007), *Die Rückkehr JHWHs: Traditions- und religionsgeschichtliche Untersuchungen zu Jesaja 40,1–11, Jesaja 52,7–10 und verwandten Texten*, WMANT 116, Neukirchen-Vluyn: Neukirchener Verlag.

Eissfeldt, O. (1962a), 'Jahwe als König', in *Kleine Schriften*, 6 vols., Tübingen: Mohr Siebeck, 1: 172–193.

—————— (1962b), 'Promises of Grace to David in Isaiah 55:1–5', in B. W. Anderson and W. Harrelson (eds.), *Israel's Prophetic Heritage: Essays in Honor of James Muilenburg*, New York: Harper, 196–207.

Emerton, J. A. (1982), 'The Translation and Interpretation of Isaiah vi. 13', in J. A. Emerton and S. C. Reif (eds.), *Interpreting the Hebrew Bible: Essays in Honour of E. I. J. Rosenthal*, Cambridge: Cambridge University Press, 85–118.

Evans, C. A. (1986), 'Isaiah 6:9–13 in the Context of Isaiah's Theology', *JETS* 29: 139–146.

–––––– (1988), 'On the Unity and Parallel Structure of Isaiah', *VT* 38: 129–147.

Firmage Jr, E., J. Milgrom and U. Dahmen (2004), '*rwm*', in *TDOT* 13: 402–409.

Flynn, S. W. (2006), 'Where Is YHWH in Isaiah 57,14–15?', *Bib* 87: 358–370.

–––––– (2014), *YHWH Is King: The Development of Divine Kingship in Ancient Israel*, VTSup 159, Leiden: Brill.

Foster, B. R. (1997), 'Epic of Creation (1.111): Enuma Elish', in W. W. Hallo and K. L. Younger (eds.), *The Context of Scripture*, vol. 1: *Canonical Compositions from the Biblical World*, Leiden: Brill, 390–404.

France, R. T. (1968), 'The Servant of the Lord in the Teaching of Jesus', *TynBul* 19: 26–52.

Gabler, J. P. (2004), 'An Oration on the Proper Distinction Between Biblical and Dogmatic Theology and the Specific Objectives of Each', in B. C. Ollenberger (ed.), *Old Testament Theology: Flowering and Future*, tr. J. Sandys-Wunsch and L. Eldredge (1831), SBTS 1, Winona Lake: Eisenbrauns, 497–506.

Gentry, P. J., and S. J. Wellum (2012), *Kingdom Through Covenant: A Biblical-Theological Understanding of the Covenants*, Wheaton: Crossway.

Gignilliat, M. (2008), 'Who Is Isaiah's Servant? Narrative Identity and Theological Potentiality', *SJT* 61: 125–136.

Goldingay, J. (1987), *Theological Diversity and the Authority of the Old Testament*, Grand Rapids: Eerdmans.

–––––– (1999), 'The Compound Name in Isaiah 9:5(6)', *CBQ* 61: 239–244.

–––––– (2001), *Isaiah*, NIBC, Peabody: Hendrickson.

–––––– (2003), *Old Testament Theology: Israel's Gospel*, vol. 1, Downers Grove: IVP Academic.

–––––– (2013), 'Isaiah 56–66: An Isaianic and Postcolonial Reading', in A. T. Abernethy, M. G. Brett, T. Bulkeley and T. Meadowcroft (eds.), *Isaiah and Imperial Context: The Book of Isaiah in Times of Empire*, Eugene, Ore.: Pickwick, 151–166.

–––––– (2014), *The Theology of the Book of Isaiah*, Downers Grove: InterVarsity Press.

Goldingay, J., and D. Payne (2006a), *Isaiah 40–55: A Critical and Exegetical Commentary*, vol. 1, ICC, Edinburgh: T. & T. Clark.

────── (2006b), *Isaiah 40–55: A Critical and Exegetical Commentary*, vol. 2, ICC, Edinburgh: T. & T. Clark.

Goldsworthy, G. (1981), *Gospel and Kingdom*, Exeter: Paternoster.

Gorman, M. J. (2009), *Elements of Biblical Exegesis: A Basic Guide for Students and Ministers*, rev. and exp. ed., Peabody: Hendrickson.

Goswell, G. (2013), 'Royal Names: Naming and Wordplay in Isaiah 7', *WTJ* 75: 97–105.

────── (2014), 'Isaiah 16: A Forgotten Chapter in the History of Messianism', *SJOT* 28: 91–103.

────── (2015), 'The Shape of Messianism in Isaiah 9', *WTJ* 77: 101–110.

Gray, J. (1979), *The Biblical Doctrine of the Reign of God*, Edinburgh: T. & T. Clark.

Gray, M. (2006), *Rhetoric and Social Justice in Isaiah*, LHBOTS 432, London: T. & T. Clark.

Grayson, K. (1996), *Assyrian Rulers of the Early First Millennium BC II (858–745 BC)*, RIMA 2, Toronto: University of Toronto Press.

Green, J. B. (1997), *The Gospel of Luke*, NICNT, Grand Rapids: Eerdmans.

Gregory, B. C. (2007), 'The Postexilic Exile in Third Isaiah: Isaiah 61:1–3 in Light of Second Temple Hermeneutics', *JBL* 126: 475–496.

Greidanus, S. (1999), *Preaching Christ from the Old Testament: A Contemporary Hermeneutical Method*, Grand Rapids: Eerdmans.

Hägglund, F. (2008), *Isaiah 53 in the Light of Homecoming After Exile*, Tübingen: Mohr Siebeck.

Hamborg, G. R. (1981), 'Reasons for Judgment in the Oracles Against the Nations of the Prophet Isaiah', *VT* 31: 145–159.

Hamilton, J. (2008), '"The Virgin Will Conceive": Typological Fulfillment in Matthew 1:18–23', in D. M. Gurtner and J. Nolland (eds.), *Built upon the Rock: Studies in the Gospel of Matthew*, Grand Rapids: Eerdmans.

Harris, M. J. (1992), *Jesus as God: The New Testament Use of Theos in Reference to Jesus*, Grand Rapids: Baker.

Hartley, J. E. (2003), 'Holy, Holiness', in *DOTP*, 420–431.

Hayes, E. R. (2012), 'The One Who Brings Justice: Conceptualizing the Role of "The Servant" in Isaiah 42:1–4 and Matthew 12:15–21', in I. Provan and M. J. Boda (eds.), *Let Us Go Up to Zion: Essays in Honour of H. G. M. Williamson on the Occasion of His Sixty-Fifth Birthday*, VTSup 153, Leiden: Brill, 143–151.

Hayes, K. M. (2002), *'The Earth Mourns'*: *Prophetic Metaphor and Oral Aesthetic*, Academia Biblica 8, Leiden: Brill.

Hays, C. B. (2013), 'The Date and Message of Isaiah 24–27 in Light of Hebrew Diachrony', in J. T. Hibbard and H. C. P. Kim (eds.), *Formation and Intertextuality in Isaiah 24–27*, Ancient Israel and Its Literature 17, Atlanta: SBL, 7–24.

Hays, R. B. (1989), *Echoes of Scripture in the Letters of Paul*, New Haven: Yale University Press.

Hengel, M., with D. P. Bailey (2004), 'The Effective History of Isaiah 53 in the Pre-Christian Period', in B. Janowski and P. Stuhlmacher (eds.), *The Suffering Servant: Isaiah 53 in Jewish and Christian Sources*, tr. D. P. Bailey, Grand Rapids: Eerdmans, 75–146.

Hermisson, H.-J. (2004), 'The Fourth Servant Song in the Context of Second Isaiah', in B. Janowski and P. Stuhlmacher (eds.), *The Suffering Servant: Isaiah 53 in Jewish and Christian Sources*, tr. D. P. Bailey, Grand Rapids: Eerdmans, 16–47.

Heskett, R. (2007), *Messianism Within the Scriptural Scrolls of Isaiah*, LHBOTS 456, London: T. & T. Clark.

Holladay, W. (1978), *Isaiah: Scroll of a Prophetic Heritage*, Grand Rapids: Eerdmans.

House, P. R. (1993), 'Isaiah's Call and Its Context in Isaiah 1–6', *CTR* 6: 207–222.

Houston, W. (1993), 'The Kingdom of God in Isaiah: Divine Power and Human Response', in R. S. Barbour (ed.), *The Kingdom of God and Human Society: Essays by Members of the Scripture, Theology and Society Group*, Edinburgh: T. & T. Clark, 28–41.

Hugenberger, G. P. (1995), 'The Servant of the Lord in the "Servant Songs" of Isaiah: A Second Moses Figure', in P. E. Satterthwaite, R. S. Hess and G. J. Wenham (eds.), *The Lord's Anointed: Interpretation of Old Testament Messianic Texts*, Grand Rapids: Baker, 105–140.

Irsigler, H. (1991), 'Gott als König in Berufung und Verkündigung Jesajas', in F. V. Reiterer (ed.), *Ein Gott, eine Offenbarung: Beiträge zur biblischen Exegese, Theologie und Spiritualität. Fss. N. Füglister*, Würzburg: Echter Verlag, 127–154.

Iser, W. (1980), *The Act of Reading: A Theory of Aesthetic Response*, Baltimore: Johns Hopkins University Press.

Jang, S.-H. (2012), 'Hearing the Word of God in Isaiah 1 and 65–66: A Synchronic Approach', in R. Boer, M. Carden and J. Kelso (eds.), *The One Who Reads May Run: Essays in Honour of Edgar W. Conrad*, LHBOTS 553, New York: T. & T. Clark, 41–58.

Janowski, B. (2004), 'He Bore Our Sins: Isaiah 53 and the Drama of Taking Another's Place', in B. Janowski and P. Stuhlmacher (eds.), *The Suffering Servant: Isaiah 53 in Jewish and Christian Sources*, tr. D. P. Bailey, Grand Rapids: Eerdmans, 48–74.

Janzen, J. G. (1994), 'On the Moral Nature of God's Power: Yahweh and the Sea in Job and Deutero-Isaiah', *CBQ* 56: 458–478.

Jenkins, A. K. (1989), 'The Development of Isaiah Tradition in Isaiah 13–23', in J. Vermeylen (ed.), *The Book of Isaiah. Le livre d'Isaïe: Les oracles et leurs relectures. Unité et complexité de l'ouvrage*, Leuven: Peeters, 237–251.

Jenner, K. A. (2011), 'Jerusalem, Zion and the Unique Servant of Yhwh in the New Heaven and the New Earth: A Study on Recovering Identity Versus Lamenting Faded Glory (Isaiah 1–5 and 65–66)', in A. L. H. M. van Wieringen and A. van der Woude (eds.), *'Enlarge the Site of Your Tent': The City as Unifying Theme in Isaiah. The Isaiah Workshop – De Jesaja Werkplaats*, OtSt 58, Leiden: Brill, 169–189.

Jensen, J. (1973), *The Use of tôrâ by Isaiah: His Debate with the Wisdom Tradition*, CBQMS 3, Washington, D. C.: Catholic Biblical Association of America.

Johnson, D. G. (1988), *From Chaos to Restoration: An Integrative Reading of Isaiah 24–27*, JSOTSup 61, Sheffield: Sheffield Academic Press.

Kaiser, O. (1974), *Isaiah 13–39*, tr. R. A. Wilson, OTL, Philadelphia: Westminster.

Kelle, B. E. (2012), 'Israelite History', *DOTP*, 397–422.

Kennedy, J. M. (2004), 'Yahweh's Strongman? The Characterization of Hezekiah in the Book of Isaiah', *PRS* 31: 383–397.

Kim, H. C. P. (2013), 'City, Earth, and Empire in Isaiah 24–27', in J. T. Hibbard and H. C. P. Kim (eds.), *Formation and Intertextuality in Isaiah 24–27*, Ancient Israel and Its Literature 17, Atlanta: Society of Biblical Literature, 25–48.

King, A. M. (2015), 'A Remnant Will Return: An Analysis of the Literary Function of the Remnant Motif in Isaiah', *JESOT* 4.2: 145–169.

Knierim, R. (1968), 'The Vocation of Isaiah', *VT* 18: 47–68.

Koole, J. L. (1997), *Isaiah III: Isaiah 40–48*, vol. 1, HCOT, Leuven: Peeters.

———— (1998), *Isaiah III: Isaiah 49–55*, vol. 2, HCOT, Leuven: Peeters.

———— (2001), *Isaiah III: Isaiah 56–66*, vol. 3, HCOT, Leuven: Peeters.

Köstenberger, A. J. (2012), 'The Present and Future of Biblical Theology', *Them* 37: 445–464.

Laato, A. (1988), *Who Is Immanuel? The Rise and the Foundering of Isaiah's Messianic Expectations*, Åbo: Åbo Academy.

——— (1992), *The Servant of YHWH and Cyrus: A Reinterpretation of the Exilic Messianic Programme in Isaiah 40–55*, Stockholm: Almqvist & Wiksell International.

——— (1998), *'About Zion I Will Not Be Silent': The Book of Isaiah as an Ideological Unity*, ConBOT 44, Stockholm: Almqvist & Wiksell International.

——— (2012), *Who Is the Servant of the Lord? Jewish and Christian Interpretations on Isaiah 53 from Antiquity to the Middle Ages*, Studies in Rewritten Bible 4, Winona Lake: Eisenbrauns.

Laberge, L. (1982), 'The Woe-Oracles of Isaiah 28–33', *EgT* 13: 157–190.

Landy, F. (1999), 'Strategies of Concentration and Diffusion in Isaiah 6', *BI* 6: 58–86.

Laniak, T. S. (2006), *Shepherds After My Own Heart: Pastoral Traditions and Leadership in the Bible*, NSBT 20, Downers Grove: InterVarsity Press.

Leclerc, T. L. (2001), *Yahweh Is Exalted in Justice: Solidarity and Conflict in Isaiah*, Minneapolis: Fortress.

Lee, S. (1995), *Creation and Redemption in Isaiah 40–55*, Jin Dao Dissertation Series 2, Hong Kong: Alliance Bible Seminary.

Lessing, R. R. (2010), 'Yahweh Versus Marduk Creation Theology in Isaiah 40–55', *Concordia Journal* 36: 234–244.

——— (2011), 'Isaiah's Servants in Chapters 40–55: Clearing up the Confusion', *Concordia Journal* 37: 130–134.

Levenson, J. D. (1984), 'The Temple and the World', *JR* 64: 275–298.

——— (1985), *Sinai and Zion: An Entry into the Jewish Bible*, New York: Harper Collins.

Liebreich, L. (1954), 'The Position of Chapter Six in the Book of Isaiah', *HUCA* 25: 37–40.

——— (1956), 'The Compilation of the Book of Isaiah', *JQR* 46: 259–277.

Lim, B. H. (2010), *The 'Way of the LORD' in the Book of Isaiah*, LHBOTS 522, Edinburgh: T. & T. Clark.

Lind, M. C. (1980), *Yahweh Is a Warrior: The Theology of Warfare in Ancient Israel*, Scottdale: Herald.

——— (1997), 'Political Implications of Isaiah 6', in C. C. Broyles and C. A. Evans (eds.), *Writing and Reading the Scroll of Isaiah: Studies of an Interpretive Tradition*, VTSup 70.1, Leiden: Brill, 317–338.

Longenecker, R. (1975), *Biblical Exegesis in the Apostolic Period*, Grand Rapids: Eerdmans.

Longman III, T., and D. G. Reid (1995), *God Is a Warrior*, Grand Rapids: Zondervan.

Lund, O. (2007), *Way Metaphors and Way Topics in Isaiah 40–55*, FAT 2, Tübingen: Mohr Siebeck.

Lynch, M. J. (2008), 'Zion's Warrior and the Nations: Isaiah 59:15b–63:6 in Isaiah's Zion Traditions', *CBQ* 70: 244–263.

McCann Jr, J. C. (2003), 'The Book of Isaiah – Theses and Hypotheses', *BTB* 33: 88–94.

MacDonald, N. (2008), *Not Bread Alone: The Uses of Food in the Old Testament*, Oxford: Oxford University Press.

———— (2009), 'Monotheism and Isaiah', in D. G. Firth and H. G. M. Williamson (eds.), *Interpreting Isaiah: Issues and Approaches*, Downers Grove: InterVarsity Press, 43–61.

———— (2012), ' "The Eyes of All Look to You": The Generosity of the Divine King', in K. Ehrensperger, N. MacDonald and L. S. Rehmann (eds.), *Decisive Meals: Table Politics in Biblical Literature*, LNTS 449, New York: T. & T. Clark, 1–14.

Magonet, J. (1986), 'The Structure of Isaiah 6', in *Proceedings of the Ninth World Congress of Jewish Studies. Jerusalem, August 4–12, 1985. Division A. The Period of the Bible*, Jerusalem: World Union of Jewish Studies, 91–97.

Maier, C. M. (2008), *Daughter Zion, Mother Zion: Gender, Space, and the Sacred in Ancient Israel*, Minneapolis: Fortress.

Marlow, H. (2011), 'The Spirit of Yahweh in Isaiah 11:1–9', in D. G. Firth and P. D. Wegner (eds.), *Presence, Power and Promise: The Role of the Spirit of God in the Old Testament*, Downers Grove: InterVarsity Press.

Mason, S. D. (2007), 'Another Flood? Genesis 9 and Isaiah's Broken Eternal Covenant', *JSOT* 32: 177–198.

Mathewson, D. (2005), 'Isaiah in the Book of Revelation', in S. Moyise and M. J. J. Menken (eds.), *Isaiah in the New Testament*, London: T. & T. Clark, 189–210.

Mettinger, T. N. D. (1982), 'YHWH SABAOTH – The Heavenly King on the Cherubim Throne', in T. Ishida (ed.), *Studies in the Period of David and Solomon and Other Essays*, Winona Lake: Eisenbrauns, 109–138.

———— (1997), 'In Search of the Hidden Structure: YHWH as King in Isaiah 40–55', in C. G. Broyles and C. A. Evans (eds.), *Writing*

and Reading the Scroll of Isaiah: Studies of an Interpretive Tradition,
VTSup 70.1, Leiden: Brill, 143–154.

Metzger, M. (1985), *Königsthron und Gottesthron. Thronformen und Throndarstellungen in Ägypten und im Vorderen Orient im dritten und zweiten Jahrtausend vor Christus und deren Bedeutung für das Verständnis von Aussagen über den Thron im Alten Testament,* AOAT 15, 2 vols., Neukirchen-Vluyn: Neukirchener Verlag.

Millar, W. R. (1976), *Isaiah 24–27 and the Origin of Apocalpytic,* HSM 11, Missoula: Scholars Press.

Miller, J. M., and J. H. Hayes (2006), *A History of Ancient Israel and Judah,* 2nd ed., Louisville: Westminster John Knox.

Miller, P. D. (1973), *The Divine Warrior in Early Israel,* HSM 5, Cambridge, Mass.: Harvard University Press.

Moberly, R. W. L. (2001), 'Whose Justice? Which Righteousness? The Interpretation of Isaiah v 16', *VT* 51: 55–68.

—— (2003), ' "Holy, Holy, Holy": Isaiah's Vision of God', in S. C. Barton (ed.), *Holiness Past and Present,* London: T. & T. Clark, 122–140.

Möller, K. (2004), 'The Nature and Genre of Biblical Theology', in C. G. Bartholomew, M. Healy, K. Möller and R. Parry (eds.), *Out of Egypt: Biblical Theology and Biblical Interpretation,* Scripture and Hermeneutics Series 5, Grand Rapids: Zondervan, 41–64.

—— (2013), *Old Testament Theology: Reading the Hebrew Bible as Christian Scripture,* Ada: Baker Academic.

Morgan, C. W., and R. A. Peterson (eds.) (2012), *The Kingdom of God,* Theology in Community, Wheaton: Crossway.

Motyer, J. A. (1993), *The Prophecy of Isaiah: An Introduction and Commentary,* Downers Grove: InterVarsity Press.

Naudé, J. (1997), '*qdš*', in *NIDOTTE* 3: 877–887.

Neufeld, T. R. Y. (1997), '*Put On the Armour of God':* The Divine Warrior from Isaiah to Ephesians, JSNTSup 140, Sheffield: Sheffield Academic Press.

Nel, P. J. (1997), '*mšl*', in *NIDOTTE* 2: 1136–1137.

North, C. R. (1948), *The Suffering Servant in Deutero-Isaiah: A Historical and Critical Study,* London: Oxford University Press.

Oh, A. S.-H. (2014), *Oh, That You Would Rend the Heavens and Come Down: The Eschatological Theology of Third Isaiah (Isaiah 56–66),* Eugene, Ore.: Pickwick.

Ollenburger, B. C. (1987a), 'Isaiah's Creation Theology', *ExAud* 3: 54–71.

——— (1987b), *Zion the City of the Great King: A Theological Symbol of the Jerusalem Cult*, JSOTSup 41, Sheffield: JSOT Press.

Olley, J. W. (1999), '"Trust in the Lord": Hezekiah, Kings and Isaiah', *TynBul* 50: 59–77.

Ortlund, E. N. (2010), *Theophany and Chaoskampf: The Interpretation of Theophanic Imagery in the Baal Epic, Isaiah, and the Twelve*, Gorgias Ugaritic Studies 5, Piscataway, N.J.: Gorgias.

Oswalt, J. N. (1986), *The Book of Isaiah: Chapters 1–39*, NICOT, Grand Rapids: Eerdmans.

——— (1997), 'Righteousness in Isaiah: A Study of the Function of Chapters 55–66 in the Present Structure of the Book', in C. G. Broyles and C. A. Evans (eds.), *Writing and Reading the Scroll of Isaiah: Studies of an Interpretive Tradition*, VTSup 70.1, Leiden: Brill, 177–191.

——— (1998), *The Book of Isaiah: Chapters 40–66*, NICOT, Grand Rapids: Eerdmans.

——— (2005), 'Isaiah 24–27: Songs in the Night', *CTJ* 40: 76–84.

——— (2006), 'The Nations in Isaiah: Friend or Foe; Servant or Partner', *BBR* 16: 41–51.

Pao, D. (2002), *Acts and the Isaianic New Exodus*, Grand Rapids: Baker.

Parpola, S. (2004), 'The Leftovers of God and King: On the Distribution of Meat at the Assyrian and Achaemenid Imperial Courts', in C. Grottanelli and L. Milano (eds.), *Food and Identity in the Ancient World*, History of the Ancient Near East 9, Padova: S. A. R. G. O. N., 281–312.

Paul, S. (2011), *Isaiah 40–66: A Commentary*, Grand Rapids: Eerdmans.

Polan, G. J. (1986), *In the Ways of Justice Toward Salvation: A Rhetorical Analysis of Isaiah 56–59*, New York: Lang.

Polaski, D. C. (2001), *Authorizing an End: The Isaiah Apocalpyse and Intertextuality*, BIS 50, Leiden: Brill.

Provan, I., V. P. Long and T. Longman III (2003), *A Biblical History of Israel*, Louisville: Westminster John Knox.

Rad, G. von (1991), *Holy War in Ancient Israel*, tr. M. J. Dawn, Grand Rapids: Eerdmans.

——— (2005), *Old Testament Theology*, vol. 1, Peabody: Prince.

Rainey, A. F., and R. S. Notley (2014), *The Sacred Bridge: Carta's Atlas of the Biblical World*, 2nd ed., Jerusalem: Carta.

Reimer, D. (1997), 'ṣdq', in *NIDOTTE* 3: 744–769.

Rendtorff, R. (1993a), 'The Composition of the Book of Isaiah', in M. Kohl (tr. and ed.), *Canon and Theology: Overtures to an Old Testament Theology*, OBT, Minneapolis: Fortress, 146–169.

———— (1993b), 'Isaiah 6 in the Framework of the Composition of the Book', in M. Kohl (tr. and ed.), *Canon and Theology: Overtures to an Old Testament Theology*, OBT, Minneapolis: Fortress, 170–180.

———— (1993c), 'Isaiah 56:1 as a Key to the Formation of the Book of Isaiah', in M. Kohl (tr. and ed.), *Canon and Theology: Overtures to an Old Testament Theology*, OBT, Minneapolis: Fortress, 181–189.

Reumann, J. (1992), 'Righteousness (Early Judaism)', in *ABD* 5: 736–742.

Roberts, J. J. M. (1983a), 'The Divine King and the Human Community in Isaiah's Vision of the Future', in H. B. Huffmon, F. A. Spina and A. R. W. Green, *The Quest for the Kingdom of God: Studies in Honor of George E. Mendenhall*, Winona Lake: Eisenbrauns, 127–136.

———— (1983b), 'Isaiah 33: An Isaianic Elaboration of the Zion Tradition', in C. L. Meyers and M. O'Connor (eds.), *The Word of the Lord Shall Go Forth: Essays in Honor of David Noel Freedman in Celebration of His Sixtieth Birthday*, Winona Lake: Eisenbrauns, 16–25.

———— (1997), 'Whose Child Is This? Reflections on the Speaking Voice in Isaiah 9:5', *HTR* 90.2: 115–129.

Rowley, H. H. (1952), *The Servant of the Lord and Other Essays on the Old Testament*, London: Lutterworth.

Sacon, K. K. (1974), 'Isaiah 40:1–11 – A Rhetorical-Critical Study', in J. J. Jackson and M. Kessler (eds.), *Rhetorical Criticism: Essays in Honor of James Muilenburg*, Pittsburgh: Pickwick, 99–116.

Sawyer, J. F. A. (1996), *The Fifth Gospel: Isaiah in the History of Christianity*, Cambridge: Cambridge University Press.

Schibler, D. (1995), 'Messianism and Messianic Prophecy in Isaiah 1–12 and 28–33', in P. E. Satterthwaite, R. S. Hess and G. J. Wenham (eds.), *The Lord's Anointed: Interpretation of Old Testament Messianic Texts*, Grand Rapids: Baker, 87–104.

Schmid, K. (2005), 'Herrschererwartungen und-aussagen im Jesajabuch: Überlegungen zu ihrer synchronen Logik und zu ihren diachronen Transformationen', in K. Schmid (ed.), *Prophetische Heils- und Herrschererwartungen*, SBS 194, Stuttgart: Katholisches Bibelwerk, 37–74.

Schultz, R. L. (1995), 'The King in the Book of Isaiah', in P. E. Satterthwaite, R. S. Hess and G. J. Wenham (eds.), *The Lord's Anointed: Interpretation of Old Testament Messianic Texts*, Grand Rapids: Baker, 141–165.

—— (2005), 'Isaiah, Book of', *DTIB*, 336–344.

—— (2009), 'Nationalism and Universalism in Isaiah', in D. G. Firth and H. G. M. Williamson (eds.), *Interpreting Isaiah: Issues and Approaches*, Downers Grove: InterVarsity Press, 122–144.

Scobie, C. H. H. (1991), 'The Challenge of Biblical Theology', *TynBul* 41: 31–61.

Scott, R. B. Y. (1936), 'The Relation of Isaiah, Chapter 35, to Deutero-Isaiah', *AJSL* 52.3: 178–191.

Scullion, J. J. (1992), 'Righteousness (OT)', in *ABD* 5: 724–736.

Seifrid, M. A. (2001), 'Righteousness Language in the Hebrew Scriptures and Early Judaism', in D. A. Carson, P. T. O'Brien and M. A. Seifrid (eds.), *Justification and Variegated Nomism*, vol. 1, Grand Rapids: Baker Academic, 415–442.

Seitz, C. R. (1988), 'Isaiah 1–66: Making Sense of the Whole', in C. R. Seitz (ed.), *Reading and Preaching the Book of Isaiah*, Philadelphia: Fortress, 105–126.

—— (1991), *Zion's Final Destiny: The Development of the Book of Isaiah. A Reassessment of Isaiah 36–39*, Minneapolis: Fortress.

—— (1993), *Isaiah 1–39*, Interpretation, Louisville: Westminster John Knox.

—— (1998), *Words Without End: The Old Testament as Abiding Theological Witness*, Grand Rapids: Eerdmans.

—— (2001), *Figured Out: Typology and Providence in Christian Scripture*, Louisville: Westminster John Knox.

—— (2004), '"You Are My Servant, You Are the Israel in Whom I Will Be Glorified": The Servant Songs and the Effect of Literary Context in Isaiah', *CTJ* 39: 117–134.

—— (2007), *Prophecy and Hermeneutics: Toward a New Introduction to the Prophets*, STI, Grand Rapids: Baker Academic.

—— (2011), *The Character of Christian Scripture: The Significance of a Two-Testament Bible*, STI, Grand Rapids: Baker Academic.

Seri, A. (2006), 'The Fifty Names of Marduk in "Enûma eliš"', *JAOS* 126: 507–519.

Shead, A. G. (2012), *A Mouth Full of Fire: The Word of God in the Words of Jeremiah*, NSBT 29, Nottingham: Inter-Varsity Press.

Smelik, K. A. D. (1986), 'Distortion of Old Testament Prophecy: The Purpose of Isaiah XXXVI–XXXVII', *OTS* 24: 70–93.

Smith, G. V. (1982), 'The Concept of God/the Gods as King in the Ancient Near East and the Bible', *TrinJ* 3: 18–38.

—— (2007), *Isaiah 1–39*, NAC 15a, Nashville: B&H.

—— (2009), *Isaiah 40–66*, NAC 15b, Nashville: B&H.

Smith, J. K. A. (2009), *Desiring the Kingdom: Worship, Worldview, and Cultural Formation*, Cultural Liturgy 1, Grand Rapids: Baker Academic.

——— (2013), *Imagining the Kingdom: How Worship Works*, Cultural Liturgy 2, Grand Rapids: Baker Academic.

Smith, P. A. (1995), *Rhetoric and Redaction in Trito-Isaiah: The Structure, Growth and Authorship of Isaiah 56–66*, VTSup 62, Leiden: Brill.

Stansell, G. (1996), 'Isaiah 28–33: Blest Be the Tie that Binds (Isaiah Together)', in R. F. Melugin and M. A. Sweeney, *New Visions of Isaiah*, JSOTSup 214, Sheffield: Sheffield Academic Press, 68–103.

——— (2009), 'The Nations' Journey to Zion: Pilgrimage and Tribute as Metaphor in the Book of Isaiah', in A. J. Everson and H. C. P. Kim (eds.), *The Desert Will Bloom: Poetic Visions in Isaiah*, Atlanta: Society of Biblical Literature, 233–255.

Steck, O. H. (1991), *Studien zu Tritojesaja*, BZAW 203, Berlin: de Gruyter.

——— (2000), *The Prophetic Books and Their Theological Witness*, tr. James D. Nogalski, St Louis: Chalice.

Stovell, B. M. (2012), *Mapping Metaphorical Discourse in the Fourth Gospel: John's Eternal King*, Linguistic Biblical Studies 5, Leiden: Brill.

Strange, D. (2004), 'A Little Dwelling on the Divine Presence: Towards a "Whereness" of the Triune God', in T. D. Alexander and S. Gathercole (eds.), *Heaven on Earth: The Temple in Biblical Theology*, Carlisle: Paternoster, 211–229.

Strawn, B. A. (2007), '"A World Under Control": Isaiah 60 and the Apadana Reliefs from Persepolis', in J. L. Berquist (ed.), *Approaching Yehud: New Approaches to the Study of the Persian Period*, Atlanta: Society of Biblical Literature, 85–116.

Stromberg, J. (2000), *The Prophetic Books and Their Theological Witness*, tr. J. D. Nogalski, St Louis: Chalice.

——— (2009), 'An Inner-Isaianic Reading of Isaiah 61:1–3', in D. G. Firth and H. G. M. Williamson (eds.), *Interpreting Isaiah: Issues and Approaches*, Downers Grove: InterVarsity Press, 261–272.

——— (2011a), *An Introduction to the Study of Isaiah*, T. & T. Clark Approaches to Biblical Studies, London: T. & T. Clark.

——— (2011b), *Isaiah After Exile: The Author of Third Isaiah as Reader and Redactor of the Book*, Oxford Theological Monographs, Oxford: Oxford University Press.

Stuhlmueller, C. (1959), 'The Theology of Creation in Second Isaias', *CBQ* 21: 429–467.

Sweeney, M. A. (1987), 'New Gleanings from an Old Vineyard: Isaiah 27 Reconsidered', in C. A. Evans and W. F. Stinespring, *Early Jewish and Christian Exegesis Studies in Memory of William Hugh Brownlee*, Atlanta: Scholars Press, 52–66.

——— (1988), 'Textual Citations in Isaiah 24–27: Toward an Understanding of the Redactional Function of Chapters 24–27 in the Book of Isaiah', *JBL* 107: 39–52.

——— (1996), *Isaiah 1–39: With an Introduction to Prophetic Literature*, FOTL, Grand Rapids: Eerdmans.

——— (1997), 'The Reconceptualization of the Davidic Covenant', in J. van Ruiten and M. Vervenne (eds.), *Studies in the Book of Isaiah: Festschrift Willem A. M. Beuken*, BETL 132, Leuven: Peeters, 41–61.

——— (2014), 'Eschatology in the Book of Isaiah', in R. J. Bautch and J. T. Hibbard (eds.), *The Book of Isaiah: Enduring Questions Answered Anew. Essays Honoring Joseph Blenkinsopp and His Contribution to the Study of Isaiah*, Grand Rapids: Eerdmans, 179–195.

Thompson, M. E. W. (2002), 'Vision, Reality and Worship: Isaiah 33', *ExpTim* 113: 327–333.

Tiemeyer, L.-S. (2006), *Priestly Rites and Prophetic Rage: Post-Exilic Prophetic Critique of the Priesthood*, FAT 2.19, Tübingen: Mohr Siebeck.

——— (2010), *For the Comfort of Zion: The Geographical and Theological Location of Isaiah 40–55*, VTSup 139, Leiden: Brill.

——— (2012), 'The Coming of the Lord – an Inter-Textual Reading of Isa 40:1–11; 52:7–10; 59:15b–20; 62:10–11 and 63:1–6', in C. C. Broyles and C. A. Evans (eds.), *Writing and Reading the Scroll of Isaiah: Studies of an Interpretive Tradition*, VTSup 70.1, Leiden: Brill, 233–244.

Treat, J. R. (2014), *The Crucified King: Atonement and Kingdom in Biblical and Systematic Theology*, Grand Rapids: Zondervan.

Treier, D. J. (2008), *Introducing Theological Interpretation of Scripture: Recovering a Christian Practice*, Grand Rapids: Baker Academic.

Trimm, C. (2012), 'Recent Research on Warfare in the Old Testament', *CBR* 10: 171–216.

Vanhoozer, K. J. (ed.) (2005a), *Dictionary for Theological Interpretation of the Bible*, Grand Rapids: Baker Academic.

——— (2005b), *The Drama of Doctrine: A Canonical-Linguistic Approach to Christian Theology*, Louisville: Westminster John Knox.

────── (2006), 'Imprisoned or Free?: Text, Status, and Theological Interpretation in the Master/Slave Discourse of Philemon', in A. K. M. Adam, S. E. Fowl, K. J. Vanhoozer and F. Watson (eds.), *Reading Scripture with the Church: Towards a Hermeneutic for Theological Interpretation*, Grand Rapids: Baker Academic, 51–94.

Wagner, T. (2012), *Gottes Herrlichkeit: Bedeutung und Verwendung des Begriffs kābôd im Alten Testament*, VTSup 151, Leiden: Brill.

Walton, J. H. (1987), 'Isa 7:14: What's in a Name?', *JETS* 30: 289–306.

Ward, J. M. (1968), 'Servant Songs in Isaiah', *RevExp* 65: 433–446.

Waschke, E.-J. (2004), 'Jesaja 33 und seine redaktionelle Funktion im Protojesajabuch', in M. Witte (ed.), *Gott und Mensch im Dialog: Festschrift für Otto Kaiser zum 80. Geburtstag*, vol. 1, BZAW 345, Berlin: de Gruyter, 517–532.

Watson, F. (1997), *Text and Truth: Redefining Biblical Theology*, Edinburgh: T. & T. Clark.

Watts, J. D. W. (2005), *Isaiah 1–33*, rev. edn, WBC 24, Nashville: Thomas Nelson.

Watts, R. E. (1997), *Isaiah's New Exodus in Mark*, rev. edn 2001, Grand Rapids: Baker Academic.

────── (2004), 'Immanuel: Virgin Birth Proof Text or Programmatic Warning of Things to Come (Isa 7:14 in Matt 1:23)?', in C. A. Evans (ed.), *From Prophecy to Testament: The Function of the Old Testament in the New*, Peabody: Hendrickson, 92–113.

Webb, B. G. (1990), 'Zion in Transformation: A Literary Approach to Isaiah', in D. J. A. Clines, S. E. Fowl and S. E. Porter (eds.), *The Bible in Three Dimensions: Essays in Celebration of Forty Years of Biblical Studies in the University of Sheffield*, JSOTSup 87, Sheffield: JSOT Press, 65–84.

────── (1996), *The Message of Isaiah: On Eagles' Wings*, Leicester: Inter-Varsity Press.

Webster, E. C. (1986), 'A Rhetorical Study of Isaiah 66', *JSOT* 34: 93–108.

Wegner, P. D. (1992a), *An Examination of Kingship and Messianic Expectation in Isaiah 1–35*, Lewiston: Mellen.

────── (1992b), 'A Re-Examination of Isaiah IX 1–6', *VT* 42: 103–112.

Weinfeld, M. (1992), 'Justice and Righteousness – *mišpāṭ ûṣĕdāqâ* – the Expression and Its Meaning', in H. G. Reventlow and Y. Hoffman (eds.), *Justice and Righteousness: Biblical Themes and Their Influence*, JSOTSup 137, Sheffield: JSOT Press, 228–246.

Wenham, G. J. (1972), '*bĕtûlāh*, "A Girl of Marriageable Age"', *VT* 22: 326–347.

Westermann, C. (1969), *Isaiah 40–66: A Commentary*, OTL, Louisville: Westminster John Knox.

Whybray, R. N. (1975), *Isaiah 40–66*, NCBC, Grand Rapids: Eerdmans.

―――― (1978), *Thanksgiving for a Liberated Prophet: An Interpretation of Isaiah Chapter 53*, JSOTSup 4, Sheffield: JSOT Press.

Wilcox, P., and D. Paton-Williams (1988), 'The Servant Songs in Deutero-Isaiah', *JSOT* 42: 79–102.

Wildberger, H. (1991), *Isaiah 1–12*, tr. T. H. Trapp, CC, Minneapolis: Fortress.

―――― (1997), *Isaiah 13–27*, tr. T. H. Trapp, CC, Minneapolis: Fortress.

―――― (2002), *Isaiah 28–39*, tr. T. H. Trapp, CC, Minneapolis: Fortress.

Williamson, H. G. M. (1978), 'Sure Mercies of David: Subjective or Objective Genitive?', *JSS* 23: 31–49.

―――― (1994), *The Book Called Isaiah: Deutero-Isaiah's Role in Composition and Redaction*, New York: Oxford University Press.

―――― (1997), 'Isaiah 6,13 and 1,29–31', in J. van Ruiten and M. Vervenne (eds.), *Studies in the Book of Isaiah: Festschrift Willem A. M. Beuken*, BETL 132, Leuven: Peeters, 119–128.

―――― (1998a), 'Messianic Texts in Isaiah 1–39', in J. Day (ed.), *King and Messiah in Israel and the Ancient Near East: Proceedings of the Oxford Old Testament Seminar*, JSOTSup 270, Sheffield: Sheffield Academic Press, 238–270.

―――― (1998b), *Variations on a Theme: King, Messiah and Servant in the Book of Isaiah*, Didsbury Lectures 1997, Carlisle: Paternoster.

―――― (1999), '"From One Degree of Glory to Another": Themes and Theology in Isaiah', in E. Ball (ed.), *In Search of True Wisdom: Essays in Old Testament Interpretation in Honour of Ronald E. Clements*, JSOTSup 300, Sheffield: Sheffield Academic Press, 174–195.

―――― (2006), *A Critical and Exegetical Commentary on Isaiah 1–5*, ICC, London: T. & T. Clark.

Willis, T. M. (1991), 'Yahweh's Elders (Isa 24,23): Senior Officials of the Divine Court', *ZAW* 103: 75–85.

Winkle, D. W. van (1985), 'The Relationship of the Nations to Yahweh and to Israel in Isaiah XL–LV', *VT* 35: 446–458.

Wright, C. J. H. (2006), *The Mission of God: Unlocking the Bible's Grand Narrative*, Downers Grove: IVP Academic.

Wright, J. L. (2008), 'Military Valor and Kingship: A Book-Oriented Approach to the Study of a Major War Theme', in B. E. Kelle and

F. R. Ames (eds.), *Writing and Reading War: Rhetoric, Gender, and Ethics in Biblical and Modern Contexts*, Leiden: Brill, 33–56.

——— (2010a), 'Commensal Politics in Ancient Western Asia: The Background to Nehemiah's Feasting (Part I)', *ZAW* 122: 212–233.

——— (2010b), 'Commensal Politics in Ancient Western Asia: The Background to Nehemiah's Feasting (continued, Part II)', *ZAW* 122: 333–352.

Yamada, S. (2000), *The Construction of the Assyrian Empire: A Historical Study of the Inscriptions of Shalmaneser III (859–824 BC) Relating to His Campaigns to the West*, Culture and History of the Ancient Near East 3, Leiden: Brill.

Young, E. J. (1965), *The Book of Isaiah*, vol. 1, NICOT, Grand Rapids: Eerdmans.

BIBLIOGRAPHY

Index of authors

Index of Scripture references

237

Titles in this series:

An index of Scripture references for all the volumes may be found at
http://www.thegospelcoalition.org/resources/nsbt

Printed and bound by CPI Group (UK) Ltd, Croydon, CR0 4YY

13/04/2025

14656474-0002